By the Sweat of the Brow

—

By the Sweat of the Brow

Literature and Labor in
Antebellum America

Nicholas K. Bromell

The University of Chicago Press
Chicago and London

Nicholas K. Bromell is associate professor of English at the
University of Massachusetts, Amherst.

The University of Chicago Press, Chicago 60637
The University of Chicago Press, Ltd., London
© 1993 by The University of Chicago
All rights reserved. Published 1993
Printed in the United States of America
02 01 00 99 98 97 96 95 94 93   1 2 3 4 5

ISBN: 0–226–07554–0 (cloth)

Library of Congress Cataloging-in-Publication Data
Bromell, Nicholas Knowles.
    By the sweat of the brow: Literature and labor in antebellum
America / Nicholas K. Bromell.
        p.   cm.
Includes bibliographical references and index.
    1. Amerian literature—19th century—History and criticism.
2. Working class writings, American—History and criticism.
3. Slaves' writings, American—History and criticism.   4. Slavery
and slaves in literature.   5. Working class in literature.   6. Work
in literature.   I. Title.
PS217.W66B76   1993
810.9′920623—dc20   93-17247
                                                         CIP

To the Memory of

John A. Moore

Contents

Part Four: Writing the Work of Slaves

Part Five: Toward an Ontology of Labor

Acknowledgments

———

Many persons have helped me learn about work, think about work, and write this work about work. My mother and father initiated me. Arthur Rosenthal taught me more by example than he can possibly imagine. Jay Fliegelman got me started, seeing promise in this project when it had none. Along the way, I was given dollops of encouragement I desperately needed from Bruce Laurie, Gary Kulik, Brook Thomas, Gillian Brown, Larry Buell, and Arnold Rampersad. The Charlotte Newcombe Foundation provided a fellowship, the English Department at the University of Massachusetts gave me some time, and the American Antiquarian Society offered its wonderful library and most helpful staff. Above all, though, I would like to thank my co-worker in life, Laura Doyle, from whose own work I have liberally helped myself.

Introduction:
"Ain't That Work?"

> "Tom contemplated the boy a bit and said:
> 'What do you call work?'
> 'Why, ain't that work?'
> Tom resumed his whitewashing and answered carelessly:
> 'Well, maybe it is, and maybe it ain't.
> All I know is, it suits Tom Sawyer.'"
> —*Tom Sawyer* (1876)[1]

One does not require an expert's knowledge of the antebellum period of United States history to know that during the middle three decades of the century the nature of the work many Americans performed changed drastically. Several generations of labor historians have documented the ways a spreading market economy and the concomitant development of industrial modes of production turned many independent artisans into wage laborers. More recently, historians have provided detailed accounts of the way these forces also transformed the work performed by many lower- and middle-class women. It is well known, too, that this period witnessed the emergence of professionalism as we know it today. Finally, these were also the years when the spread of slavery into the western territories forced Americans to decide whether that particular mode of work was consistent with democratic ideals and conducive to national prosperity. Artisanal work, agricultural work, factory work, domestic work, professional work, slavery: on each of these topics the historical bibliography for the antebellum decades is immense. Taken as a whole, they indicate powerfully that during these years the nature and meaning of work were anxiously discussed and contested as new ideological formations were developed to explain and justify new work practices.[2]

1

The aim of this book is, first and foremost, to uncover the ways antebellum writers participated in this broad cultural contestation of the meaning of work; it examines the way these writers represent and deal with work in their texts and, more important, the way their concern with work influences their own artistic practice and shapes the works they write. Second, this book is a cultural study that follows the path marked out by Daniel Rodgers in his study of the transformation of the work ethic during the years of American industrialization.[3] It aims to uncover the major paradigms through which Americans constructed and reconstructed their ideas about the nature and meaning of work in these turbulent years. Finally, this book hopes to contribute to what one might call "work studies" (as distinct from the more familiar field of labor history) by helping to establish work as an important subject of cultural criticism and by exploring the complex processes through which work is both valorized and erased by the cultures of capitalism.

This project began with my observation that, in the United States, at least, work takes place everywhere yet appears to find cultural representation almost nowhere. One can think instantly of exceptions: photographs by Lewis Hine, films by Charlie Chaplin, fiction by Louis Auchincloss and Tillie Olsen, poems by Robert Frost, and so on. But when one considers that work is the primary mode through which adult identity is constructed ("What do you do?" being the question most likely to fix one's social position), one cannot but notice that very few novels or plays or films actually explore the work experience—be it the work of a banker, a housewife, a factory hand, or a salesman. This absence becomes more conspicuous when one considers the foundational status of work in bourgeois ideology: according to John Locke, it is the sole source and justification of private property; according to Adam Smith and David Ricardo, it is the primary creator of economic value. Even critics of capitalism have taken for granted the central importance of work. As is well known, Karl Marx claimed that work was man's "species characteristic." Max Weber proposed that although specific work practices may be largely the product or effect of certain economic forces, ideological interpretations of work (specifically, the work ethic) contribute powerfully to the formation of those economic forces in the first place. But while capitalism's advocates and critics alike argue for work's importance to a capitalist culture, where does work find representation in that culture? In how many paintings, sculptures, poems, plays, stories, novels (or TV shows, movies, and advertisements) do we find not just workers (from bus driver Ralph Cramden to Doctor Clifford Huxtable) but men and women *working*?

Jacob Riis's *How the Other Half Lives* (1890), for example, contains hundreds of images of working men, women, and children, but Riis almost invariably photographs them when they are not at work. Walter A. Wyckoff's *The Workers: An Experiment in Reality* (1898) describes dozens of workers but pays very little attention to their work—either to its outward, formal, visible characteristics or to its inner subjectivity, to the experiences of such work. In *Mechanic Accents,* similarly, Michael Denning ingeniously uncovers working-class "concerns and accents" within the popular fiction consumed by the working class, but he is unable to find a single representation of the work actually performed by that class.[4]

Even when we are shown workers working, moreover, we seem as much excluded from as allowed into a full comprehension of their work. In Lewis Hine's *Men at Work* (1932) and *Women at Work* (1981), for example, the photographs cut into and disrupt the flow of the work activity, presenting it as an isolated moment, as a tableau; the very essence of work as a continuous activity, as motion, seems missing. Worse, Hine's portraits seem staged (as many of them in fact were); the worker seems to be *acting,* not working. And even in the few images (most of them in *Women at Work*) when we sense that we really are seeing work, not a posed simulation of work, we are unprepared to unpack what we see. In "Garment Workers" #106 (72:159:436mp), for example, two women bend over their needles, stitching men's suit jackets. We see boxes of buttons in front of them, a rack of suits over their shoulders, and part of the back of a man who seems to be arranging the finished jackets. From the photograph we can infer that the women's workplace is cramped, that they have relatively little freedom of movement (less than the man behind them), and that women of different ages (and perhaps, to judge by their clothes, different ethnicities or backgrounds) did such work side by side. But we seem to be circling around, rather than gaining access to, the work itself. We are given almost no information about the formal characteristics of such work (how many minutes at a time did the women bend over each jacket without looking up? how many jackets did they sew in a day? how often did they stand up? did they eat lunch—or dinner, or breakfast—at their seats?) and we are left utterly ignorant of the experiential qualities of such work (how much concentration did it entail? did the women talk, daydream, and think while they worked—and if so, about what kinds of things? What satisfactions, if any, did the women gain from such work? In what ways was the work painful? and so on.) That we are unable to decode this photograph is less a reflection of Hine's limitations than of our own. We are not used to encountering and responding to representations of work.[5]

Given the widespread transformations of work that occurred during the antebellum decades, the relative invisibility of work in the literature of the so-called American Renaissance is especially striking. Again, one thinks of apparent exceptions—Whittier, Melville, a few of Whitman's poems—but these are exceptions, not the rule.[6] Nor have some fifty years of historicist (whether "old" or "new") scholarship succeeded in bringing to light the way work might have been a major concern of antebellum writers. Even the dominant historicism of the last ten years, which is a historicism deeply informed by Marxism, has been signally uninterested in the subject of work. Instead, it has focused almost exclusively on economic exchange, applying with rich results a Marxism of the marketplace but omitting to discuss in much detail the very activity which brings a market (and all other cultural products, for that matter) into being: work.

My purpose is not so much to explain as to help remedy this absence of work from American culture's representations of itself; the first step in making work visible is simply to learn to look for the ways that it *is* present, which is what I try to do. Nevertheless, I would offer as a provisional explanatory hypothesis that work is a concept, and a word, that functions in American culture primarily as a blank, as an open space into which various meanings can be inserted. Frank Lentricchia has written that "it is precisely the ontological emptiness . . . [of such a word]—it is always differentially, or contextually defined—which permits it to be undecidable, unresolvably ambiguous at an abstract level of epistemological analysis, and yet at a concrete level, historically sedimented, set in place, stabilized, appropriated by a particular class, even though such settings, stabilizations, and appropriations will in turn be upset by other classes, other times."[7] Work is deliberately left open, then, its meaning unfixed, because it is a crucial site of conflict and change. In a culture whose foundational values and activities are comprised by work ("But do your work, and I shall know you," writes Emerson; "Do your work, and you shall reinforce yourself "[8]), the specific meaning of work remains fluid and inclusive, and specific representations of work—explorations of what work is and descriptions of how it feels—are allowed to appear but seldom to cohere into an authoritative whole. At the same time, this very fluidity means that work's meaning will always be contested as one class, or group, or profession, tries to establish a privileged claim to work's fountain of values.

What this suggests then, is not that work is absent from culture, but that it is relatively invisible there. Its invisibility is not a natural condition but a precarious achievement. Again and again, attempts will be made within the culture to indicate and represent work, to claim that work is one thing and not another, but the culture as a whole will allow these indications and representations only a provisional reality. I would suggest, specifically, that a pluralistic culture maintains the blankness of work not so much by censoring representations as by filtering and controlling the reception of those representations. If this is true, then the prevalence of what I have called a marketplace Marxism in cultural studies is hardly surprising: it deflects our attention away from the subject of work at the moment we come closest to it.

This is not to say that work has remained entirely outside the purview of literary studies of the antebellum period. F. O. Matthiessen repeatedly circles around the subject in *American Renaissance*.⁹ Perry Miller's chapter on "The Protestant Ethic" in *The New England Mind: From Colony to Province* helpfully stated the obvious, and Henry Nash Smith's important essay on "Emerson's Problem of Vocation" must have contributed to Sherman Paul's emphasis on Thoreau's vocational anxieties in *The Shores of America*. Meanwhile, William Charvat's essays, collected in *The Profession of Authorship in America,* broke the ground that later was to be cultivated so fruitfully by Michael T. Gilmore, Walter Benn Michaels, and others. Perhaps because the belated discovery of antebellum women writers coincided with and made possible a broader definition of literature, the presence of work in these women's writings, both as subject and as a formative concern, has received considerably more attention. Mary Kelley's "At War with Herself: Harriet Beecher Stowe as Woman in Conflict within the Home" and later her *Private Women, Public Stage;* Kathryn Kish Sklar's *Catharine Beecher: A Study in American Domesticity;* and Gillian Brown's "Getting in the Kitchen with Dinah" (to name just a few) all deal with the problematic relation between work and writing in texts by antebellum women writers. To these and many other critical studies I am deeply indebted.¹⁰

Suggestive and important as these studies are, however, they all tend to treat work glancingly, as incidental rather than central to their concerns—which may be about the work ethic, or about the psychology of vocational choice, or about the impact of a market economy upon a writer's practice, or about the construction of individualism, and so on. For example, Smith's and Paul's highly illuminating accounts of Emerson's and Thoreau's vocational crises make plain that both writers faced agonizing choices about what kind of work they would perform. But for Smith and Paul, the drama is one of choice among options, (such as, pulpit, or politics, or farming, or writing), not one in which the very nature of these options as work is skeptically scrutinized and in which, finally, the reliability of "work" as a transparent and reliable category of human experience is cast in doubt. Similarly, Charvat's and Gilmore's analyses of the ways antebellum writers responded to the spread of a market economy focus much more on these writers' representations of the market than on the work these writers perform in making such representations. In general, literary historians share with labor historians an assumption that we already know what work is and that we can therefore trace its transformations with relative ease. Work remains, by and large, a neutral and transparent counter positioned here and there in order to explain something else.

This book, as I have already indicated, begins with the assumption that work is not already fully understood and ready for deployment in discussions of the ways writers respond to economic change. It assumes that work as a category of human experience is a complex and always contested social construction, a construction for which superficially vague and fluid openness conceals myriad specificities that sometimes mesh and more often clash. Beneath our hazily held assumptions—that "work" means all purposive human activity, or some such generality— lie precise differentiations among and valuations of different kinds of work. Moreover, the meaning of work—that is, both the definition of what work is and the values ascribed to it—is neither fixed nor static. It is changed by economic forces (as Marx argued) and (as Weber maintained) it also contributes its own force to economic change.

My attempt to map the meanings of work in the antebellum period has proceeded from two starting points: from general, theoretical efforts to disclose the nature of work and from contemporaneous, antebellum sources which speak directly or indirectly on the subject. Theory—I am thinking primarily of the writings of Marx, Charlotte Perkins Gilman, Martin Heidegger, Herbert Marcuse, Hannah Arendt, and Elaine Scarry—has been useful to me not as a master key that unlocks the meaning of work in every period of time, but as a stimulus to thought and as a reminder that work is an extraordinarily rich, though still hardly understood, category of thought and experience. The helpfulness of these writers to me consists less in their accounting for the historical origins and causes of antebellum thinking about work (a subject that lies outside the scope of this study), than in their elaborating and making explicit what may be only implied by that thinking. For example, Marcuse's amalgamation of Freud and Marx lies behind my claims that the distinction between mind and body also entails a distinction between discipline and desire. Similarly, I several times employ Hannah Arendt's distinction between work and labor because I think it articulates a discrimination that was felt, but never put quite so clearly, by a number of nineteenth-century writers (especially Thoreau). I make the same use of Marx's notion of alienated labor. Charlotte Perkins Gilman's writings on work have helped me give a more abstract, or philosophical, cast to the preceding generation of women's writings on domestic labor. Heidegger's essay on "The Origin of the Work of Art" shadows my discussion at many points, as does Elaine Scarry's meditation on work in *The Body in Pain*. But because my subject is literary studies, and because my primary aim has been to bring to light the ways work's meanings were contested and constructed at a specific historical moment, I have deliberately refrained from fashioning these quite different understandings into a monolithic conception of work. By the same token, though it deals with and relies upon social and political history, this book is primarily a study in literary history. It does not attempt to uncover causal links between events and ideas, but to analyze the language of antebellum writers and to discern within that language the operation, and the affirmation or rejection, of paradigmatic understandings of work.[11]

My principal finding is that during the antebellum period work was understood primarily by way of a distinction between manual and mental labor, which in turn rested upon an assumed dichotomy of mind (and soul) and body. Virtually all antebellum attempts to account for the nature and meaning of work (including professional work, domestic labor, artisanry, factory labor, writing, and so on) rested, finally, on increasingly unstable notions about the natures of, and relations between, the mind and the body. When Theodore Parker writes that "the duty of labor is written on man's body," or when Melville writes that a ship's carpenter's "brain, if he ever had one, must have early oozed into the muscles of his fingers," or when the Lowell mill girls title their collection of literary work *Mind Among the Spindles*, or when John Neal distinguishes the knowledge of ideas from the knowledge of "things," all are attempting to represent and evaluate work in terms of their understanding and valuation of mind and body. The use of these terms is by no means limited to literary figures. On the contrary, it even more powerfully structures the discourse on work generated by reformers, politicians, political economists, and labor advocates. In his *Political Economy* (1841), Alonzo Potter refers to the "decisive fact, that by far the most productive labour of all is that of the *mind*, which is not susceptible of compulsion." By contrast, labor advocate William Heighton relies on the same distinction but makes the opposite claim when he writes that "an employer who does not regularly apply his hands to daily toil, is an accumulator and not a producer of wealth." The paradigm underlies also the antebellum discourse on maternal labor and woman's separate sphere. While some writers emphasize the disembodied, spiritual nature of such work, others seem to betray their awareness that maternal labor is ineluctably embodied. Mrs. A. J. Graves, for example, writes that woman "was placed in this world to fill a station embracing far higher duties than those of a mere domestic laborer. She has been endowed with intellectual faculties and moral influence, . . ." But Graves also maintains that "women who spend their days in idleness and folly, are by far more deserving of contempt than she whose time and thoughts are occupied in the necessary manual labors of her nursery and kitchen . . ." Finally, the paradigm functions centrally also in antebellum efforts to understand slavery and in particular to understand the relation between slavery and race. The escaped slave might be delivered from the hard physical labor of slavery, but not from the bodily racial identity racism and race consciousness promote. Racism consigned the freed black to an identity determined by bodily characteristics, which is why escaped slave Henry Bibb pledges "ever to contend for the natural equality of the human family, without regard to color, which is but fading *matter,* while *mind* makes the man."[12]

Because work was defined in terms of the mind and the body, and because work in turn was (as indeed it remains) a primary ideological constituent of class and gender identity, the many different facets of the antebellum discourse about work are always simultaneously what we would now call political, social, psychological, and philosophical in nature. (This complexity of work—the fact that it is the site or intersection of so many concerns—is what makes work studies so complex an endeavor and what distinguishes it from, say, labor studies, or marketplace studies, both of which have tended to treat work primarily as a political or economic phenomenon.[13]) Two brief examples may serve to show how these various considerations inform and complicate the subject of work in this period.

When Emerson writes that "a manly innocency shows in the face, form, and whole deportment of a mason, a smith, a joiner, a laborer, while his muscles are strained, and his face earnestly addressed to his work," he expresses both admiration and envy of the (apparently) deeply embodied nature of the mason's work (compared to his own).[14] He admires the innocence and he is envious not just of the health, but of the apparently eroticized labor this man enjoys; in Emerson's view, physical labor gives free play to a man's "animal spirits" and does not require the "prudence," "concentration," and "continence" that discipline the mental labor of the writer or professional man. Moreover, the mason's innocence is marked by and reflects an enviable gender authenticity. The manliness of his face and labor implies that mental labor is in essence effeminate, a fear Emerson and other male writers of the period frequently betray, as when Emerson writes that "the faults and vices of our literature and philosophy, their too great fineness, effeminacy, and melancholy, are attributable to the enervated and sickly habits of the literary class."[15] Thus, Emerson's casual remark about the mason points back toward his own psychological anxieties and to gender uncertainties which he associates with his work.[16]

At the same time, the political and social dimensions of Emerson's thinking about work become clear when we remember that Emerson's admiration and envy did not prompt him to emulate the mason. Emerson is certain that "the amount of manual labor which is necessary to the maintenance of a family indisposes and disqualifies [one] for mental exertion."[17] Mental laborers lead one kind of life and pay a certain price for it; manual laborers lead a different life and pay a different price. In either case, the rewards and the prices are at once social (class status), economic (income), psychological (release or repression of desire), and physiological: "Ask the digger in the ditch to explain Newton's laws," Emerson writes; "the fine organs of his brain have been pinched by overwork. . . . [H]e has but one future, and that is already predetermined in his lobes, and described in that little fatty face, pig-eye, and squat form."[18]

The philosophical implications of Emerson's distinctions are almost too visible to require mention. The fact that one kind of work is performed by the mind, another by the body, means not just that the performers of those different kinds of work will be separated from one another by their different physiological and psychological makeup and their different class position. It means also that their products will be fundamentally, ontologically different. The mind will work with ideas, the body with things; and the thrust of Emerson's early philosophical project will be to assert the superiority and indeed the greater reality of the former. There is a strain in Emerson that celebrates the literature of the "near and low"; in language that prefigures Theodor Adorno's insistence that we must recognize the material basis of culture, Emerson writes that "we must have a basis for our higher accomplishments, our delicate entertainments of poetry and philosophy, in the work of our hands."[19] But Emerson's predominant tendency is to affirm that these accomplishments are in fact "higher" and that while the "basis" must be there, it must also be put in its place. "A work of art is something which the Reason created in spite of the hands."[20] Conversely, when his disciple Thoreau concludes the opening sentence of *Walden* by claiming that he "lived by the labor of [his] hands only," he is signaling a desire to close the ontological gap between body and mind, things and ideas, laboring and thinking, which Emerson sought to affirm.

The power of the distinction between manual and mental labor to structure the antebellum writer's understanding of his or her own work is visible also in what is perhaps the period's most famous meditation on the nature of artistic creativity—Hawthorne's description in *The Scarlet Letter* of "the deserted parlor, lighted only by the glimmering coal fire and the moon," as a "neutral territory . . . where the Actual and the Imaginary may meet, and each imbue itself with the nature of the other." In this room, the moonlight "spiritualizes" all the objects in the room so that they "lose their actual substance" and become "things of intellect." But the tendency of the Imagination's moonlight to "spiritualize" matter is counterbalanced by the power of the Actual and its fire-light, "which mingles itself with the cold spirituality of the moonbeams and communicates, as it were, a heart and sensibilities . . . to the forms which fancy summons up."[21] Hawthorne makes no mention here of any kind of labor—although the scene functions in part to contrast his performance as a Custom-House official with his labor as a literary man. Nevertheless, Hawthorne not only employs metaphors that figure the process of literary composition as kinds of work (as when he refers to his "intellectual forge" and his "intellectual machinery") but, more important, his language here is saturated with significances found also in the antebellum discourse about the nature and meaning of work. Especially in the context of Hawthorne's earlier reference to a "fellowship of toil and impracticable schemes" at Brook Farm, the language echoes William Ellery Channing's claim in "On the Elevation of the Laboring Classes" that "matter was made for spirit" and that "we were placed in the material creation not to be its slaves, but to master it, and to make it a minister to our highest powers." It echoes also the words of judges at the Fifth Exhibition of the Massachusetts Charitable Mechanic Association who write that in the technology displayed there, from "the smallest implement, up to the noble steam-engine . . . was to be seen the controlling power, which Mind is capable of exercising over Matter." Most closely, it echoes Owen Warland's project of "spiritualizing machinery" in "The Artist of the Beautiful" and Hawthorne's account of Brook Farm as a failed attempt to "spiritualize labor" where "the clods of earth . . . we so constantly belabored and turned over and over, were never etherealized into thought. Our thoughts, on the contrary, were fast becoming cloddish. Intellectual activity is incompatible with any large amount of physical activity."[22] My point is not that Hawthorne was reflexively "influenced" by the discourse concerning the nature of work and the difference between manual and mental labor—instances of which appeared, in *The Dial, The Democratic Review,* and *The New-England Magazine* (magazines Hawthorne knew and published in). My point, rather, is that the distinction between mental and manual labor, resting upon an assumed dichotomy of mind and matter, was the paradigm that structured virtually all antebellum thinking about work, including the work of writing. Consequently, when Richard Brodhead points out that Hawthorne's narrative method in *The Scarlet Letter* "works against a clear distinction between mental and physical reality,"[23] it is worth remembering that this distinction is also one between two kinds of work, and that it is the distinction against which George Ripley brought the Brook Farm experiment to bear.

As these brief examples suggest, the fact that work helps constitute class and gender identity, and in turn is constituted itself by the different meanings assigned to "mind" and "body," means that making explicit the many implications folded into the antebellum discourse on work requires both patience and assistance. I have been greatly assisted not only by the theoretical works mentioned above, but by the research of many social and cultural historians of the antebellum period. However, even with their help I fear that this book never would have been completed had I not made an important methodological discovery—that the visibility of cultural representations of work is greatest wherever the work of representing work announces itself. That is, work as a representation becomes more visible when we can see also the work which made that representation. Although literary texts seem to be especially self-conscious of this dynamic, of the relation between the work (writing) that makes representations and the work represented therein, it is more immediately obvious to the naked eye in nonliterary texts that baldly make a power play to appropriate and define work. For example, when Edward Everett addresses an audience of workingmen on the subject of a workingman's party, and attempts to establish himself as an authority on work's nature and meaning, the work he is doing of representing (that is, capturing the meaning of) work manifests itself quite plainly. It is in texts like these that the paradigmatic operation of the dichotomy between manual and mental labor is most discernible, and it is in the often florid rhetoric of such texts that the political and philosophical dimensions of that dichotomy are most unequivocally revealed. For this reason, the method I employ in what follows is to use such texts (on manual labor, on domesticity, on slavery) not so much to contextualize as to open up the more conventionally literary texts I examine. In turn, these literary texts often are suffused with a self-consciousness about the work that brought them into being, an awareness of aesthetic practice, that can be employed to illumine what remains hidden in, and from, the former texts. Indeed, I have found that because writing is, after all, work, a writer's reflections on his or her practice or aesthetics can be read as labor, or rather work, theory; conversely, because a writer is embedded in a culture and surrounded by other workers (be they iron-puddlers or lawyers, mill girls or doctors), his or her writerly work will be to some extent shaped by the norms that define all these kinds of work at that time. To study work, then, is to be able to move from one kind of activity to another, one kind of text to another, with relative ease—and, I hope, with illuminating results. Certainly it is my aim to make possible new readings of important literary texts by showing what happens when we read a literary work (as product) *through* literary work (as activity). At the same time, it is my hope that this book will repay a debt. By showing that literary texts can have evidentiary validity and richness in exposing buried ideological constructions of work, I hope to return to labor and social historians some of what I have learned from them.

1
The Works of Mind and Body

1

Manual Labor and the Problem of Literary Representation

"The working man handles *things*. The professional man *plies* words."
—James J. Davis, *The Iron Puddler* (1922)[1]

"The duty of labor is written on man's body, in the stout muscle of the arm and the delicate machinery of the hand."
—Theodore Parker, "Thoughts on Labor" (1841)[2]

For about three decades, roughly between 1830 and 1860, politics and aesthetics converged for the American writer in two questions: what is the nature of my work as a writer and what should be the relation of that work to the work performed by others? Pursued into the realm of aesthetics, these questions prompted writers to revise accepted notions of creativity and to rethink both the aims and means of their artistic practice. Pursued into the realm of politics, these questions entailed confronting and evaluating the division of labor—a division which, under the pressures of industrialization, was becoming ever more finely calibrated. They required the writer to think of himself or herself not just as a producer who is located in the marketplace, but as a worker who occupies the realm of necessity in which so many readers labor.

From the outset, these questions were posed in terms of a distinction between manual and mental labor. For example, when George Ripley wrote to Ralph Waldo Emerson in December 1840, inviting him to join the Brook Farm community, he described their project as an effort "to combine manual and mental labor" and to "unite the thinker and worker as far as possible in the same individual."[3] Although Emerson, as is well known, declined the invitation, he supported the project's aim. In "Man the Reformer," a lecture delivered to the Mechanics' Apprentices' Library Association on 25 January 1841, he spoke favorably of the "doctrine, that the manual labor of society ought to be shared among all the members" and characteristically added therapeutic and philosophic reasons why every man should perform some manual labor.

> The use of manual labor is one which never grows obsolete, and which is inapplicable to no person. A man should have a farm or mechanical craft for his culture. We must have a basis for our higher accomplishments, our delicate entertainments of poetry and philosophy, in the work of our hands.[4]

Ripley and Emerson were neither the first nor the last New England writers to approach the nature of work in general and of writing in particular by way of this distinction between "thinker" and "worker," "head" and "hands." Nor were they unusual in finding manual labor attractive both politically and practically—politically insofar as they accepted the "doctrine" that the world's burden of manual labor should be "shared" by all, including mental laborers, and practically insofar as they felt that as writers they might personally benefit from manual labor. "When I go into my garden with a spade," Emerson writes, "and dig a bed, I feel such an exhilaration and health, that I discover that I have been defrauding myself all this time in letting others do for me what I should have done with my own hands" (p. 150). As early as 1832, a Society for the Promotion of Manual Labor in Literary Institutions had been founded in New York and in 1833 it published its *First Annual Report,* a collection of testimonials by distinguished authorities, most of them men of science. All of them argued that the performance of manual labor could help those who worked with their minds to live better lives and think better thoughts. Dr. John Bell was typical in advancing the Lockean thesis that the mind had much to gain from the varied sense impressions made available through manual labor. "The addition of agricultural and mechanical employment to theoretical learning cannot but enrich the mind with a large stock of ideas and imagery, and enable it to indulge in new and varied combinations of known facts and opinions, and afford it much greater facilities for striking out fresh paths for invention and discovery." In 1856, L. A. Hine advanced essentially the same argument in *A Plea for Harmonic Education:* ". . . the mind receives all its vigor from the body. . . . And yet all our colleges, academies, and high schools almost entirely neglect the body, as if it were too gross for their notice."[5]

On 23 July 1843, to point to another example, Horace Greeley took a break from what he called "the fierce turmoils and hot strifes" of newspaper work to deliver a commencement address called "The Relations of Learning to Labor" at Hamilton College. Warning of the dangers of a life devoted exclusively to "intellectual culture," Greeley urges his audience to see that "to a true and healthful development of the Man, . . . a constant participation in Manual Labor [is] indispensable."[6] A course of manual labor undertaken in college, Greeley suggests, is the best way to teach "our Young Men the nature of their own frames, and the shocking violence they do to that nature by overtaxing its powers, and then drugging it with narcotics and stimulants to reanimate them." In other words, manual labor helps discipline the body and regulate the energies which would otherwise seek outlet in sexual and social dissipation. And for Greeley, the inclusion of manual labor in the college curriculum serves a political purpose as well:

> The division of the Race into two unequal, contrasted classes—the few Thinkers, the many Workers—has been and is the source of many and sore evils, including the loss of the fitting and manly independence of each. . . . Not till we have emancipated the Many from the subjection of taking their thoughts at second-hand from the Few, may we hope to accomplish much for the upraising of the long trampled masses. Not till we have emancipated the Few from the equally degrading necessity of subsisting on the fruits of physical toil of the Many, can we secure to the more cultivated and intellectual their proper ascendancy over the less affluent in mental wealth.

This social division of labor, as Greeley understands it, has the immediate psychosocial consequence of unmanning workers by depriving them of their "manly independence." More subtly, its degradation of the "trampled masses" actually curtails "the proper ascendancy" of mental laborers over those "less affluent in mental wealth." That is, mental workers will be "secure" in their ascendancy only when they can maintain and demonstrate a suitable manliness to the masses—a manliness, he implies, that is enfeebled by an exclusive devotion to mental labor. In sum, the mental laborer's disciplining of his own body prepares him also for the work of disciplining—through persuasion not coercion—the masses of manual laborers.

As all these examples indicate, in the 1830s and 1840s a number of New England writers felt obliged to understand and adjust their work in relation to the work performed by those who worked with their hands. They felt that their labor as writers, which they assumed to be a form of mental labor, was part of a more general division of labor, one in which the "many Workers" performed "physical toil" while the "few

Thinkers" parasitically subsisted on them. For personal as well as political reasons—and these, I have suggested, often contradicted one another—they felt challenged to resist this ontological distinction in work which gave rise to a social separation of classes. "Things will never come to their proper level," wrote Theodore Parker, "so long as Thought with the Head, and Work with the Hands are considered incompatible."[7] In 1852, Charles Eliot Norton summarized this movement, though too facilely, when he wrote that "the distinguishing characteristic of the literature of the present age is the attention which it bestows to that portion of society which is generally called 'the lower classes.'. . . From the folio report to the novel, the essay, and the poem, the claims of labor and the laborer are set forth with various power, but with a single object."[8]

The sources of this impulse were complex, and while it is not my aim here to elaborate fully the socioeconomic and intellectual history that lies behind it, a brief account is in order. Most immediately, these writers were responding to the fact that what we would now call a rapidly industrializing market economy was dramatically changing the nature of the work many persons performed. Following the War of 1812, mounting pressure for "internal improvements" sparked an impressive expansion of transportation facilities. By 1850, some 3,500 miles of inland waterways had been constructed. In the 1840s, railroad mileage tripled to 9,000 miles and jumped fivefold more in the 1850s.[9] As capital became more fluid and transportation facilities improved, increasing numbers of people found it worth their while to produce goods (cloth, for example, and agricultural products) for exchange in the market rather than for use in the household or for barter. By the same token, as the market economy expanded, individual households experienced a growing need for cash in order to make purchases. New England farmers in particular felt the pinch. Unable to compete with western farmers, yet strapped for cash, many left the land and went to look for work elsewhere. Often, one or more members of the household left to become wage earners. Meanwhile, industrial entrepreneurs were building factories that brought advantages of scale into their competition with small workshops and artisans, often forcing the latter out of business and into the factory as wage earners. The demand for workers in the mills, and for school teachers, drew many young women away from the now rapidly obsolescing economic unit of the household farm to earn both wages and a measure of independence away from home. As all of these changes stimulated greater demand for legal, financial, and technical expertise, the period also saw the emergence and rapid rise to power of the professions and a professional (or "learned") class. At the same time, as these changes destabilized social life and eroded the relatively fixed and settled nature of the New England village, the New England ministry became subject to competitive market laws and had to fundamentally rethink the nature of the ministerial calling.[10]

In sum, from the weaver or shoemaker who was forced to relinquish the independence of artisanal work in his or her own workshop and go to work as a wage hand; to the young woman who left the farm chores that had occupied generations of her forebears and went to work in a mill town; to the young graduate of Harvard who found that the ministry or the law was not quite the settled, gentlemanly calling it had been for his father and grandfather, many Americans were finding that the traditional nature of their work, and the meaning ascribed to it, were undergoing rapid and profound change.

To the writer, not the least important aspect of this change was a transformation of the meaning of literary work; the opening of markets was creating a wider demand for the printed word and making it possible for men and women who did not have independent means to write for a living. For example, between 1820 and 1830, American writers published 109 works of fiction in this country; by 1850, this number rose to a thousand, by which time the total value of all books published and sold in the United States had risen fivefold to some $12.5 million.[11]

There were also less immediate sources for the interest in work—their own, and that of others—that seized hold of so many writers in this period. First, as New Englanders they inherited a theological, or ethical, tradition that emphasized man's duty to work for the glory of God and the good of the community. This tradition, or ethic, promoted work as a secular activity devoted, finally, to spiritual ends. Man was obliged to work hard in a "calling" ordained by God and to regard the fruits of that work not as personal gain but as a concrete manifestation of his success in conforming his life to God's purposes. "If thou beest a man that lives without a calling," admonished John Cotton, "though thou has two thousand years to spend, yet if thou hast no calling, tending to publique good, thou art an uncleane beast."[12] Zwingli's benediction made the same point, less grimly: "In the things of this life, the laborer is most like to God."[13]

Although by 1830 the moral imperatives of Calvinism had lost some of their force, a modified form of the work ethic remained strong, particularly among the middle class. As Daniel Rodgers has shown, the new work ethic put less emphasis on work as a "calling" that served to glorify God and more on work as a publicly "useful" activity that brought both material reward and psychological and moral sustenance to the worker.[14] Thomas Carlyle was perhaps the first, and certainly the most influential, promoter of the new ethic. In "Signs of the Times," and again in *Past and Present,* Carlyle celebrated the "perennial nobleness, and even sacredness" of work by calling attention in particular to its nearly mystical role in constituting individual identity.[15] For Carlyle, work, more than any other activity, is the means whereby each individual has an opportunity to discover and actualize himself. "Labour is Life: from the inmost heart of the Worker rises his god-given Force, the sacred celestial Life-essence breathed into him by Almighty God" (p. 190). A person who does not find his proper work, or who does not work at all, loses not just a means of serving humanity and advancing himself; he loses the opportunity to exist, to be himself. But this self-creative power of work is, after all, just another expression of work's more general creativity. Work is creative "Force," and as such it establishes a fraternity between writer and laborer by dissolving their social differences in the alembic of their common activity: "He that works, whatsoever be his work, he bodies forth the Form of Things Unseen; a small Poet every Worker is" (p. 197).

As educated men concerned with political affairs, Ripley, Emerson, and Greeley would have been familiar also with a political-economic discourse which, beginning with John Locke's *Second Treatise of Civil Government* and extending through Adam Smith and David Ricardo, established labor as the most fundamental determinant of economic value. "Labour alone," wrote Smith, ". . . never varying in its own value, is alone the ultimate and real standard by which the value of all commodities can at all times be estimated and compared. It is their real price; money is their nominal price only."[16] While by the early 1820s Smith's general economic theory was highly regarded by American political economists, both his labor theory of value and his invidious distinction between productive and unproductive labor presented them with an embarrassing problem: both appeared to lend important theoretical and ideological support to increasingly vocal and powerful working-class advocates while at the same time calling into question the value and respectability of a number of trades and professions monopolized by the upper class. "'That labour is the sole source of wealth,'" wrote the English political economist John Cazenove in 1832, "seems to be a doctrine as dangerous as it is false, as it happily affords a handle to those who would represent all property as belonging to the working class . . .'"[17]

During the second and third decades of the century, a number of American political economists affiliated with the upper class followed the trail marked by their counterparts in Britain and attempted either to recast Smith's theory or to deny it outright. Caleb Cushing, for example, who was a tutor at Harvard and an associate of Edward Everett's, was highly critical of the theory in his *Practical Principles of Political Economy*. In *Notes on Political Economy* (1826), similarly, J. N. Cardozo claimed that "the notion . . . that capital is nothing but accumulated labour, is as erroneous as the idea that labour is the sole element and regulator of value."[18] But Cushing's and Cardozo's task was not easy. They and like-minded thinkers were setting themselves in opposition not only to the political energies mobilized by Andrew Jackson and the Democratic Party but also to a belief closely associated with Republican ideology and consecrated by Benjamin Franklin, who had written: "'Trade in general being nothing else but the exchange of labor for labor, the value of all things is most justly measured by labor.'"[19] In the United States, then, Smith's labor theory of value remained powerful. But if it helped establish the social, economic, and political importance of work, it at the same time posed an inescapable question many rushed to answer: what, exactly, was "labor," or "work"?

Of course, Smith's distinction between productive and unproductive labor provided the beginning of an answer:

> There is one sort of labour which adds to the value of the subject on which it is bestowed: there is another which has no such effect. The former, as it produces value, may be called productive; the latter, unproductive labour. (p. 330)

A productive laborer, Smith went on to explain, was one who worked upon what we would now call a raw material and made it into "some particular subject or vendible commodity, which lasts for some time after the labour is past." The unproductive laborer, by contrast, was one who made nothing vendible and durable—the menial servant, for example, who waited on his master's person but added nothing of value to his property. The same could be said of many public servants, and one senses a certain bemusement as Smith ranks among the unproductive "some of the gravest and most important, and some of the most frivolous of all professions: churchmen, lawyers, physicians, men of letters of all kinds, buffoons, musicians, . . ." (p. 330) and so on.

Not surprisingly, Smith's invidious distinction was taken up by early labor advocates who could use it to claim that common laborers were more productive of national wealth than many members of the upper class. For example, in 1830 one group of Vermont workingmen complained that "while those who subsist by labor, who are in fact the *producers* of the wealth of the country, are becoming poorer, the *non-producers,* who are *consumers* of that wealth, are *pari passu,* growing richer."[20] These polemicists seldom singled out industrialists as targets, but aimed at merchant capitalists and members of the learned professions who "lived by their wits." Their work—if indeed they worked at all—was intrinsically deceitful, an easy and invisible process that created no product:

> All who can do so resort to some means of living without hard work, the learned professions are crowded, and combinations are formed by that portion of society who have money and leisure, or who live by their wits, to increase and maintain their own relative importance, whilst the more industrious and useful portion of the community . . . are reduced to constant toil, stripped of the better part of their earnings, holding a subordinate, if not degraded position in society, and frequently despised by the very men, women, and children, who live upon the fruits of their labor.[21]

Of course, such claims did not go uncontested by representatives of the learned, or professional, classes. Writing in the *North American Review* in 1824, for example, Jared Sparks argued, "All labor is productive, which promotes the end it designs, and when this end is a benefit to the laborer himself, it has value, and so far as it ministers to the wants or comforts of society, or any members of society, it is productive."[22]

At stake in all of these claims is possession of the words "labor" and "work." The struggle over their meaning is part of a political struggle, for whoever can claim to be society's foremost workers can lay claim also to social and political prerogatives. Important though they were, however, the terms "productive" and "unproductive" were perhaps too fluid and indeterminate adequately to structure antebellum thinking about the nature of work. They were quickly supplanted by the more powerful distinction between manual and mental labor. Perhaps because it appeared to be more concrete and commonsensical, perhaps because it had deep roots in a theological disjunction of body and mind, spirit and matter, this distinction soon came to dominate the entire range of antebellum discourse about the meaning of work.

Because antebellum writers understood work primarily by way of the distinction between manual and mental labor, their discussions of work almost inevitably entailed correlative questions about the relation of body to mind, matter to spirit. If the issue of work had, for them, closely related aesthetic and political aspects, it also involved considerations that were psychological, physiological, and religious in nature. All of these aspects of the antebellum debate over the meaning of work will be pursued in later chapters. In these pages, however, I want to focus specifically on the way this discourse about work was used to define the relation between classes. I begin with this subject partly because I believe that history emerges most fundamentally out of class struggle and economic change, but also because the antebellum discourse about the way work constitutes class employs so vivid a rhetoric of mind and body. Here we can uncover and elaborate the implications of this rhetoric with relative ease, which in turn will permit us to see more clearly how that rhetoric functions also when the work in question is that of mothering, for example, or that of slavery.

*

Beginning in about the second or third decade of the century, class distinctions in the United States (or at least in New England) were felt to rest less on differences in wealth and social background and increasingly on differences in the work persons performed. The paradigm that organized these differences was the distinction between manual and mental labor, and on this distinction rested also the social distinction between the laboring and learned (or professional) classes. To put it crudely, the "laboring classes" were seen to consist of men and women who worked primarily with their bodies (for which the hand served often as synecdoche) while the "learned classes" were thought to consist of those who worked primarily with their minds (a term that was often identified with "soul").23

In the 1820s and 1830s, when manual workers began to press claims for greater political and social equality, middle-class writers responded in various ways, but almost all of them argued or assumed that the distinction between manual and mental labor rested on a "deeper" and more sacred distinction between body and mind. Indeed, this metaphysical distinction became the ideological foundation of a social and political hierarchy. This is why, in many antebellum addresses and lectures on the subject of working-class rights, a strictly political or economic rhetoric gives way to a more philosophical, or religious, rhetoric about the relation of mind to body, spirit to matter.

Edward Everett's famous "Lecture on the Working Men's Party," delivered at the Charlestown Lyceum in 1830, and thereafter frequently reprinted and reviewed, offers a prime example of this kind of response to working-class agitation. Everett, a Boston blueblood turned "friend of the working-man," is a particularly interesting figure because he stood at the border of two worlds—politics and intellectual life—and served as a channel through which several kinds of discourse about labor mixed with and modified each other. After a distinguished career as a professor of Greek at Harvard, Everett was editor of the *North American Review* for three years and then entered politics, eventually becoming Governor of Massachusetts. In the early 1830s, he played a major role in efforts to enlist workers in a "Workingmen's Party," which in fact had little interest in advancing the workingmen's cause.

In his "Lecture," Everett argues that society should accord more respect to work, including manual labor, and at the same time he affirms the suitability of a class structure based on the distinction between manual and mental labor. "Man is by nature an active being," Everett begins. "He is made to labor."[24] Thus, a workingmen's party "is founded in the very principles of our nature" (p. 8). Everett goes on to construct a highly organicist model of civilized society in which many "different kinds of workmen" work for and depend upon each other in "one harmonious society" (p. 14). This model, in turn, is supported by another, by "the very structure and organization of man" as "a being consisting of a body and a soul." For Everett, the distinction between body and soul is absolute, founded on a presumably inarguable difference between "matter" and "spirit":

> What is body? It is material substance; it is clay, dust, ashes. . . . Matter, in its appearance to us, is an unorganized, inanimate, cold, dull, and barren thing. . . . And we say, that the body of man is formed of the clay or dust; because these substances seem to us to make the nearest approach to the total privation of all the properties of the intellect. . . . It is soul, which thinks, reasons, invents, remembers, hopes, and loves. (p. 15)

Everett does admit that "the humblest laborer, who works with his hands, possesses a soul" (p. 16); and that "there is no operation of manual labor so simple, so mechanical, which does not require the exercise of . . . intellectual powers" (p. 17). But what he wishes to emphasize is, first, that manual labor is primarily material in that it works on "cold, dull, and barren" matter, while mental work is, of course, spiritual, the work of a soul "which thinks, reasons, invents, remembers, hopes, and loves." Second, Everett claims that "the Creator" has allotted to different individuals different proportions of mind and body and has thereby established both physiological and metaphysical bases for a social hierarchy: "Though all men are alike composed of body and soul, yet no two men, probably, are exactly the same in respect to either; and provision has been made, by the Author of our being, for an infinity of pursuits and employments, calling out, in degrees as various, the peculiar powers of both principles" (p. 18). Thus, the primary division of labor into mental work and manual labor is the natural consequence of "the very structure and organization of man" (p. 14). This means that every man who works "is entitled to the good fellowship of every other member of the community" (p. 31)—to good fellowship, but not to equal regard. For clearly, if to be human is, finally, to think, reason, invent, love, and so on, then those who work with their minds are more human than those who work with their bodies. After praising each of the professions in turn, Everett concludes by underlining again the metaphysical basis for the social superiority of the learned classes. Just as it is the "reasoning soul" which "makes man superior to the beasts that perish; so it is this, which, in its moral and intellectual endowments, is the sole foundation for the only distinctions between man and man, which have any real value" (p. 31).

Perhaps the most famous single antebellum address to workingmen by a representative of the middle classes was William Ellery Channing's "Lecture on the Elevation of the Laboring Classes." For Channing, too, the distinction between manual and mental labor has to be dealt with in terms of the "mind" or "soul" and the "body" or "matter." By "elevation," Channing says, he certainly does not mean "an outward change of condition," a "release from labor," the acquisition of "political power," or "struggling for another rank."[25] What he does mean is an "Elevation of Soul." And here Channing feels obliged to refute those who would maintain that the workingman is too "plainly designed to work on matter" to become "spiritual":

> This objection will be considered by and by; but I would just observe in passing, that the objector must have studied very carefully the material world, if he supposes, that it is meant to be the grave of the minds of most of those who occupy it. Matter was made for spirit, body for mind. The mind, the spirit, is the end of this living organization of flesh and bones, of nerves and muscles. . . . We were placed in this material creation, not to be its slaves, but to master it, and to make it a minister to our highest powers. . . . To maintain, then, that the mass of men are and must be so immersed in matter, that their souls cannot rise, is to contradict the great end of their connexion with matter. (p. 167)

Well-intentioned as he might be, Channing does not see that he cannot affirm the hierarchy of the "mind" over the "body," "spirit" over "the material world," "souls" over "flesh and bones, . . . nerves and muscles," and at the same time "elevate" the men and women who work with their hands into the ranks of those who work with their minds. Or rather, he can attempt to do so, but his attempt will have to achieve a miraculous metamorphosis: manual labor must be somehow be intellectualized, spiritualized, etherealized. There is certainly some value in such a proposal. At the very least, it suggests that Channing was dimly aware that manual labor is seldom *entirely* manual, and that carpenters, for example, probably use their mathematical faculties more than, say, a typical minister. But Channing cannot conceive that immersion "in matter," in the life of the body and its senses, might hold intrinsic value for any man or woman. For him, matter is merely a "slave" which the

mind or spirit (the terms are always interchangeable) is to "master."
Manual work can be made valuable, therefore, only insofar as it can be
made mental:

> Labor becomes a new thing, when thought is thrown into it, when the
> mind keeps pace with the hands. . . . The more of mind we carry into toil,
> the better. Without a habit of thought, a man works more like a brute or
> machine, than like a man. (p. 176)

The next step of this logic is ineluctable. If "soul" and "mind" are
closely associated and held in opposition to "matter" and "body"; and
if Christian values uphold the superiority of one to the other; then a
class hierarchy based on the distinction between mental and manual labor receives justification so profoundly inarguable that it passes into the
realm of common sense. Theodore Sedgwick, for example, writes:

> The more ideas, the more mind a man has, the better for him; all agree
> to that; so, also, the more a man *labours* with his mind, which is mental
> labour, the higher he is in the scale of labourers: all must agree to that
> whether they will or no. This is a real distinction in nature, and can no
> more be got rid of by laws, customs, and form of government, than the
> complexion of the face, or color of the eyes. . . . It is upon this ground,
> that there ever have been, and ever will be, high and low, rich and poor,
> masters and servants.[26]

*

How did those who actually worked with their hands and bodies think
about and experience their labor? Of course, the bias of the historical
record makes this a hard question to answer, but it is possible to draw
some useful and valid inferences from the numerous addresses delivered
by working-class advocates to largely working-class audiences. The chief
characteristic of these addresses is a repeated insistence that manual labor is more "productive" of wealth than other kinds of labor. As we
have seen, the formal source of this distinction between productive and
unproductive labor is Adam Smith's *Wealth of Nations;* but Smith himself does not suggest that *manual* labor is distinctively productive. That
equation is first made by the working-class advocates themselves. What
did they mean by it?

The simple answer is that workers felt that the most effective rhetorical weapon at their disposal was this arrow plucked from the quiver of
capitalism's Bible. By persuasively claiming to be the real producers of a
nation's wealth, manual workers aimed to get a fairer share of the mone-
tary value of such wealth. They aimed also to get a wider social respect

for their labors. While these motives were undoubtedly operative, and perhaps dominant, another meaning can be uncovered in the term "productive." To those who worked with their hands and shaped various materials—soil, stone, leather, cloth, metal, and so on—the term signified the visibility and tangibility of their product. The things they made could be seen, touched, hefted, smelled. Moreover, the work they performed was also relatively visible: one could see the effort of the digger leaning into his spade, of the seamstress bent over her needle. Their work was inscribed in and expressed by the attitudes of their bodies. Mental work, by contrast, was invisible, and most of the things it produced could neither be seen nor touched. One cannot see the brain thinking; one cannot see and feel the profit turned by a favorable exchange or the decision rendered by a judge. From the perspective of those who work with their hands, mental labor and its products are at best a kind of magic and at worst a sham. As Emerson observed in "Doctrine of the Hands," "Our manual labor has this advantage over the liberal employments, that the thing must be done. In the learned professions a man may for an occasion affect to know what he knows not, or pretend to do what he does not, and of his omission his client is not competent to judge."[27]

This view is never, to my knowledge, articulated explicitly by antebellum labor advocates. It can be detected, however, in the rhetorical figures they employed. For example, William Heighton, a shoemaker of Philadelphia, asks his audience to understand the difference between wealth and money by imagining "a man placed on some barren or desolate island, . . . surrounded on all sides with heaps of gold and silver."[28] Can we conceive of such a man as being wealthy, Heighton asks, when he can neither eat, nor drink, nor clothe himself with what he has? Heighton's definition of true wealth, clearly, is that it must be able to provide for the body. And his account of the labor that can produce such wealth places equal emphasis on the body—that is, on the materiality of the means, the substance, and the ends of labor. He asks his audience to imagine the same man on another island, without any money—

> and in their stead possessing in fertility and abundance all other useful mineral, vegetable, and animal productions of the earth, here it is evident that he would *be able* to save himself from hunger, nakedness, and destitution THROUGH THE LABOUR OF HIS OWN HANDS, in gathering the fruits, in entrapping and killing animals, in collecting and preparing the raw materials, scattered around in every direction. . . . It is not gold or silver then, nor the natural productions of the earth *of themselves* that constitute

wealth, but THE LABOUR OF MEN'S HANDS in collecting, arranging, preparing, and making them in every respect ready to be immediately
appropriated to the necessities and convenience of man. (p. 3)

This "productive" labor of a man's body or "hands," Heighton goes
on to say, "is that which produces or brings into existence some real,
tangible article of wealth; as, for instance, a loaf of bread, a coat, a table,
etc." (p. 6). Conversely, what is the source or "fountain" of wealth,
Heighton asks in another speech, by which the rich accumulate their
great holdings? "That fountain, need I tell you, consists of the *marrow
and the bones, the blood and the muscles of the Industrious classes, the
ONLY authors and producers of all the luxuries and wealth which the rich
are enabled to accumulate . . .*"[29]
In Heighton's terms, there is really no such thing as mental labor.
Mental labor, being unproductive of visible, "tangible" artifacts is
merely a mask for "idleness." Again and again he contrasts those who
work with their "hands" with those who do not work at all but merely
"accumulate." After listing the many advantages a wealthy man would
derive from his investment of surplus capital in a public improvement,
Heighton concludes: "And last, but not least, all these advantages are
acquired by the rich man without any labour or toil; without any struggle from day dawn til dark to *create* them, or wearing out his life and his
energies to procure a living for his family." This theme is central to his
argument. ". . . the Trading class," he claims, ". . . are UNPRO-
DUCERS; with their own hands they *shape* no materials, *erect* no property, *create* no wealth" (p. 11). Productivity is identified with physicality, materiality, visibility—of the process and of the products.
Productivity is, finally, centered in the human body, for which the hand
serves as a synecdoche. It is the body that must be fed and clothed by
labor; it is the body's labor that can produce such necessities; it is the
worker's body—his "marrow," "bones," "blood," and "muscle"—that
gets spirited away or appropriated by the idle capitalist.
What, then, does Heighton propose? Does he call for a reevaluation
of the body, and of the skills of the hand, relative to the mind and its
skills? Not at all. When Heighton and other labor advocates turn from
their analyses of the difference between manual and (by implication)
mental labor to develop a political and social program, they focus exclusively on "education," on "intelligence," on "mental culture"—that is,
on mentality. The "main cause of the poverty and degradation" that has
afflicted the working classes, says Heighton, "is WANT OF INTEL-
LIGENCE." The crucial remedy, therefore, is a "general diffusion of
knowledge through the working class."[30] Seth Luther, another artisan

who was also a popular working-class lecturer, makes the same point. The wealthy classes who produce nothing have conspired "to prevent the 'common people,' the lower orders, by which our higher orders mean farmers, mechanics, and laborers, from *thinking, reasoning,* and watching the movements of these same higher orders."[31] The remedy, again, is education. "If we wish to live in a community, peaceably, orderly, free from excess, outrage and crime, we must use our exertions for the general diffusion of education, of intelligence, among every class of our citizens" (p. 6).

This emphasis on the need for education is in part a veiled warning to the upper classes and in part a recognition that antebellum manual laborers have been deprived of the time and opportunity to educate themselves about the means and ends of political power. But it points also to what one might call the sealed-off quality of manual labor, to the fact that its values and perspectives do not get reported or articulated in a discourse dominated by employers and capitalists. Heighton, and Luther especially, mean much more by "education" and "self-culture" than practical political savvy; they mean access to and control of what we would now call "ideology." For example, they repeatedly point to the way the wealthy classes have seized control of language itself. "To hide existing, or anticipated and *inevitable* evils, of the kind resulting from like causes, our ears are constantly filled with the cry of *National* wealth, National glory, *American* System, and American industry" (p. 16). "We are authorized to say," Luther continues, "to any man . . . who represents the population employed in cotton mills to be a happy and contented people, . . . that the statements to that effect are false" (p. 22). This is clearly a battle of representation against self-representation. And in the exhortatory tone of Heighton's and Luther's addresses, one senses a recognition on their part that they have to persuade manual laborers to take advantage of such opportunities for education as are already open to them. They seem to recognize that manual laborers commonly have participated in an ideological erasure of their work's interiority, its experiential characteristics and values, sealing themselves off from thought *of a certain kind*. Their passionate addresses aim principally to persuade manual laborers to break through this seal, to develop for themselves a different way of thinking, to develop, indeed, the mentality that characterizes the life and work of the idle, but powerful, rich.[32]

The manual worker's need for and resistance to "education" points to the fact that the knowledge the worker *does* possess is not recognized or valued by society as a whole. The pain of the manual laborer, and of those like Heighton and Luther who speak for him, is that within the language of representation then available, the value of manual labor has no voice. It is, to anticipate Melville's and Thoreau's words, at once "stolid" and "bottomless." What the manual laborer knows is a knowledge of the body, a knowledge that puts itself into actions, not into words. Antebellum apprentices did not go to school to learn a craft; they learned in the workplace, by working. One does not learn how to make a good joint or to lay a solid course of bricks merely by reading a book (though the many antebellum textbooks for apprentice mechanics suggest that reading was helpful); one learns by doing.[33]

This apparently unwordable knowledge of the manual laborer can only be gestured toward; it seems, by its very nature, to resist or elude articulation. Novelist and art critic John Neal, in his Address to the Maine Charitable Mechanics' Association (1838), can help his audience lay claim to such knowledge, but only by way of a series of rhetorical questions:

> What makes the difference, after all, between one class and another? . . . *Education*. . . . And what sort of Education, Sir! That which is obtained only at colleges or schools? or that which is obtained in the streets and thoroughfares, the high-ways and the workshops of the world, where all the faculties of Man are obliged to be strengthened? . . . Is not the accomplished blacksmith, or shipwright, or fisherman, or tailor, or shoemaker, an *educated* man? . . . Then why is he not an educated Man? Simply because the few that have spent their lives in the acquisition of learning . . . have agreed to call a particular learning, knowledge; . . . and to distinguish those who happen to be acquainted with this particular sort of learning, . . . the *educated;* and all others—no matter how profoundly imbued they may be, with all other knowledge, the knowledge of God or Man, or the knowledge of things,—*uneducated?*[34]

But of course many genuine friends of the working class, including Heighton and Luther, were among those who defined "knowledge" and "education" in a way that excludes "the knowledge of things." To them, such knowledge could not be put into words and, more problematically, seemed to prevent workers from acquiring the kind of knowledge that could be articulated.

Thus, the problem of composing a language of the laboring body is a problem of representation and of self-representation. As Mark Erlich, a carpenter himself, has observed in his history of the trade in Massachusetts, while there are "many physical monuments to the craft and skill" of carpenters, "the descriptive or analytic monuments" are lacking.

> 'We work more with our hands,' says John Greenland [a carpenter whom Erlich interviewed]. 'We are far more gifted with our hands than we are

with our heads.' Greenland's observation unfairly minimizes the poetry and intelligence built into the trade and the people who carry it out. But he is right in the sense that the trade has no tradition of documenting the experiences of the men (and now increasingly women) who pass on a language, culture, and set of skills from one generation to the next.[35]

*

There are a number of ways to account for the absence of such a "tradition" and the silence of the laboring body. In *Intellectual and Manual Labor: A Critique of Epistemology*, Alfred Sohn-Rethel suggests that the voicelessness of manual work can be explained in that it confronts an epistemology that has no place for it. The epistemology of bourgeois culture understands the mind as a self-sufficient, purely rational mode of understanding, one that can derive the fundamental laws of logic and being from abstract thinking:

> The theory of "pure mathematics" and of "pure sciences" triumphs in the fact that it owes no debt to manual labor. Indeed, Kant's task was to explain how these two disciplines were possible on an *a priori* basis in the mind. . . . This meant singling out the part of our being which is underivable from our physical and sensorial nature, and which carries the possibilities of pure mathematics and pure science.[36]

The knowledge of the manual worker, by contrast, does not derive from abstract thinking. "The artisan or individual manual worker masters his production not through abstract knowledge, but by practical 'know-how' and by the expertise of his hands" (p. 112). Intellectual and manual worker thus face one another across a seemingly impassable divide: each defines the very ground of knowing in terms that exclude the knowledge of the other.

Sohn-Rethel's critique is valuable, but it oversimplifies somewhat the epistemological assumptions of European culture—at least as these would have influenced antebellum American writing about work. Kant's emphasis on establishing an *a priori* basis for knowledge in the mind is counterbalanced by Locke's emphasis on the epistemological primacy of the senses. As is well known, Locke depicted the mind as a relatively passive recipient of sense impressions and argued that all human knowledge is derivable from the engagement of our senses with the material world. It is less well known that Locke himself valued manual labor because it was a disciplined and enjoyable mode of such engagement. In *Some Thoughts Concerning Education* (1693), Locke writes that "skill not only in languages, and learned sciences, but in painting, turning, gardening, tempering, and working in iron, and all other useful arts, is worth the having." Another proponent of the value of the senses (that is, of the body) as a source of knowledge was Jean-Jacques Rousseau. In *Emile*, for example, he argues that a student "will learn more by one hour of manual labor, than he will retain from a whole day's verbal instructions." Thus, it is not accurate to say that "western" or "bourgeois" epistemology is entirely hostile to the senses in general and to manual labor in particular. We should see, rather, that the senses and the body are a subject of controversy, a site of contest. Epistemological assumptions do not make it impossible, only difficult, to express the values of manual labor.[37]

There is another reason why manual workers have been reluctant to analyze and describe their work, especially in writing. A long tradition, going back at least to the guild system of the late Middle Ages, encourages the manual laborer to be silent about skills because diffusion of knowledge about them might threaten his livelihood. The worker knows that scarcity creates value. He knows that it is his knowledge of a skill that puts bread in his mouth; to give away this knowledge is to bring into being workers who will compete with him. "My people had been workers in metal from the time when the age of farming in Wales gave way to the birth of modern industries," writes James Davis. "They were proud of their skill, and the secrets of the trade were passed from father to son as a legacy of great value, and were never told to persons outside the family."[38] The need for secrecy leads to the development of a code that has a value of its own. The manual worker remains close-lipped about his work. He who would learn to do it must be quick with eye, mind, and hand—quick to observe how it is done, quick to coordinate observation with physical action. No patient instructor will tell him again and again how to perform the task. Through this code, craft secrets are protected and, at the same time, an almost natural process of selection is established to promote the gifted and obstruct the less competent learners.

We can identify another aspect of the problem of giving voice to manual labor by recognizing that in some ways it is actually more representable than mental labor. As we shall see, this was a problem a number of antebellum writers came up against when they attempted to defend mental labor and its productivity and to resist the claim of Heighton and others that "workers" consisted only of those who worked with their bodies. Calvin Colton, for example, in *The Rights of Labor* (1846) asserts that "laborers" does not mean only those who "make hard hands and hard fists, by striking hard blows; who wipe the sweat from the brow of toil, in any vocation, in doors or out, on land or water." The term should include also those who "apply their powers and faculties, of body or mind; their hands, or their heads, or their fingers; their invention or their skill; their hearts, or their intellect."[39] Colton's rhetoric is a veritable inventory of the terms in the dichotomized debate over the relation between, and relative values of, mental and manual labor: "toil," "mechanic," "hands," "fingers," "sweat," "body," "mind," "head," "intellect," "faculties," "learned." All are one, he claims. But his rhetoric betrays what we might call its own intrinsic loyalty to the concrete, to the material, and hence to the body and its labor. Colton's articulated emphasis is balanced, but his rhetorical energies flow more abundantly toward one set of terms than the other—toward the "hard hands and hard fists" of those who strike "hard blows" and "wipe the sweat from the brow of toil" not toward the relatively abstract and invisible labors of "legislators, magistrates, judges, clerks" and so on. This is the first of many instances in which we shall see that while the abstract values of mentality and spirituality are more easily stated, bodily labor clothes itself more readily in concrete, figurative language. In other words, abstract labor makes abstract sense, but that sense cannot be argued through concrete, picturesque, figurative language without crossing over into the realm and values of the body and its labor. Conversely, while bodily labor, being so much more visible, can be more easily represented in figurative language, its values cannot find expression in abstract terms without crossing over and borrowing from the realm of mentality and mental labor. All verbal efforts—whether by manual laborers or by middle-class ideologues and artists—to come to terms with the meaning of work will be colored and confused by these predispositions of their language.

Finally, another explanation of the sealed-off character of manual labor might be that we are apt to misread the few verbal articulations it does produce. The diary of Edward Jenner Carpenter, an apprentice cabinetmaker in Greenfield, Massachusetts, is, I think, representative of the few such journals by workingmen that we have. Typical entries remark upon the weather, his health, and the amount of work accomplished that day. "Monday June 24th. A warm day, but considerable airy. I got up this morning about half past 4 o'clock and went to work on a coffin we got it done about half past eight I then finished my secretary which took till most noon I then looked out some stuff for another, but concluded to make some press boards to press paper with for L. Merriam and Co., which I have not finished yet."[40] Nowhere do we find even a flicker of interest in recording how he felt about or understood the work of a cabinetmaker.

But perhaps we are asking the wrong questions entirely. When Carpenter writes, for example, that "I then finished my secretary which took till most noon," his sentence does tell us something about his activity. It may be that what I have called the "absence of self-reflection" about work in such texts is actually a discrepancy between the information he provides and my curiosity about the experience of such work. In other words, we cannot know what that sentence spoke to him. It may be that, austere and even empty as it seems, it nevertheless carried for him the smell of sawdust, the sound of the saw, the ache in his arm, the sense of accomplishment at the end of the day, and so on. What we do know, however, is that the sentence carries none of these meanings for us. And here, I think, it is important to specify more clearly this "us" and "we." We are, by and large, men and women who perform what is conventionally known as mental work. We read, we think, we write. To us, the world and work of the Greenfield carpenter are something of a mystery; and to those of us who have become interested in that world and work, the carpenter's laconic diary entries are frustratingly inadequate, indeed virtually empty of significance. But this does not mean that they were empty for him—or that they need be for other readers.

The reasons for manual labor's resistance to verbal representation, then, are many. The worker seeks to protect his skills and knows that the best way to do so is to keep them embodied rather than to articulate them. The epistemological assumptions of bourgeois culture are divided on the subject of the body and its skills: Locke and his followers value the senses as a source of knowledge, while Kant and later idealists seek to establish the autonomy of the mind through a radical, ontological independence from matter and the body. Finally, even when the manual laborer does write down his or her experience of work, many readers may not be able to interpret accurately the meaning of the words. To all these reasons, some Marxist critics would add another: the experiential qualities of manual labor are not brought into the light of bourgeois culture because such culture establishes itself on the concealment of manual labor. That is, such culture defines itself as something that can come into being only when necessity has been left behind. Only the manual labor that is performed voluntarily, as a kind of hobby, can find expression in such culture.

*

The literary representation of the interior, experienced qualities of manual labor would seem to require both the development of a language of the laboring body and a collapse of the distinction between writing as mental work and the physical work it seeks to represent. Both of these projects, as we shall see, were undertaken by a number of antebellum writers.[41] Their motives were varied, their success uneven, but their formulation of the problem in terms of the distinction between "mind" and "hand" was remarkably consistent. In February 1849, for example, A. J. H. Duganne, author of dime novels and popular economic and political works, delivered his poem "The Gospel of Manual Labor" before the Boston Mechanic Apprentices Library Association. The gospel is presented as a dream vision in which the narrator sees the world portioned out to "cold" science on the one hand and to "Mammon" on the other, and feels that neither can "save mankind."[42] In despair he cries out for a revelation and hears a voice command him to "Arise and Work." Transported back through time, he beholds Adam expelled from Eden:

> His tearful eye saw but the iron soil—
> His soul despairing sank beneath the curse of Toil.
> But Toil was not his curse! The Eternal's plan,
> Shrouded in mystery, was the good of Man! (p. 8)

The "good" does not immediately manifest itself, however. As the narrator traverses centuries of history, he sees that in age after age laborers have been doomed to suffer. He sees that although laborers built the great monuments of every civilization, their memory has perished. The ruins of Greece, Rome, and Egypt carry a lesson for us. Why, he asks, when we gaze on their ruins, do we "reck not the forgotten builder?"

> It is because the soul which was in him
>   Who built, hath passed into his work. It is
>   Because the eternal life which had been his,
> Was trodden out by kings from soul and limb
>   That with it they might build these monuments
>   To their own glory.—Human soul and sense
> Was sacrificed to matter—and stones became
> Instead of man, the altars of a nation's fame. (pp. 12–13)

This Ruskinian notion that the souls of manual laborers have passed into their work is powerful, but ambivalent. It suggests that the bodily knowledge and the physical movements of the worker can become the medium, or vehicle, for the transmission of spirit from one material frame (the body) to another (the artifact). As such, Duganne's vision is close to conventional aesthetic theories that ascribe precisely such powers to the artist's creative imagination. But Duganne emphasizes the destructive and degrading aspect of this process. Because the workers have no control over the process, they are used up in it. When Duganne tries to envision what such control would look like, he resorts to the familiar hierarchies of mind and spirit over body and matter:

O, had those hecatombs of souls—this mass
  Of living labor been together welded!—
  Had one great mental monument been builded!—
Then had that rescued and united whole
Templed creation with a deathless human soul! (p. 13)

Duganne's poem does not explain how "united" labor would achieve the preservation of the worker's soul in the artifacts he creates. Nor does the poem emerge from, or reconcile, its divided loyalties to body and mind. While the articulated argument of the poem certainly upholds the superiority of mind, and seeks to redeem labor by investing it with attributes of mentality, the poem's rhetorical energies often move in the opposite direction, toward an affirmation of the body.

Nations are built of Men. The mighty frame
  Of that huge skeleton—a state—
  Given we it with priest or potentate
Is ever more the same:
Bones, sinews, flesh, and blood of human kind
  Moulded together and made one
By that tremendous charm—the Mind; . . . (p. 14)

Thus, the dense physicality of the body lends itself to poetic articulation in "bones," "sinews," "flesh," and "blood"; the mind, on the other hand, remains abstract and poetically empty, a "tremendous charm," even while it retains an assumed superiority. The substance of manual labor can be indicated, but its value cannot be affirmed, by the language Duganne has at his disposal.

The difficulty of representing manual work as it is felt and understood and valued by manual workers is equally plain in *Moby-Dick*, that novel which at first glance seems to consist largely of workers performing work, but which on closer inspection turns out to render seamen and their labors practically invisible.[43] It is true that Melville describes a harvesting process in most of its particulars; readers put down his book feeling that they have *seen* whales harpooned, towed, sliced open, and reduced to oil in the try-works of the *Pequod*. But the passages in *Moby-Dick* devoted to a description of this work are almost invariably cast in a passive voice that effectually detaches work activities from the men performing them. For example, "Cutting In" relates that the "hawser-like rope . . . *was* then conducted," that "the block . . . *was* attached," that a "semicircular line . . . *is* cut," that "the hook *is* inserted," that "the blubber . . . *is* stripped off," and that "thus the work proceeds; . . ." [my emphasis]. Melville does provide one or two glimpses of actual men actively working—"Starbuck and Stubb . . . began cut-

ting" and "One of the attending harpooners . . . dextrously slices"—
but these are exceptions. Much more often, Melville renders manual
work as a process composed of unlocated actions rather than as a drama
of men straining their muscles and wielding their tools.[44]

In other passages apparently devoted to a description of work,
Melville sometimes embodies that work in an actual workman, but always in order to specify a vehicle for an elaborate metaphor, or to
ground a flight of metaphysical fancy, or to illustrate a moral homily.
Thus, Ishmael's work of standing watch serves as an occasion for warning about the dangers of transcendental speculation (pp. 158–59).
Similarly, Ishmael's and Queequeg's work with the "monkey-rope" offers Ishmael a chance to reflect upon the interconnectedness of all beings (p. 320). Melville very seldom allows physical work to stand forth
as a subject in its own right. He does not attempt to open up the interior of such work, to account for the worker's feelings and intentions as
he performs such work. Indeed, Melville's rhetoric about his own intentions in writing *Moby-Dick* makes clear that although he regards manual
work and workers as legitimate subjects for his fiction, he also feels that
they are subjects in need of transfiguring elaboration. He writes that he
will "weave round" his sailors "tragic graces"; that he will "ascribe" to
them "high qualities, though dark"; that he will "touch" the "workman's arm with some ethereal light" and reveal the "democratic dignity" "shining in the arm that wields a pick or drives a spike" (p. 117).
But what he will not do, apparently, is delineate that arm in all its rich,
dense corporeality—an arm of muscles, tendons, veins, an arm trained
to particular tasks, an actual arm of an actual man.

The nearest thing to an exception to this rule sheds some light on
Melville's policy. The carpenter is the only man aboard the *Pequod*
whose work as he performs and experiences it is opened to us by way of
the narrator's gaze. But what Ishmael sees is an enigma, or paradox. On
the one hand, as the ship's jack-of-all-trades, the carpenter is manifestly
a skilled workman, which "would seem to argue some uncommon vi-
vacity of intelligence." But this is "not precisely so. For nothing was this
man more remarkable, than for a certain impersonal stolidity as it were;
impersonal, I say; for it so shaded off into the infinite surround of
things, that it seemed one with the general stolidity discernible in the
whole visible world; . . ." The carpenter's work, while guided by intelligence of some sort, cannot be fathomed or understood by the intelligence of the literary mind. It remains obdurate, sealed off from understanding or analysis—as "stolid" as the material world it manifestly
works so well. "You might almost say," writes Melville, "that this
strange uncompromisedness in him involved a sort of unintelligence;

for in his numerous trades, he did not seem to work so much by reason or by instinct, or simply because he had been tutored to it, or by any admixture of all these, even or uneven; but merely by a kind of deaf and dumb, spontaneous literal process."

The import of this meditation on the carpenter's work is clear: manual labor is "deaf and dumb" because it does not speak itself in words, preferring to remain as silent as the earth itself. Moreover, his work is a puzzle to the narrator's mind precisely because it cannot be captured by such categorical terms as "intelligence" and "unintelligence." The carpenter is a paradox and an enigma standing athwart the distinction between mental and manual labor, his "stolidity" affirming and his skill destabilizing it. Ishmael can make sense of him only by way of a complementary paradox: "He was a pure manipulator; his brain, if he ever had one, must have early oozed into the muscles of his fingers."

If, as the example of the carpenter suggests, the interiority of manual labor by its very nature baffled the antebellum American literary mind and resisted verbal articulation, it becomes less surprising that Melville so consistently refrains from attempting to represent it in *Moby-Dick*. However, if Melville's skepticism was sound, it would have posed a grave challenge to the many antebellum calls for a democratization of literature and culture. It would have belied, for example, the claim that "Poetry, forsaking the knight in his bower, the baron in his castle, has taken up her abode, 'for better for worse,' with the artificer and the husbandman."45 How could a literature "of the near, the low, the common," to use Emerson's words, truly be representative if it was unable to represent the working men and women who, putatively, constituted the very backbone of the republic?46

Henry David Thoreau, another antebellum writer who was troubled by this apparent illegibility of the laboring body, likewise predicates his understanding of work on ontological distinctions between "brain" and "muscle," "spirit" and "matter," the "animal" and the "intellectual." But Thoreau, more obviously than Melville, also registers a skepticism about the validity of this convention, or paradigm. *Walden*'s account of the woodcutter Therien, for example, introduces him as a man who appears to consist of body, of matter. "In him the animal man was chiefly developed. . . . But the intellectual and what is called spiritual man in him were slumbering as in an infant."47 However, Thoreau's qualifying phrase—"and what is called"—carefully implies that what passes for spiritual may not really be so; and that true spirituality might as readily be found in the coarse and sweaty body of a woodcutter as in the fastidious intellectuality of a Harvard scholar.

Like the *Pequod*'s carpenter, Therien cannot be contained within the conventional, mutually exclusive categories of "manual" and "mental," "animal" and "learned," "body" and "mind." His "thinking" is "immersed in his animal life"—it is bound up with and inseparable from the sensuous life of his body—and it is for this very reason his own, original and thus valuable. But because he cannot be understood in terms of these categories, Therien cannot be represented in a discourse predicated on them. This is why his person, although full of "thought," produces almost nothing which "can be reported"—that is, represented in a written text, including the text of *Walden*.

In sum, both Melville and Thoreau locate the difficulty of representing the interiority, or experienced qualities, of manual work in the "muddy" opacity or "stolidity" of the body. Their writings also question, even as they themselves rely on, the root source of the problem—namely, an assumed ontological distinction between mind and body. As with all binary categories, these terms are mutually exclusive. Since mind and body repel one another like oil and water, they cannot illuminate or know each other. Wherever intelligence seeks to shed light on the body, the body seems to become a different thing—no longer purely itself, but now an outpost or colony of mind. Words, as Therien suggests, "kill" it. When Melville and Thoreau scrutinize manual laborers, they collide with the problem posed, and created, by this dichotomy; at the same time, however, their firsthand knowledge of both the laborer and labor compels them to question its validity. If the carpenter's "brain" has "oozed into the muscles of his fingers," does this mean that he is mindless or that his body possesses an inscrutable and unwordable intelligence? If Therien's "thought" cannot be "reported," does the fault lie in a defect of his "mind" or in the inadequacy of society's mode of understanding his body and his work?

The relation of literary to manual labor was taken up and explored at length by both Thoreau and Melville, especially, as we shall see, in two of their relatively youthful books—*Redburn* and *A Week on the Concord and Merrimack Rivers*—and with quite different outcomes. But it is necessary first to understand fully that the problem posed by the opacity of manual labor to written articulation was a matter not only of literary, but of political importance. As we shall see in the next chapter, the inscrutability of manual labor Melville and Thoreau questioned was actually an achievement, an important part of the process by which the degradation of skilled manual work by the division of labor and mechanization was made ideologically acceptable—indeed, desirable.

2

The Meaning and Demeaning of Manual Labor at the Exhibitions of the Massachusetts Charitable Mechanic Association

―――――――

"In our Mechanics Fair, there must be not only bridges, ploughs, carpenters' planes, and baking troughs, but also some few finer instruments,—rain gauges, thermometers, and telescopes; and, in society, besides farmers, sailors, and weavers, there must be a few persons of purer fire kept specially as gauges and meters of character; . . ."

—R. W. Emerson, "The Transcendentalist" (1841)[1]

At a "Public Dinner given to Henry C. Carey, Esq. at the LaPierre House, April 27th, 1859," the successful ironworker turned manufacturer, Joseph Harrison, Jr., took issue with Noah Webster's definition of the "'mechanic arts'" as "'those in which the hands are more concerned than the mind . . .'" "I think I am right in inferring that the venerable lexicographer was not a mechanic," he observed with irony. But Harrison's indication that the "mind" is concerned in the mechanic arts is quickly followed by an acknowledgement that both "manual" and "mental skill" have been largely replaced by mechanical contrivances:

"thirty-five years ago . . . ," he says, "hammer, chisel, and file, hand-lathe, drill-brace, and screw-stock were almost the only instruments used in working iron, after it came from the foundry and forge. Now, machines are made to fashion iron into almost every form by other means than man's power and skill—manual and even mental skill being in a great degree superseded by these machines." Having witnessed and profitably participated in this mechanization of what was formerly a craft-based industry, Harrison appears to be entangled, unconsciously, in three quite different sets of values. The dominant is that of the capitalist manufacturer who has no personal stake whatever in the characteristics or quality of the work experience, be it mental, manual, or some combination of both. The intermediary set of values is that of an enterprising mechanic who has managed to translate his bodily know-how into technical improvements in the means of production and thereby launched his quite spectacular career. The subordinated, and almost entirely repressed, set of values is that of the man who knows that craft work does entail considerable "manual skill" and whose rhetoric lingers with nostalgic affection over the tools he once gripped and knew so well.[2]

Harrison's speech, and his career, epitomize the range of meanings "mechanic" could have in the antebellum period. Each manual worker had to situate him or herself somewhere on this spectrum and choose a meaning that, to use Michael Denning's term, "accented" his or her experience of what was valuable in work.[3] Was it the potential for invention—for that almost miraculous transformation of bodily knowledge into an abstract principle that could then be mechanized—that had most appeal? Was it a delicate balance between, a kind of reciprocal give and take between, the skill of the mind and the skill of the hand? Or was it the loss (or subordination) of mentality in the manifold sensuality of physical labor that made it valuable?

The appeal of invention was strong. To be a mechanic/inventor was, after all, to turn the tables on the professional classes and on all others who derived a sense of social superiority by laying claim to what Greeley called "mental affluence." The mechanic inventor not only transformed bodily knowledge into concepts and abstractions, but in so doing he provided mankind with artifacts of immense practical value. Mechanics' and apprentices' associations, composed primarily of carpenters, shoemakers, masons, and the like, frequently invoked Newton, Franklin, and Fulton as their symbolic founders and fathers. The libraries of these institutions almost invariably stocked such works as John Connell's *Biographical Sketches of Distinguished Mechanics* (1852), L. Smiles's *Industrial Biography* (1864), H. Howes's *Memoirs of the Most Eminent Mechanics* (1842), Edward Foucaud's *The Book of Illustrious Mechanics* (1847), and so on. Timothy Claxton's *Memoirs of a Mechanic* (1839), for example, relates how a humble apprentice whitesmith rose to become an illustrious inventor. While the prefaces to these volumes often use "mechanic" in the broadest possible sense to include anyone who performs skilled manual labor, the contents focus exclusively on inventors—for example, Samuel Slater, Eli Whitney, and Thomas Blanchard. Foucaud writes: "I have thought it a great and honorable task, to write the history of the mechanic, the humble and modest annals of the working-man, who has devoted all his faculties to manual labor; . . . The *Illustrious Mechanics* will contain an account of the laborer at his work-bench, tools in hand, and every piece of handicraft whose object has been the improvement of any one art will be here recorded."[4] But Foucaud's conventional catalog of illustrious inventors provides nothing of the kind. The "humble and modest . . . working-man" at his "work-bench, tools in hand" never appears. One wonders whether the apprentice carpenter, say, or the master cooper who perused this volume in his association library was irked or pleased by this erasure. One wonders, too, how many mechanic readers understood that these great inventors were the technological founders of the industrialism that was at that moment absorbing and degrading the skilled labor of many workers.[5]

I do not mean to imply that the term "mechanic" never referred to workers who could plausibly imagine themselves becoming, like Joseph Harrison, inventors and industrialists. Although they constituted a minority in the membership lists of the mechanics associations I have studied, machinists do appear there. Moreover, if there is one kind of book we can be certain was directed toward, and consumed by, mechanics of the period, it is the technical manual or treatise—works like Henry T. Brown's *Five Hundred and Seven Mechanical Movements* (1868), J. Wilson's *The Mechanic's and Builder's Price Book* (1856), Robert Riddell's *Mechanics' Geometry* (1874), I. R. Butts's *The Tinman's Manual and Mechanics' Handbook* (1860). A mere glance at these volumes imparts one crucial lesson: the distinction between manual and mental labor was more ideological than actual. Not just machinists, but carpenters, masons, and a host of other skilled tradesworkers had to perform mental calculations of considerable complexity. Another genre—what we might call textbooks in mechanics—make the point even more forcefully. Works like Henry Kater's and Dionysius Lardner's *Treatise on Mechanics* (1831) and James Pilkington's *The Artist's and Mechanics Repository and Working Man's In-*

formant (1839) are detailed introductions to and expositions of physics, chemistry, and mathematics. At the same time, as their titles and frontispieces make clear, these works present themselves to "working men"—a term laden with political and social significations and strongly associated with manual workers. It would seem that even when these texts have every reason to cut loose from the material and bodily aspects of the work their readers performed—to evolve into a realm of pure mentality, like literature, law, or theology, or like the physical sciences today—these texts stubbornly cling to symbols and suggestions of manual labor.

This subordinated, but firm, allegiance to the body stands in marked contrast to the views of those who promoted "mechanism," or "mechanical philosophy"—the ideological justification of the emerging industrial order. As Timothy Walker makes clear in the classic exposition of those views, *Defense of Mechanical Philosophy,* the virtues of mechanism as a means of reducing labor are predicated upon a presumed worthlessness of the body:

> So long as we are doomed to inhabit bodies, these bodies, however gross and unworthy they may be deemed, must be taken care of. . . . A certain amount of labor, then, must be performed expressly for the support of our bodies. But at the same time, as we have a higher and nobler nature, which must also be cared for, the necessary labor spent upon our bodies should be as much abridged as possible, to give leisure to the concerns of this better nature.[6]

For Walker, the "gross and unworthy" body is merely a source of "animal wants" (p. 124). It contributes nothing of value to life or society, but rather siphons off precious resources from our "higher and nobler nature." To him it is inconceivable that the laboring body might have knowledge—craft skills with economic value and work experiences worth preserving for their own sake. His rhetoric empties the mechanic's physical labor of value so that it may be replaced, with no loss, by the efficiencies of mechanism.

The contest between these two views of the body—epitomized as a struggle to define "mechanic" either as an inventor whose work is primarily mental, or as an artisan whose work is primarily physical—was staged repeatedly and dramatically at the exhibitions of the Massachusetts Charitable Mechanic Association between 1837 and 1860. Here, large and small manufacturers, skilled and unskilled laborers, masters and journeymen came together to exhibit their products to each other and to the general public. Here, also, was waged a contest—silent on one side, bombastic on the other—to establish the cultural significance of the exhibitions and of the artifacts displayed therein. As one orator pronounced, the exhibitions were "a vital, earnest instrument of instruction":

> We call it an Exhibition. But that does not describe the thing. It is more. It is an educator. The whole scene is a vital, earnest instrument of instruction. It is an argument. It is a treatise. It is a poem. It is an illustrated textbook. It is one of the people's quick-witted, extemporized, unencumbered universities.[7]

The first Exhibition, which opened on 18 September 1837, was presented as a celebration of American artisanry in general. It included "contributions of articles from every department of industry—of choice specimens of American ingenuity and skill—rare and valuable domestic productions, natural or artificial,—the delicate and beautiful handiwork of females—useful labor saving machines, implements of husbandry, and new models of machinery, in all their varieties."[8] The exhibits were grouped in thirty-five categories, including, for example, "Glass, Earthen, and Stone Wares," "Philosophical Apparatus," "Coopers' Work, Boats, and Pump and Blockmakers' Tools," and "Cordage and Twine." The categories are not listed in any discernible order, though it is worth noting that the first is "Fine Arts" and the last "Machinery and Inventions." Also notable is the exhibition's organization of space: visitors entered Faneuil Hall and found "tables laden with the most delicate fabrics," "ample galleries filled with cabinet wares," "the most elegant productions of the loom and the artist," and an entire wall "adorned with woman's tasteful work, equalled only by her own loveliness." Visitors then crossed a bridge to Quincy Hall and "viewed the fine array of machinery and tools—the helps and means of the mechanic. . . .

> Here were sources of protracted enjoyment to all who could fathom the mysterious applications of wheels and screws and levers. The steam engine was busily at work in forcing other machinery to accomplish, in a few moments, the most tedious and difficult hand labor:—while other machines, worked by hand, showed the facility with which modern ingenuity could supplant the more simple but time-exhausting processes of previous ages. (p. 10)

The segregation of "Machinery and Inventions" from all other artifacts suggests not only that these were the largest single group, but that in the minds of the organizers they formed a distinctly different category of made thing. Moreover, the organizers infused a certain drama or teleology into the exhibition by having spectators pass through the hand-made artifacts in Faneuil Hall and cross a bridge to get to the machines and inventions which were at once more modern, more engrossing, and more spectacular. Splendid as the displays in Faneuil Hall might have been, they were inert, even dead compared to the living, moving machines found in Quincy Hall. Finally, the writer of the catalog adverts blandly to an irony that hardly could have been lost on the artisans whose artifacts served as the introduction, or threshold, to the gorgeous display of machinery: many of these machines were intended to "perform the most tedious and difficult hand labor," to "supplant the more simple but time-exhausting processes of previous ages"—in short, to mechanize the skills and replace the work of the artisans themselves.

The underlying antagonism between handwork and machinery remains relatively subdued in the Exhibition of 1837. As we shall see, however, the enmity intensifies as time passes. Gradually, the exhibitions serve far less to celebrate artisanry in general than to applaud one particular kind of artisanry—the invention of new machines, especially labor-saving machines. This trend is openly voiced, as we shall see, by the addresses delivered at and published to accompany the exhibitions. It is also reflected in the composition and organization of the artifacts displayed and in the distribution of medals among various kinds of work. In this contest over the substance and meaning of the exhibitions, the promoters of a new industrial order clearly have the upper hand—even in an organization dominated, numerically, by artisans. At the same time, however, the lists of artifacts and the descriptions accompanying them also tell another story—one in which the values of manual labor express themselves through handmade things and even spill into and express themselves through the words of the addresses. Beneath the more obvious efforts of those who would empty manual labor of its meaning and value we find some evidence of manual laborers telling their version of things and finding the locus of their values and feelings in the skill of the hand, the sentience of the body.

The single most telling indication of the artisans' commitment to their values is the abundance and range of artifacts they submitted—and continued to submit—to the exhibitions. While Quincy Hall displayed impressive machines that awed the public, many artisans nevertheless saw fit to display such seemingly humble artifacts as:

An oval Harness Cask—mahogany top and brass hoops—complete workmanship in every respect, reflecting high credit upon the maker. *A Silver Medal* (p. 35)

Two ships' Steering Wheels—on the plan commonly in use—the workmanship and finish are of the highest order, surpassing all others presented. *A Silver Medal* (p. 36)

A stalk of Rye, tall and prolific. (p. 48)

One case of Saw Sets and other useful inventions. The greater part of Mr. Akin's tools have been long in use, and have approved themselves to the various mechanics who have used them. They must hold a high rank. *A Silver Medal* (p. 67)

One boxwood Grooving Plough—very superior; Carpenters' Planes, of various kinds. (p. 66)

Horse shoe. (p. 69)

To read any of the exhibition catalogs from cover to cover is to encounter hundreds of such entries and to find again and again such encomiums as "good workmanship," "excellently made," "beautifully wrought," "first rate quality," "highly credible to the maker," "a very perfect piece of work," and so on. For many artisans, clearly, the exhibitions were valuable opportunities to display their skill and craftsmanship and to have their work appraised and applauded by the discerning eye of other artisans.

It is worth noting that many items ("horse shoe," "two coils of rigging,") receive no praise but are left to speak for themselves—for better or worse. It is worth noting also that many products (Mr. Akin's tools, for example) are praised because they have stood the test of time; they are functional and their functionality has been demonstrated. Other items receive praise because they represent an advance or "improvement," but this criterion for distinction does not dominate. Indeed, if any one characteristic of the artifacts displayed at the first exhibition receives special notice, it is their beauty; the judges are frequently pleased by an *aesthetic* dimension of the artifacts, by their makers' commitment to a level of workmanship that exceeds the strict requirements of necessity. For example, in 1837 the judges of coopers' work commended: "One oval Harness Cask, bird's eye maple, with copper hoops, and an improvement of a screw set, for screwing it to the vessel's deck—a beautiful specimen of skill in this manufacture, and must be highly approved for strength, durability, and beauty—a fit ornament to any ship" (p. 35). That year, the judges of Philosophical Apparatus were equally impressed by beauty. They praise "Two Electrical Machines,—highly finished and powerful instruments. One is the most beautiful machine that the Committee have seen; the manner in which it is mounted, and the arrangement of the battery, are ingenious and render it a very *convenient,* as well as beautiful instrument" (p.

28). They also praise an air pump which, "as a specimen of beautiful workmanship, is inferior to no instrument of the kind in the collection" (p. 28). In sum, across a wide variety of trades, the judges singled out for special praise those artifacts which were exceptionally well made and which displayed a degree of "finish" or "workmanship" that surpassed the requirements of necessity.

On crossing the bridge from Faneuil to Quincy Hall, visitors to the first exhibition found an enormous quantity and bewildering variety of artifacts displayed as "New Inventions, Machinery, Steam Engines, and Apparatus." The 126 exhibited items included, for example:

Miniature Steam Engine. A beautiful specimen of workmanship, so nicely adjusted as to be set in motion by the breath. (*A Diploma*, p. 87)

Machine for Tennoning, Boring, and Mortising. This is not claimed by Mr. Boyd [the inventor] as an original machine, but has been much improved by him since it came into his possession. It cuts a tennon of any width or thickness with the most perfect accuracy, either of hard or soft wood, in less time than could be imagined; and although, from Mr. Boyd's avocations during the Fair being such as to prevent his paying any attention to the machine, yet it was occasionally set at work by others, and all who saw it were pleased with its simplicity and accuracy of performance. Considering its ability to bore and cut mortises, we should think no carpenter or cabinet maker would be without it. We think it deserving of more celebrity than it has yet obtained. (pp. 88–89)

Boom Derrick. This is an improvement upon Holmes' Boom Derrick. We think Mr. Savage's improvement has added much to its convenience. In the construction of heavy masonry, and in all stone or marble yards, or public works, it is almost indispensable. It is the arm and hand of a giant, capable of lifting the largest weights, and placing them at the will of its mover. We cannot dismiss this article, without stopping to pay a small tribute to the memory of him who first introduced this and many other valuable machines to use, for the benefit of our mechanics—Almoran Holmes—a man without education, without friends, who from the humblest walks of life raised himself into notice. Many of our builders are now reaping the fruit of his talent, without knowing to whom they are indebted. *A Silver Medal* (p. 93)

Model of the Main Mast of a line of battle ship. Of this model it is not necessary for the Committee to say more, than that Mr. Harris was the maker of the masts of Old Ironsides, and of most of the vessels built afterwards on this station, until one of his apprentices was taken into the Navy Yard, as master builder of spars for our public ships.

This little model is an exact representation of the mast of the largest size; and we believe that, to the faithfulness of the work of Mr. Harris, all our old naval commanders can bear witness. (pp. 93–94)

Card Sticking Machines. These machines are not claimed as original inventions, but as modifications on Whittemore's machines, by which they are made more simple, compact, and less liable to derangement, and consequently, ensuring better work with less labor than any machines now in use.

The Committee, without pretending to decide upon the claim to originality in the improvements introduced, feel themselves authorized to say, that they have never seen better cards than those made by these machines, and the testimony of those who have used them would bear them out in a still stronger expression; and the beautiful accuracy of the machine, at work during the exhibition,—its sensitiveness in instantly rejecting an imperfect tooth, would almost induce a belief that it was possessed of consciousness. A thorough knowledge of the laws of motion must have been necessary to one who would improve these machines; this we believe Mr. Earl to possess, and he is a skillful workman, as well as an able designer, as is shown in the finish of these beautiful machines. *A Silver Medal* (pp. 96–97)

As these examples suggest, the first exhibition's display of machinery and inventions was by no means limited to machines with industrial and labor-saving applications. Of the 126 items displayed, only fourteen were unquestionably intended for large-scale manufacturing purposes; seven seem to have been made for artisans in small shops, three for domestic manufacturing, and fourteen for carpentry and the building trades. Moreover, the category itself was clearly flexible enough to include such works as Isaac Harris's model of a Main Mast and E. Brown's Portable Shower Bath ("There should be one in every family" [p. 97]). When we examine the distribution of medals, we find a similar diffusion and flexibility: six silver medals were awarded to machines with industrial manufacturing applications, three silver medals went to machines designed for the building trades, one silver was given to a silk spinning machine for domestic use, and two silver (and the only gold) to measuring instruments that were probably of more use to artisans than to industrialists. Most significantly, the judges in this category, too, explicitly recognize and reward the values of artisanal craft work. They praise Mr. Earl, for example, because he is "skillful workman, as well as an able designer, as is shown in the finish of these beautiful machines" (p. 97). The judges are at least as interested in the aesthetic aspects of the artifacts—in their look, polish, and finish—as they are in their function. They do not hesitate to award a silver medal to "Specimens of Wrought Granite" whose "wreathes and leaves are distinctly and perfectly cut, without flaws or mendings, and evince great skill in the manipulation, as well as correct taste on the design" (p. 100). Notice, too, how the judges at once distinguish between conception ("designer"/"design") and execution ("workman"/"manipulation") and praise the worker who can do both. Finally, the descriptions are couched in an informal, almost chatty tone. There is plenty of time to digress in praise of Mr. Holmes and Mr. Harris. And a description of two fire engines, alluding to the competition among volunteer fire companies, asks: "By the by, where was Bisbee's beautiful machine? Have the Tigers metamorphised her into their Race Boat? We *guess* if they pull her as fast as we have seen them throw water from the pipe of their engines, *they* must pull hard who beat them" (p. 96).

When we turn to Edward Everett's *Address,* however, we find (not surprisingly) a markedly different tone and attitude. His speech is an eloquent effort to seize control of the meaning of the first exhibition; it aims, specifically, to expunge the values of manual labor in order to justify the abstraction of such labor by industrial manufacturing. After all, only when manual labor has no intrinsic *quality* can it be abstracted and considered merely in terms of *quantity*—that is, as so much mere stuff to be measured and minimized by labor-saving machines.

Everett's starting point is familiar: God has given Man the prerogative of exercising "control over matter and inferior animals."[9] The mind's control over matter "is principally effected through the medium of the mechanic arts, taking that term in its widest acceptation" (p. 6). The hallmark of civilized nations is their employment of mechanics to subdue matter and to surpass the imperatives of the mere body. "We have some means," Everett points out, "of judging what man was before any of the useful arts was discovered, because there exist on the surface of the globe many tribes and races nearly or quite destitute of them; as, for instance, the native inhabitants of this continent" (p. 8). The American Indian, then, stands forth as an example to civilized nations of the condition they have left behind. But this condition, Everett admits, has certain compensations, among them a superior development of the body and its skills: "it is a somewhat humiliating reflection, that, in many things dependent on the human organs and senses,—unaided by the arts,—the savage greatly excels the most improved civilized man" (p. 9). (Thoreau, as we shall see in a later chapter, makes precisely the same observation but places altogether different value on it: he is drawn to and emulates the bodily knowledge of the Indian because he is disgusted by civilization's mania for "improvements.")

After thus deftly associating superior bodily skills and knowledge with "the savage," Everett goes on to celebrate the advance of technology over the outworn processes of artisanal and unskilled manual work:

> But the great difference between savage and civilized life consists in the
> want of those more improved arts [that is, the invention of labor-saving
> machinery],—the products of which we have been contemplating,—by
> which no inconsiderable quantity of human power and skill can be trans-
> ferred to inanimate tools and machinery, and perpetuated in them;—the
> arts whereby the grasp of the hand, which soon wearies, can be trans-
> ferred to the iron grasp of the vise, the clamp, the bolt, that never tire;
> the arts by which stone, and metal, and leather, and wood, may be made
> to perform the offices of poor flesh and blood. (p. 10)

Everett's logic is impeccable: Because man has been ordained by God
to subdue matter, the employment of his mind in doing so is his wor-
thiest endeavor. Because superior bodily knowledge is the mark of a re-
tarded condition, progress demands that it be supplanted by mental labor and by the work of machines. Significantly, Everett does not
distinguish between skilled and unskilled manual labor. Both "human
power *and skill*" (my emphases) should be "transferred to inanimate
tools and machinery." Because the body's skills are useful only to the
savage who, dependent upon them, refuses to walk the path to civilization, the body itself is expendable. The "grasp of the hand"—and once
again the hand appears as the key synecdoche for embodied knowledge—can be replaced by the vise; "poor flesh and bone" will give way
to "stone, metal, leather, and wood."

Everett appears to be blind to the ironies latent in his argument. How
otherwise could he address an audience of artisans and applaud "the
iron-fingered artificers in yonder mill?" Although some in the audience
certainly were employers and masters of journeymen and apprentices,
others must have bridled when Everett celebrated the new machines as
ideal employees—"subject to absolute control without despotism,—laboring night and day for their movers . . . an orderly population, to
which mobs and riots are unknown" (p. 12). But Everett's apparent na-
ivete should not blind *us* to the subtle ways he obscures these ironies,
consistently seeking to enlist mechanics in their own undoing, to twist
his celebration of "the useful arts" into an argument that empties manual labor of all value. Discussing the virtues of the spinning-wheel and
other labor-saving devices, for example, Everett erases all differences between them and other tools (for example, vises and bolts). In his mind,
the inventor of a machine that replaces the power and skill of an artisan
is no different from the inventor of a tool that makes the artisan's work
more efficient. "Yes, the men who, in the infancy of the arts, invented
the saw or plane, the grindstone, the vise, or the hand-mill; and those
who, in later periods, have contributed to the wonderful system of modern machinery, are entitled to rank high among the benefactors of man-

kind,—the fathers of civilization,—the creators, I had almost said, of nations" (p. 14). In sum, by arguing that "mind, acting through the mechanic arts, is the vital principle of modern civilized society" (p. 15); by
enlisting "the useful and mechanic arts" in the cause of "intellectual progress"; and by asserting that "all art . . . is a creation of the mind of
man;—an essence of infinite capacity for improvement" (p. 22), Everett
makes even skilled manual labor expendable. The hand of the artisan and
the "poor flesh and bone" of the unskilled worker, their "power" and
their "skill" are destined to serve "intellectual progress" and thus to create the machinery that will eventually supplant them.

Powerful as Everett's rhetoric is, it nevertheless registers some appreciation for the very values it aims to deny. Everett must praise the Indian's bodily skill in order to suggest that such skill actually impedes
progress. He must give even matter its due:

> Mind, all the time, is the great mover; but surrounded,—encased,—as it
> is with matter, acting by myriad material organs, treading a material
> earth, incorporated and mingled up with matter,—I do not know that
> there is anything but pure, inward thought, which is not dependent upon
> it; and even the capacity of the mind for pure thought is essentially af-
> fected by the condition of the material body, and by external circum-
> stances acting upon it. (p. 6)

Moreover, even when the values Everett opposes are not articulated, we
can infer their presence from the existence of Everett's argument. Everett never explicitly *says* that mechanical skill might in fundamental
ways be a bodily skill or "know-how," but in his insistence, repeated by
many others, that mechanical skill is mental, we catch a glimpse of that
possibility. Everett and others like him must have felt that such a view
was maintained by certain people—else why would they have brought
such rhetorical energies to bear against it?

Most significantly, Everett also acknowledges what I have called the
"sealed-off" quality of manual labor, its opacity to intellectual analysis
and understanding. Admitting that it might never be "possible to write
the secret history of the mechanic arts," Everett betrays the unease
many intellectuals feel when confronted by artisanal work they cannot
fathom. Moreover, Everett here means not the mechanic arts in general,
but mechanical invention in particular; by his own lights, invention is
the imposition of mind over matter, a thoroughly rational process, and
theoretically it should be entirely susceptible to analysis and description.
But such is not the case: "the astonishment and admiration with which
we should survey the wonders of modern machinery, are impaired by
not knowing, . . . the stages through which it has passed, and the men-

tal efforts which have been expended in improving it." The reason why many of these steps and stages are not known and remain a "secret history" is that they are the result not of ratiocination, but of experience, sentient knowledge, tinkering, know-how. They have never been put into words, and they cannot be recovered through inference.

Ten years later, visitors to the Fifth Exhibition of the Massachusetts Charitable Mechanic Association would have found that Everett's insistence on the superior values of Mind had made headway against the silent values of artisanal mechanics. Compared to the first exhibition, the fifth gives far more emphasis to invention in general and to the invention of labor-saving machines in particular. The dominance of these values is signalled instantly by the placement of the category "Machinery, New Inventions, Iron and Brass Castings, and Railroad Iron" at the front rather than the back of the catalog.[10] Moreover, now this category is the only one given its own long introduction, which explicitly articulates the values the public should find in the entries. According to the judges, these

> plainly evinced a healthy and vigorous state of mind in those who are engaged in the improvement of machinery. . . . There was a wide display of useful inventions, each bearing the impress of thought and design, and all possessing their degree of capacity to multiply and cheapen many of the comforts of life, to diminish the rigors of manual labor, and thence increase the wealth and happiness of the people. From the smallest implement, up to the noble steam-engine which imparted life to all in communication with it, was to be seen the controlling power, which Mind is capable of exercising over Matter. (p. 2)

In the 1837 exhibition, manifestly ideological rhetoric had been confined to the address, leaving the lists of categories and entries relatively neutral. Now, however, the ideology of industrialism enters into and permeates the entire catalog. In their introduction to the category of "Machinery, etc." the judges go even further than Everett in attempting to enlist mechanics in the new industrial order and to persuade them that the real meaning of their work leads logically to the creation of "operative," or labor-saving, machinery. "The invention of operative machinery," they write, "to take the place of and perform, in whole or in part, the offices of the human hands, must be the business of men of superior genius" (p. 2). The young mechanics in the association should not only note that they can lay claim to the lofty title of "genius" if they invent such machinery, but they should also be aware that their work of invention is, finally, charitable rather than mercenary. "To make gain, is a laudable motive with the mechanician; but to soften the hand of labor, to wipe the sweat from the brow of toil, to diminish the blows of the hammer, and to give to manual labor another hour of repose, is a higher aim" (p. 2).

The fifth exhibition's increased emphasis on invention and improvement is reflected also in new and narrower criteria for the winning of medals. The gold medal, the organizers announce, "will be given only in particular cases, for some very valuable invention or improvement." The silver "will be given for very superior manufactured or wrought articles" (p. viii). Thus, while the gold is now altogether out of reach of the artisan devoted to traditional craftsmanship, the silver is made as available, or perhaps more available, to the manufacturer of superior articles either "manufactured or wrought." Not surprisingly, within the category "Machines, etc." the majority of silver and gold medals are awarded to machines and inventions with industrial applications and labor-saving characteristics. The Roving Speeder, for example, "is recommended as being capable of doing more work, in a better manner, than any other now in use, besides requiring less labor and attention" (p. 9).

Outside the category "Machines, etc.," however, in the pages of the catalog devoted to all other kinds of artifacts, we find a much less uniform affirmation of the values of industrialism. Artisans continue to display hundreds of items that make no attempt to improve on traditional designs and techniques of fabrication. The judges of these categories of artifact continue to praise scores of items for their superior workmanship, beauty, and so on. Indeed, some judges actually dissent from the now-dominant written ideology of the exhibition. The judges of "Cabinet Furniture, Chairs, etc." for example—

> respectfully report, that, while most of the Mechanic Arts in this City and Country, have advanced to a state of perfection, . . . they regret to say, that the manufacturing of cabinet furniture and chairs . . . —having in view excellence of workmanship in particular, and comparing the present time with a quarter of a century since—has materially depreciated. . . . The reasons are obvious: the prices have declined in corresponding ratio. (p. 127)

If the exhibition bears one unmistakably mechanic "accent," this is it. In this short passage we catch the dismay and bewilderment of artisans who, having at least partially subscribed to an ideology of "improvement" because it rendered so much respect to their calling, now find that "progress" actually depreciates their craft, particularly with regard to its "excellence of workmanship." When the judges explain this depreciation in terms of a decline in prices, they are surely referring to the development of labor-saving machines and large-scale production processes intended to increase the quantity while lowering the price of such commodities.

A more subtle, but perhaps even more subversive expression of disaffection from the values that had come to dominate the exhibition was voiced by the judges of "Carpenters' Work and Masons' Work and Tools . . ." This committee, composed of Pelham Bonney, John Temple, and Thomas Boyd, report that they found their duties "less arduous" than they had anticipated. The reason, they surmise, is partly

> the small number of articles submitted to their inspection, but mainly from the fact, that the departments, to which these articles belong, are those of prime necessity, and therefore, less of imagination and taste are therein displayed. They are mostly those, which were of the first necessity, and therefore have been the longest subject to the skill, and ingenuity of mankind. Hence not much that could be called new, was to be expected, but only superior workmanship. But even in this last category, the articles are generally deficient. (p. 136)

It would be easy to read this passage as yet another expression of the new values. The work of carpenters and masons displays little of "imagination and taste," those hallmarks of "culture," precisely because it is rooted in "necessity"—that is, in the realm of what Adorno calls "the merely existent" or "the reproduction of life."[11] Moreover, this long engagement in the realm of necessity has made the work of carpenters and masons highly traditional, even hostile to improvement. This department or category is therefore unlikely to display that fascination with the "new" so recommended by the exhibition's organizers. In fact, the three judges confess that they have been unable to award any medals in this category "because they were not able to judge, how far, on any point of merit, the articles submitted to their judgment, compared with the multitude of articles in other departments" (p. 138). Apparently, the work of carpenters and masons is too anomalous and too traditional to evaluate; the judges leave it to the organizers of the exhibition to bestow medals as they see fit.

But the rhetoric these judges employ points to another way of reading their remarks—as a sarcastic criticism of the exhibition as a whole. Perhaps the three men are speaking with tongue in cheek when they complain about the lack of "imagination and taste" in the work of carpenters and masons; perhaps we should see in their allusions to "prime necessity" and the "skill and ingenuity of mankind" expressions of craft pride in what I believe Raymond Williams has called "the aesthetics of the necessary." This way of reading the passage receives some support from the judges' caustic evaluation of a labor-saving Rabbet Plane:

For this improvement, modestly set forth as "enabling a man to do two days' work in one," the Committee sees no foundation; but they should judge, from the appearance of the plane in question, that it would take a man two days, to do a day's work with such an article; and then, we might recommend the man to favorable notice, for his ingenuity and skill, should his work be decently performed, under such disadvantages. (p. 137)

The judges' values here are clear: not only are they skeptical about mechanical improvements, but they place the worker before the machine. Although the new plane is worthless in their view, they would bestow praise on any man whose "ingenuity and skill" permitted him to do decent work with it anyway.

The possibility that these judges are disaffected and ironic becomes almost a certainty when we learn that all were craftsmen themselves. Pelham Bonney is included in the MCMA's 1849 membership list as a "Housewright" who joined the association in 1838. In the catalog for the second exhibition (1839), we read that Bonney won a silver medal for "A Black Walnut Door, of good, thorough workmanship, and neat design; worthy of approbation and encouragement, and creditable to the maker as a mechanic" (p. 47). John Templeton was a stonecutter who joined the association in 1826. Thomas Boyd was a housewright who joined in 1837. We have already seen reference made to his improved mortise and tennon cutter in the 1837 exhibition. That same year he won a silver medal for "A Door, containing six pannels, well proportioned, veneered in rose wood. A good degree of taste is exhibited by the maker in making the veneers and in the execution of the work. The beauty of the work, and the brilliancy of polish can hardly be exceeded. The maker is entitled to high commendation for his taste and skill in the manufacture, being the first of the kind within the knowledge of the Committee" (p. 65). In sum, in earlier exhibitions, Bonney and Boyd had been praised for "neat design," "taste," and a degree of innovation—precisely the qualities they now (sarcastically) claim to be *generically* inappropriate to the work of carpenters and masons. Their allusion to the small number of articles submitted and their professed inability to judge them express not condescension but disenchantment. And their complaint that the articles that year are deficient even in "superior workmanship" reflects the dismay of craftsmen who see what the new order's obsession with improvement is doing to their trade.

*

Nine years later, at the 1856 exhibition, the work of men in the building trades is not exhibited at all. Did they refuse to participate, or were they excluded? We may never know. In either case, however, the consequence is clear: the exhibition carries no work by the trades with the largest membership in the MCMA—trades which, moreover, had a tradition of radicalism going back to the Ten-Hour strikes of the twenties and thirties.

In the items displayed, in the descriptions accompanying them, in the distribution of medals, and in the *Address* delivered, the exhibition of 1856 marks a further stage on the trajectory we have been tracing. Artisanal values give way still more to the ascending ideology of industrialism. Once again the organizers narrow the criteria by which medals are to be awarded: "A gold medal . . . will be awarded only for very valuable and meritorious inventions or improvements. A silver medal, for articles of superior workmanship, new applications of material and improvements in construction." Perhaps to placate the many exhibitors whose work would be excluded by such standards, the organizers introduce a third medal, of bronze, "for articles of superior workmanship, but of less importance or utility."[12]

Reverend F. D. Huntington's *Address* at the 1856 exhibition carries the suggestive title "Hands: Brain: Heart" and develops still further the argument against the body and its skills while at the same time registering some appreciation for the very qualities it seeks to devalue. Huntington begins by asserting that the Hand, the Brain, and the Heart are the "chief elements" of the mechanician's "strength." (Note how the word "mechanic*ian*" begins to substitute for "mechanic.") Of these, "Brain and Heart are separate centres of vital systems; co-ordinate economies of the corporeal state; . . ." The hand, however, plays a subordinate role: it is "their common agent—their steward, secretary, marshal, factor, finisher" (pp. 6–7). Huntington then embarks on a panegyric of praise for the hand, but his terms are careful all the while to keep the hand in its place. That place is, of course, the body. Huntington emphasizes that the hand is deeply rooted in the body. It "begins at the roots of life. It is articulated from the clavicle of the chest" and "grows out of the midst of the man." At the same time, however, Huntington's rhetoric colonizes the hand for the industrial order by envisioning it as a kind of machine. "And when we come to the structure [of the hand] itself, with its frame-work of twenty-nine bones, its hinges and pulleys, its grooves and cords, its levers and screws of unequal lengths, its telegraph and tubes, its solids and liquids, . . . we find it the marvelous medium of man's physical commerce with the world" (p. 7). Huntington's tropes suggest that when labor-saving machines supplant the hand, machines will be supplanting other machines, not something essentially and valuably human.

Like Everett, however, Huntington cannot help paying tribute to the body. "It will be found," he acknowledges (with a sigh) "that the Hand can never be entirely displaced. Things will remain to be done by it that nothing else can do." The hand, for Huntington, is "the primal and archetypal tool." Indeed, "for complexity, for adaptation, for strength, for endurance, for delicacy, for noiseless play," it is "unrivalled and inimitable." Huntington goes beyond Everett in the self-consciousness with which he bestows this praise. Because the hand will always have its place, there is a need "not only of a sentimental recognition of its dignity, but of a muscular practice in its discipline." Huntington sounds almost Whitmanesque in his praise of sweat as the "cement that binds the social welfare":

> Christianity and republicanism together have not yet thoroughly killed out the old fallacy about manual labor, and the false shame of a brown skin. In the broad philosophy which is yet to interpret our life, every faculty and limb will be seen to be ennobled by its service. . . . It is good, amidst the fashionable fastidiousness and daintiness of our modern customs, when so many nice young men dodge behind a dry goods counter, or into the dull decencies of a profession, . . . to let some masculine calling stand forth as a witness of the wholesome law that by the literal sweat of the brow the best of men shall eat their bread; that sweat which moistens the cement that binds the social welfare together. (pp. 9–10)

But if Huntington goes beyond Everett in acknowledging the necessity of giving the Hand its due, he surpasses him also in the effort to enlist the mechanic in the new ideology. For by 1856, the tension between traditional artisanry and the new mechanism could no longer be ignored. Huntington admits that "every display like that in yonder halls" makes plain that "Hands and machines come into competition. The contrivance that does the work of a hundred hands threatens to leave the hands idle, and the mouths that match them empty" (p. 11). But Huntington invokes this "solemn social question" only to dismiss it. Only the prejudiced and irrational "timid temper" of antiprogressivism, he argues, would think of opposing the machine. After all, the machine is not really in competition with the hand. On the contrary, "the final cause of all labor-saving contrivances is to increase labor." It is the duty of mechanics like those in his audience "to come in as vindicator and interpreter, in this insane insurrection of the Hands against machines; to justify all manner of intellectual originality; to demonstrate the absolute justice of industrial laws" (p. 13). As I have suggested, Huntington can advance the argument that "labor is not finally saved, but multiplies itself, by and in the machine" only if he assumes that "labor" is an empty abstraction. To "save" or "multiply" labor makes sense only when labor has been emptied of all intrinsic meaning and reduced to mere purposeful activity.

It is hardly necessary to describe the subsequent stages of Huntington's argument—how he claims that "The hands administer; the head legislates. The hands perform; the head organizes. The hands execute; but it is the head still that originates, or invents" (p. 15). This Tayloresque separation of conception from execution has its long foreground in three decades of a rhetoric that seeks to devalue the body and its knowledge of "things." We have seen how the strategic center of this program was a subtle emptying out and then filling up of the term "mechanic." Mechanics in general were praised for their contribution to civilization; that contribution was described as essentially mental, as the exercise of the mind's control over matter; the supreme mechanic became, therefore, the inventor or "mechanician" whose work is to create machines that supplant the manual work of all other mechanics. The husk of manual labor is left behind to wither away.

Antebellum mechanics who welcomed the first two stages of this argument as long-overdue recognition of their work and of its mentality found themselves confronted by the iron logic of the third. The only way out of this trap would have been to oppose the second stage and to have argued that manual labor does not derive its essential value from its mental characteristics. But, with the language then available, this response was almost impossible to make. Manual labor does not lend itself to a defense couched in abstract terms. It goes about its business until that business is taken away. The only response the dissenting artisans of the MCMA could make was to withdraw from the exhibition altogether; few were willing to join the carpenters and masons in doing so.

2

Eros and Labor

3

The Erotics of
Labor in Melville's
Redburn

How did antebellum writers position themselves in this contest over the meanings and values of mental and manual labor? The answer, as we shall see, is complex. On the one hand, while the project of creating a "poetry for the people" and of representing manual labor was frequently celebrated in the antebellum period, it was seldom undertaken systematically and with full appreciation of its difficulties. A pattern of evasions and oversimplifications ensues, suggesting that many writers and artists contributed to the new industrial ideology even when they seemed eager to resist it. For example, in a notebook entry that recalls Emerson's rhetoric in "The American Scholar," the painter William Sidney Mount wrote that "A painter's studio is everywhere; wherever he finds a scene for a picture in doors or out. The blacksmith's shop. The shoemaker's—The Tailors—the Church—the tavern—or Hotel, the Marker—and into the dens of poverty and dissipation, high life and low life."[1] But Mount himself left no representations of "low life," much less of "dens of poverty and dissipation." His genre paintings often do take laborers as their subject, but their aim is to celebrate and romanticize labor, to soften its contours and affirm its place within the still unbroken fabric of the mythic American pastoral landscape. *Farmers Nooning* (1836), for example, depicts a circle of farmhands resting from their labors in the shade of a tree. The figures relax in different postures, they gaze in different directions, they are of different ages and even races, but they are powerfully joined by a sense of fellowship in labor and communion in nature. One leans against the tree, another sprawls in the sun, a third lolls on his belly and embraces a tuft of the hay which

61

surrounds them. No break divides the natural world from their work in it; their bucket, scythes, rakes, and haystacks all fit easily into, and in fact adorn, the landscape. These men are happy. They share a moment of eroticized leisure contiguous with and perfectly in harmony with their work—and they share it not just with each other, but with the at least temporarily leisured individual who is gazing into the painting itself.

Fourteen years later in France, Gustave Courbet began painting the *Stonebreakers*, a very different image of manual labor. Compared to that of *Farmers Nooning*, its composition is linear, not circular; two workers are fixed in a line that moves from left to right across the canvas. Perhaps because they occupy so much of the vertical and horizontal space of the painting, these laborers (a man and his young assistant) seem cut off and isolated from the rest of the world; their postures—the man kneeling with his back to the boy, the boy rooted in place by the heavy basket of stones he holds—also isolate them from one another. Bowed beneath the weight of their labor, beneath the heat of the sun they have worked under all day (as the lengthening shadows tell us), these figures are turned away from us, showing us mainly their shoulders and feet, the bulky muscle of their bodies; the activity in the painting is pure work and it shares nothing with the activity of the spectator who gazes at it. The moral of the painting, as Courbet explained, is simple: *"dans cet état, c'est ainsi qu'on commence, c'est ainsi qu'on finit."*[2]

The "achievement here," one art historian has observed, "is that Courbet gets the moral down in paint, and does not lean on anecdote or pathos. . . . There are plenty of pictures of worship, anguish, states of mind; but, for many reasons, there are few images of work. It is too obvious and obdurate for form: painters avoid it."[3] So, for slightly different reasons, do most writers of fiction. Work appears to be fundamentally antithetical to any art form the main purpose of which is to entertain, since the very aim of entertainment is to put work behind us, to open up and enrich the space provided by leisure. Work is difficult to represent also because it is by nature repetitious, not dramatic; it is difficult to include in narrative because it is a subordination to, not a mastery of, time. The great temptation always is to treat work as an "anecdote," thereby tearing it from its context of endless repetition. Finally, as we have already seen, manual labor in particular seems to resist written representation precisely to the degree that writing is conceived of as mental labor.

Nevertheless, Herman Melville sets his fourth book, *Redburn* (1849), squarely in the domain of manual labor and resolutely explores the relation between that labor and his own labor as a writer. *Redburn,* in fact, tells two distinct, but closely interwoven, stories about work.[4] The first, which covers the hero Wellingborough Redburn's voyage from New York to Liverpool, tells how the self-styled "son of a gentleman" is fashioned by hard manual labor into a wiser and tougher young man. The voyage out promises, moreover, to allow the young protagonist to achieve the sexual identity so often associated with physical labor—Emerson's "manly innocency," Greeley's "manly independence," Huntington's "masculine calling," and so on. The second, at play within the first and then dominant during the voyage home to New York, tells how this young man, who is later to write *Redburn,* discovers his vocation as a writer and comes to a fuller understanding of what literary labor actually means. The first story seems to conform to a Franklinesque notion of work as self-fashioning; the second, often ironically undercutting the first, tells how a writer discovers his proper work mainly by becoming aware of the intrinsic unreliability of language and of the extrinsic social limitations on truthful representation. Perhaps most crucially, he comes to feel that an eroticized and at times feminized free-play of the imagination is at once essential to his identity as an artist and incompatible with the disciplined work, and in his view, degraded erotic life of the common sailor. When Melville explores what I have called the "interior" values of manual labor, he finds a repression of libido that is at least as severe as that associated with enfeebling mental labor. Indeed, because he locates so much promise in the life and work of the ordinary seaman, Melville's disappointment is especially keen. In a sense, the novel seems at first to promise an optimistic double bildungsroman in which hard manual labor serves to create an authorial identity that will in turn respect and accurately represent such labor. What it delivers instead is a bleak vision of manual and literary labor as fundamentally incompatible, and of generic and marketplace constraints making honest representation of manual labor impossible. In *Redburn,* Mount's cheerful vision of the artist taking his place in a circle of harmonious, erotic, and democratized labor gives way to Courbet's vision of labor's isolation, silence, tedium, and pain.

*

Wellingborough Redburn goes to sea because his father has gone bankrupt, died, and left the family impoverished. The son of a gentleman and the great grandson of a Revolutionary War hero, Wellingborough cannot rely on this inherited identity to sustain him in the bustling world of Jacksonian America, on what Hawthorne in *The House of the*

Seven Gables calls "the fluctuating waves of our social life."[5] Amid distinctly Miltonic echoes ("the world was before me"[6]), Wellingborough goes forth to toil in the sweat of his brow and to achieve a new identity through hard physical labor.

But Melville quickly makes clear that Wellingborough's quest for identity will not be a simple forerunner of the Horatio Algeresque tale of struggle and success. As Wellingborough's ship, the *Highlander,* passes through the "Narrows" of a symbolic rebirth into the open ocean, he recalls a ramble through the Staten Island fort taken years ago with his father and uncle. It was, his description suggests, a birth, or initiation, of a quite different kind: "going in, you groped about in long vaults, twisting and turning on every side, till at last you caught a peep of green grass and sunlight, and all at once came out in an open space in the middle of the castle." Accompanied by his father and uncle, two figures of patriarchal authority and guidance, he emerges from this underworld into a paradise of green and quiet and sunlight, where the sky looks down upon him, "blue as my mother's eye." He stands at the very center of things, the *omphalos,* in the middle of the year ("June") and the middle of the day ("noon-day.") The moment reverberates in memory with an extraordinary but unrevealed importance. Then, abruptly, Wellingborough represses it. "But I must not think of those delightful days before my father became a bankrupt, and died." The security of a stable, static world presided over by a strong father and beneficent mother must give way to the hard work required by the realm of necessity: "I caught sight of that beautiful fort on the cliff, and could not help contrasting my situation now, with what it had been . . . Then I never thought of working for a living, and never knew that there were hard hearts in the world" (pp. 35–36). As the novel will make clearer, the Franklinesque achievement of a new identity through work seems to require, among its other costs, that Wellingborough "not think" of this childhood paradise where his imagination had free play under the loving "eye" of his mother. The world of physical labor is wholly and harshly masculine.

Wellingborough's voyage is an initiation, of course, and specifically it is an initiation into manual work. He is ordered to clean out the pigpen, coat the mast with "slop," scrub the decks, and perform sundry other menial tasks. He quickly realizes that in order to become a sailor, he must learn a new language and a new code of behavior. This means forsaking his "pledge of abstinence" and learning to like rum. It means understanding that conventions he has always taken for granted are no longer valid: the man in the scruffy peajacket is a mate who must be addressed as "sir"; the sailors who lounge about "with lordly indifference" do so because they are the best sailors and know their own value to the captain.

By emphasizing that Wellingborough's initiation into manual labor is also an initiation into a new set of conventions—and into the eventual realization also that *all* social standards are conventional, not natural—Melville makes clear that Wellingborough's education is also a literary education. His schooling as a sailor serves also to educate the future writer, the man who will one day write *Redburn*. This doubleness of his education is repeatedly insisted upon. For example, when Wellingborough meets a Greenlander among the crew, he discovers that the books he has read prevent him from believing that this man, so physically real and present to him, could actually have come from Greenland. "I had seen mention made of such things before, in books of voyages; but that was only reading about them, just as you read the Arabian Nights, which no one ever believes" (p. 41). The Greenlander simply *cannot* be real since he comes from Greenland, the realm of fantasy, of books.

This complicated relation between literature and life becomes ever more apparent and humorous. At the start of his voyage, Wellingborough attempts to understand his shipmates in the terms offered by his earlier reading. Because "a magazine, called the Sailors' Magazine," had represented them as "pious seamen who never swore, and paid over all their wages to the poor heathen in India," he naively regards the *Highlander*'s crew as "men of naturally gentle and kind dispositions," as "strayed lambs from the fold, . . . poor lost children, babes in the woods" (p. 47). Melville's aim here is not just to satirize: by undercutting these conventional representations of sailors, and Wellingborough's soon-to-be-dispelled faith in them, Melville makes way for the more difficult and distanced representation he, or rather his character/author Redburn, desires to provide. At the same time, however, Melville also begins to dispel the reformist fantasy that these sailors can ever be "elevated" and brought into the fold of genteel, middle-class culture. They stand on their own side of what Melville in *White-Jacket* calls "the spiked barriers" of rank.[7] As a young man who is becoming not just a sailor, but a writer, Wellingborough is beginning to understand that he can never become their comrade, that he will always remain "apart, though among them." His art, and their work, are fundamentally incompatible.

Wellingborough's understanding of the complexity of social representations and of the power of the class that names is deepened by his encounter with the sailor Jackson. Like Therien in *Walden* and the ship's carpenter in *Moby-Dick*, Jackson is an incarnation of the enigmatic—and now angry—otherness of the manual laborer. He epitomizes all that middle-class culture cannot understand and therefore dreads in the "mass," and his role in Wellingborough's education is to bring him to the brink of this knowledge. (It is crucial to Melville's narrative strategy that Wellingborough is never shown stepping over that brink, whereas the narrating voice of *Redburn* suggests that its author has.) The crux of Jackson's mysteriousness is also the source of his anger and of his power over the other members of the crew. Like Bartleby at the end of Melville's "tale of Wall Street," Jackson *knows* something:

> it was quite plain that he was by nature a marvelously clever, cunning man, though without education; and understood human nature to a kink, and well knew whom he had to deal with; and then, one glance of his squinting eye was as good as a knock-down, for it was the most deep, subtle, infernal-looking eye that I ever saw lodged in a human head. (p. 57)

What is this knowledge which Jackson possesses? He is "full of hatred and gall against every thing and every body in the world, as if all the world was one person, and had done him some dreadful harm." That hatred finds articulation, finally, when the sailor Blunt piously avers that "'all sailors are saved; they have plenty of squalls here below, but fair weather aloft.'" Jackson explodes:

> "And did you get that out of your silly Dream Book, you Greek? . . . Don't talk of heaven to me—it's a lie—I know it—and they are all fools that believe in it. Do you think, you Greek, that there's any heaven for *you?* Will they let *you* in there, with that tarry hand, and that oily head of hair?" (p. 104)

Jackson's knowledge, his "inscrutable curse," is class consciousness. It renders him an enemy of society and an isolato among the crew. The "dreadful harm" the world has done has been to consign him, despite his manifest cleverness, to the lowest rank of the social order. There his pride disdains to accept such charity as would have been bestowed by the Sailors' Magazine or by the Reverend William Ellery Channing's call for "elevation" and "amelioration."[8] Instead, he embraces his fate and sinks himself in what the middle class considers "wickedness" and "vice." If his work is brutish by their standards, then he will be a brute, an animal—a man with the eye of a "wolf, or starved tiger," "so cold, and snaky" and inhuman that he can only "howl," "shriek," and "rage" with a "fine white foam" on his lips. Karl Marx, writing just a few years earlier, had described this condition as one of "alienated labor," in which the worker "feels that he is acting freely only in his animal functions—eating, drinking, procreating, or at most in his shelter and finery—while in his human functions he feels only like an animal. The animalistic becomes the human and the human becomes the animalistic."[9] The obverse of the pale-eyed Bartleby, who could at least say "I would prefer not to," and, more damningly, "I know you" to his employer, snake-eyed Jackson cannot, or will not, speak his knowledge. Instead he rages, coughs, and finally dies "like a dog" (pp. 57–62).

Jackson is not the only victim who is rendered speechless by the social order. After Wellingborough has arrived in Liverpool, a walk through town one day takes him past a narrow street called Launcelott's Hey. There he hears a feeble wail "which seemed to come out of the earth. . . . It seemed the low, hopeless, endless wail of someone forever lost." In a ruined basement fifteen feet below street level, "crouching in a nameless squalor," is "the figure of what had been a woman" clutching two children and a baby. They are all dying of starvation. Their humanity stripped away, they have become mere "figures"; their plight is "nameless" precisely because the social order strives to keep it invisible, illegible. It has taken away their speech and virtually all their powers of communication. "They made no sign; they did not move or stir; but from the vault came that soul-sickening wail" (p. 180).

Thus, Wellingborough gradually learns the hard fact that the work men and women perform consigns them to a particular class. "There are classes of men in the world, who bear the same relation to society at large, that the wheels do to a coach." Such men "by their very vocation," that is, by their work, are "shunned by the better classes of people and cut off from all access to respectable and improving society." *Respectable and improving society* indeed. Wellingborough's irony is a forced expression of his pessimism. Jackson, his shipmates, and the poor of Liverpool are doomed to their condition because the social order is by nature hierarchical and all hierarchies must rest upon a bottom. However "indispensable" such laborers are, "No contrivance can lift them from the mire; for upon something the coach must be bottomed; on something the insiders must roll" (p. 139). When Redburn attempts, unsuccessfully, to help the starving woman in Lancelott's Hey, he is told to mind his own "business."

Yet the thrust of Redburn's double education into both manual and literary labor has been to regard the act of supplying speech to these victims as precisely his business—and a hopeless business it is, thanks to the doubled forces of property and "propriety." Strolling through town on another afternoon, he comes upon a Chartist radical giving a speech to a crowd of mechanics and artisans and he responds with a confused mix of identification and repugnance. The man's "features were good," his "whole air respectable," and he seems to Redburn to be "some despairing older son, supporting by hard toil his mother and sisters; for of such

many political desperadoes are made." He is, in short, the double of
Redburn himself, who has gone to sea to help his own mother and sisters. At the same time, the Chartist as a "political desperado" is also akin
to that "horrid desperado" of the fo'c'sle, Jackson. Their resemblance
makes clearer why Redburn has fears he himself might become a
"fiend," "something like Jackson." The awareness that class distinctions
arise out of and reaffirm the division of labor creates anger; this anger is
futile; the futility degrades and corrupts. As angry as Jackson, the Chartist speaks "with nervous appeals to his listeners," "with a rolling of eyes
and sometimes with the most frantic of gestures." Worst of all, perhaps,
his loss of respectability and self-possession is meaningless. He has no
impact. The moment he sparks the crowd's "perfect decorum and silence" into "some commotion," the police move into action, gliding
through the crowd and "politely hinting at the propriety of dispersing"
(pp. 205–6). One senses Redburn asking himself if the demeaning, self-
sacrificing, and impotent labor of the Chartist is a chilling adumbration
of the literary labor he will perform himself as a result of his experience
as a common seaman.

Shortly after *Redburn* was published, Melville wrote to his father-in-
law Lemuel Shaw that "They [*Redburn* and *White-Jacket*] are two *jobs,*
which I have done for money—being forced to it, as other men are to
sawing wood." Melville does not use this trope to ennoble literary labor; on the contrary, his intention is to emphasize his powerlessness as
a writer and, specifically, as a wage-earner in the literary marketplace.
The powerlessness has consequences: "And while I have felt obliged to
refrain from writing the kind of book I would wish to; yet, in writing
these two books, I have not repressed myself much—so far as *they* are
concerned; but have spoken pretty much as I feel."[10] In a letter written
two months later to Evert Duyckinck, Melville is more bitter:

> But I hope I shall never write such a book again. . . . What a beggarly
> 'Redburn!' And when he [an author] attempts anything higher—God
> help him & save him! . . . What madness and anguish it is, that an author
> can never—under no conceivable circumstances—be at all frank with his
> readers.[11]

As Melville sees it, an author's relation to his audience cannot be established on a basis of mutual trust, respect, and affection. On the contrary,
it is characterized by cleverness, cunning, "madness," and "anguish,"
and it requires a considerable degree of self-repression. This repression
is of a double sort. The demands of the marketplace require an author
to submit to certain middle-class standards of "propriety." At the same
time, the more his work approaches the quality of hard manual labor,

like "sawing wood" or working as a seaman, the more it entails another sort of repression—the abrupt repression of imagination and memory Wellingborough experienced as the *Highlander* sailed through the Narrows into the world of "working for a living." For Melville, as the second half of *Redburn* makes clear, the most fundamental problem of manual labor, and of "forced" literary labor, and perhaps to some degree of all conceivable labor, is that it entails repression of, or degradation of, the erotic life of the worker.

*

In Hawthorne's *The Blithedale Romance,* Miles Coverdale tries to explain, as "modestly" as possible, "several points of Fourier's system" to Hollingsworth. Teasingly, he asks "Hollingsworth's opinion as to the expediency of introducing these beautiful peculiarities into our own practice" at Blithedale. The puritanical reformer's response is explosive. In his view, Fourier has committed the "Unpardonable Sin" of choosing the "blackness of man's heart, the portion of ourselves which we shudder at, and which it is the whole aim of spiritual discipline to eradicate" as "the master-workman of his system."

> To seize upon and foster whatever vile, petty, sordid, filthy, bestial, and abominable corruptions have cankered into our nature, to be the efficient instruments of his infernal regeneration. And his consummated Paradise, as he pictures it, would be worthy of the agency which he counts upon for establishing it. The nauseous villain.[12]

The "portion of ourselves" Hollingsworth refers to with such loathing is what Fourier called man's "passional" nature, his instinctual sexual desires (what Freud later designates as "libido" and "eros.") Fourier (known to antebellum Americans principally through the writings of Albert Brisbane) had argued that work was a "torment" to man because it repressed these passions and that from this repression arose all individual psychological ills. "Every passion that is suffocated produces a counterpassion, which is as malignant as the natural passion would have been benign."[13] Fourier's aim, therefore, was to create a system of "attractive industry" that allowed each individual to perform the kinds of work he or she found personally desirable. Attractive labor would express, rather than repress, the passions. Fourier's program infuriated those middle-class reformers who valued work precisely because it could control the intemperate passions—especially the passions of the lower classes. "Thousands upon thousands are indebted to useful work," writes Timothy Shay Arthur in *Ten Nights in a Bar-Room,* "occupying many hours through each day, and leaving them with wearied bodies at night, for their safe passage from yielding youth to firm, resisting manhood."[14]

Fourier's solution might have struck people like Hollingsworth as "the Unpardonable Sin," but it appealed strongly to a number of middle-class reformers because it was able to identify and diagnose an experienced problem of work: work seemed to entail, or require, systematic repression of one's passional, sensual nature. But here a characteristic doubleness of purpose must be noted. The middle-class reformers who were drawn to Fourierism had two motives: while they most explicitly aimed to rectify the social evils of the division of labor by distributing more fairly the burden of physical labor, they also sought to palliate the psychological problems they experienced and which they associated with the mental labor performed by the learned classes.[15] Fourier's ideas appealed because they solved two problems at once: the brutifying toil of the common laborer *and* what Emerson called the "enervated and sickly habits" of the professional class.

This confluence of concerns explains why even Emerson was for a short time drawn to "The Doctrine of the Hands" (the title of an 1837 lecture). Emerson was keenly, almost morbidly, attentive to the ebb and flow of his creative energies. Like most men of his age, he subscribed to a model of psychic economy in which the quantity of energy available to the individual was limited; expenditure in one area meant depletion in another.[16] Hence it became necessary for the man who wished to work productively to conserve and husband his strength and to deploy it only in the narrow channels of his work: "the one prudence in life is concentration; the one evil is dissipation. . . . Everything is good which takes away one plaything and delusion more and drives us home to add one more stroke of useful work."[17] Such declarations and admonitions occur frequently in Emerson's journals and essays. "He who would help himself and others should not be a subject of irregular and interrupted impulses of virtue, but a continent, persisting, immovable person."[18] However, in Emerson's view the problem with this scheme's emphasis on "prudence," "concentration," and "continence," is that it amounts to systematic repression of desire, and, for the mental laborer, of bodily experience and sensuality. Mental laborers, especially writers, become "enervated" and "sickly": "I doubt not that the faults and vices of our literature and philosophy, their too great fineness, effeminacy, and melancholy, are attributable to the enervated and sickly habits of the literary class."[19] Hence, for Emerson (and for Theodore Weld, Horace Greeley, and others who wrote about professional, nonmanual work), the attractiveness of manual labor: "We must have a basis for our higher accomplishments, our delicate entertainments of poetry and philosophy, in the work of our hands."[20] Those who work with their hands and bodies do not seem to require a strict enforcement of psychic economy. Their "animal spirits" remain robust and innocent precisely because they do not have to police themselves. As we have seen, Emerson celebrates the "manly innocency" that "shows in the face, form, and whole deportment" of his (idealized) manual laborer.[21]

Thus, Emerson's concerns about work are remarkably similar to Fourier's: both pursue a fantasy of work that does not require repression of man's passional, sensual nature, that does not require careful concentration and husbanding of limited quantities of psychic energy. But for Emerson, manual labor itself does fully satisfy the needs of the literary man; the "union" of mental and manual labor proposed by Ripley is, finally, unacceptable. Although he admits that a few hours in the garden with his spade offers "exhilaration and health," he decides that for the literary mind anything more than "moderate and dainty exercise" "indisposes and disqualifies for intellectual exertion."[22] Emerson feels compelled to provide his own remedy to the apparent conflict between work (especially mental work) and desire. Like Fourier, he is a psychological determinist, believing that each person has a singular "faculty," or "talent," (the terms he substitutes for Fourier's "passions") which demands an appropriate mode of self-expression and fulfillment. Thus, his critique of "our daily employments" is that they are often "unworthy of the faculties we spend on them."[23] Similarly, the alienated young men with whom he sympathizes in "The Transcendentalist" "feel the disproportion between their faculties and the work offered them."[24] The trick is to find the work that is "worthy of" or proportioned to one's faculties, and this can be achieved only by discovering one's "talent." Indeed, borrowing from Carlyle, he offers the possibility of a man finding work so appropriate to his faculties that he becomes able to spend himself unstintingly.

> The talent is the call. There is one direction in which all space is open to him. He has faculties inviting him thither to endless exertion. He is like a ship in a river; he runs against obstructions on every side but one; on that side all obstruction is taken away, and he sweeps serenely over a deepening channel into an infinite sea.[25]

The discovery of talent obviates the need for self-control, for vigilant avoidance of "playthings" and "delusions." Now there is no fear of "dissipation" and hence no need of "concentration." Talent removes "all obstruction" and gives a person access to unlimited energy, which he can spend on "endless exertion." In particular, the erotic needs which offered themselves as a constant, dangerous, and unlawful temptation have now been channeled into and subordinated to "the useful work" he feels obliged to perform.

Melville is as sensitive as Emerson to the sacrifice of desire, or eros, that appears to be demanded by work. But, characteristically, he is less sanguine about solutions to the problem. "Bartleby," for example, is fundamentally a dramatization of an ontological opposition between Bartleby's wants (preferences) and his work's imperatives. To the demands of his employer, however "reasonable," Bartleby replies "I would prefer not to."[26] In so doing, he gives voice to the negative which the work ethic strives unceasingly to suppress: many men and women prefer not to work. Of course, most are forced to it, and most make their necessary compromises and take their inevitable punishments. Bartleby's fellow employees bend to their toil and take its pain upon, and into, their bodies. Turkey is an alcoholic whose "face blazed with augmented blazonry" after his midday drinking bout and whose work becomes "strange, inflamed, flurried," and reckless (p. 16). Nippers is a clever fellow, impatient with the drudge "duties of a mere copyist"; when he represses his frustrated ambitions for more rewarding work, they make him (and specifically his body) their victim. He suffers from "indigestion" and "nervous testiness" and can never be comfortable at his work table. "He put chips under it, blocks of various sorts, bits of pasteboard, and at last went so far as to attempt an exquisite adjustment by final pieces of folded blotting-paper. But no invention would answer" (pp. 16–17). The clerks seek to recuperate their losses, however, by small and significant acts of resistance. Turkey blots his copies in the afternoon, Nippers hisses "maledictions" and involves himself in "ward-politics." Even Bartleby's employer admits that he does not like to work very hard. Only Bartleby, however, is willing to carry the logic of resistance to its absolute, and absurd, conclusion—death.

But as Bartleby's last words ("I know you") to his employer suggest, death is perhaps less the fate of resistance to than a consequence of the functioning of the social division of labor. Although all work can be regarded as undesirable, some kinds of work—the "shit work"—are certainly more unpleasant than others. A good man at heart, Bartleby's employer has no choice but to exploit his employees if he is to avoid performing their drudge work of copying himself. His narrative makes clear what he does not permit himself to see: their work is slowly, and literally, killing them.

The deathly consequences of work's unremittent hostility to desire, and of the division of labor in particular, are nowhere more painfully represented than in Melville's "The Paradise of Bachelors, The Tartarus of Maids." The story is a grotesque elaboration of Parker's trope of "hands" and "mouths" in "Thoughts on Labor":

> this class of mouths, forgetting how hard it is to work, and not having their desires for the result of labor checked by the sweat necessary to satisfy them, but living vicariously by other men's hands, refuse to be content with the simple gratification of their natural desires. . . . Fancy must be appeased; peevishness must be quieted; and so a world of work is needed to bear the burthens which those men bind, and lay on men's shoulders, but will not lift with one of their fingers. The class of Mouths thus commits a sin, which the class of Hands must expiate.[27]

On the one hand, the lawyers of the Inns of Court appear to perform no work at all; a "class of Mouths," they do nothing but eat, and they eat not to quiet hunger but to stimulate and satisfy what Parker would have considered most "unnatural" desires. Although they are the narrator's "hosts," they are in fact parasites themselves, living off the labor, and the bodies, of others. These "others" are specified as the maids of a Berkshire paper mill, young women who sacrifice both their desires and their bodies to the insatiable appetite of the factory machine and, less visibly, to the insatiable appetite of the "class of Mouths." One has a "pallid cheek," another a "wrinkled brow," all breathe "poisonous particles" of rag, and all sacrifice the generative powers of their bodies (all are virgin "maids") to the monstrous phallus ("a vertical thing like a piston, periodically rising and falling") and spermatic power ("two great round vats . . . full of a white, wet, wooly-looking stuff, not unlike the albuminous part of an egg, soft-boiled") of the factory (pp. 328–31). Human, and specifically female, sexuality has had to make way for the enormous productivity of the machine.

In both stories, as a number of critics have pointed out, Melville is at pains to indicate that the work of writing is in some way a party to this division of labor.[28] Because the mill girls are producing paper "destined to be scribbled on," scribblers of all sorts, from lawyers to novelists, are implicated in their exploitation. Bartleby is one such scribbler, but he shares the mill girls' victimized status because he does not actually write but merely copies what his employer has written. Like Nippers, he may not write. But in both stories, the self-controlled, autonomous work of writing—which Marx would call work before it is alienated from the worker—remains out of sight. It is invisible because it has become a privilege that requires the exploitation of others. Both stories suggest that writing takes place in a realm that is independent of, though covertly dependent on, the manual labor of others—copyists on Wall Street, mill hands in a factory. Both stories suggest that for desire to flourish in one realm (the lawyer's "snug business among rich men's bonds and mortgages and title-deeds" (p. 14), the bachelors' "honey-comb" of "snug cells" (p. 319), it must be sacrificed in another. But Melville's attitude toward the conditions he represents is marked by res-ignation rather than revolutionary passion, by a quiet despair rather than a desire to reform. In particular, "Paradise/Tartarus" suggests that culture (in the narrower sense of the word) is necessarily a "luxury" and that there is no essential difference between a taste for literature and a taste for fine wines. Both come into being and thrive only within an en-closed, protected space of privilege. The writer can indicate, but not evade, these facts.

Read either as fiction or as autobiography, *Redburn* offers a narrative of the genesis of this pessimism. The novel is unsparingly grim in its de-piction of the way disciplined labor appears to destroy or degrade the erotic life of those who perform it. Wellingborough's gradual mastery of seamanship never allows him to affiliate or fraternize with the crew. He never becomes their Whitmanesque "camarado." They spurn him and, despite his criticism of prevalent social attitudes toward sailors, Redburn cannot quite shake his own disgust for them. He continues to be repelled, in particular, by what he regards as their perverted and de-graded eroticism. When on shore, his mates betake themselves to the "reeking, Sodom-like, and murderous" houses of Liverpool's Booble-Alleys. There they find syphilitic prostitutes ("infected gorgons and hy-dras") willing to perform unspeakably decadent sexual favors. Redburn is horrified, or at least claims to be: "Propriety forbids that I should en-ter into details; but kidnappers, burkers, and resurrectionists are almost saints and angels to them" (p. 191).

Certainly one of Melville's aims here is to titillate his middle-class readers with a glimpse of the dark side of working-class life à la Eugene Sue's *The Mysteries of Paris* and its innumerable imitations. But, as a pas-sage from Melville's next book, *White-Jacket,* suggests, his rhetoric's fury is excessive for this purpose. Metaphorically depicting the man-of-war as a kind of factory, Melville writes that:

> The whole body of this system [of the division of labor and authority] is emphatically a system of cruel cogs and wheels, systematically grinding up in one common hopper all that might minister to the moral well-being of the crew. . . . What too many seamen are when ashore is very well known; but what some of them become when completely cut off from shore in-dulgences can hardly be imagined by landsmen. The sins for which the cities of the plain were overthrown still linger in some of these wooden-walled Gomorrahs of the deep. . . . There are evils in men-of-war, which,

like the suppressed domestic drama of Horace Walpole, will neither bear representing, nor reading, and will hardly bear thinking of.[29]

In Melville's account, the "body" of human work has been mechanized grotesquely, hardened into "cogs," "wheels," and "iron." This division of labor, enforced by political or military authority, is in turn the cause of sexual practices which are "sins," "evils," and which, like physical labor itself, seem not to "bear representing" or "thinking of." Intentionally or not, Melville brings together here (as later in "Bartleby" and "Paradise/Tartarus") three distinct—but in his imagination inseparable—concerns: the hostility of work to eros, the degradation of eros into corrupt sexual practices ("the sins for which the cities of the plain were overthrown"), and the problem of representing what "propriety forbids." Thus here, as in Melville's letters to Shaw and Duyckinck, work's degradation of eros is linked with social repression of the writer's work of representation. The link is not so much one of cause-and-effect as of analogy. It is not so much that certain kinds of work make eros take unrepresentable form; rather, it is that the writer's self-repression hinted at in "I have not repressed myself much," in "propriety forbids that I should enter into details" and in "will neither bear representing, nor reading, and will hardly bear thinking of " is somehow *analogous* to a repression of erotic desire. The repression of self demanded by writerly work (work which is like a sawyer's) is somehow like the corruption of desire demanded by more disciplined and hierarchically ordered work.[30]

The problematic relation among these three concerns is more fully articulated in the aspect of *Redburn* that has been most puzzling to its critics—Redburn's strange and short friendship with Harry Bolton. On the one hand, Harry is the embodiment of Redburn's desire for an eroticized, masculine friendship in work—the sexualized comradarie celebrated so often by Whitman and in Melville's writings most fully imagined in the sperm-squeezing chapter of *Moby-Dick*. Bolton represents the possibility, or perhaps just the wish, that is also expressed (though more tamely) in Mount's *Farmers Nooning*: the wish that the body of the laboring man might be able to turn from toil to love, and from love back to toil, and in so doing be able to break down the barriers culture has erected between them. He represents the possibility that work might be so constructed as to no longer require the repression and sublimation of erotic energies but so as now to call them forth and flourish with them. On the other hand, Bolton also represents a return of the repressed. He is everything that Redburn has had to deny in himself since the evening the *Highlander* sailed past the fort near the Narrows. Bolton clings to his aristocratic pretensions and upper-class gentility. He appears on deck dressed "in a brocaded dressing-gown, embroidered slippers, and tasseled smoking cap" (p. 253). He shirks the work he should do and proves too cowardly to go aloft. Yet these apparent failings seem to be the inevitable consequence of his preserving an identity that is at once aristocratic, sexual, and artistic. "Charmed with his appearance," Redburn is "all eagerness to enjoy the society of this incontrovertible son of a gentleman" (p. 170)—who represents, of course, "the son of a gentleman" he used to be himself. Bolton's appearance could not contrast more strongly with that of the work-hardened, grizzled shipmates with whom Redburn has shared the fo'c'sle. "His complexion was a mantling brunette, feminine as a girl's; his feet were small; his hands were white; and his eyes were large, black, and womanly; and, poetry aside, his voice was as the sound of a harp" (p. 216). Melville's own pink-and-white rhetoric here does not so much fail, as disdain, to describe. If Bolton's actual features never materialize, it is because he is a fantasy to be invoked, not a person to be reproduced in print.

But is there room for such a fantasy in the world of work aboard the *Highlander*? Can that world make room for the effeminate, the luxurious, the poetic? Even Redburn has doubts about Harry. Though he "cherished toward Harry a heart, loving and true," he cannot suppress suspicions which "made me hold back my whole soul from him; when, in its loneliness, it was yearning to throw itself into the unbounded bosom of some immaculate friend" (p. 223).

Redburn's reservations have their source not just in Harry's apparent unwillingness and inability to join the circle of labor, but also in Harry's so attractive, but also threatening, sexuality. For just as Redburn tries, and fails, to initiate Harry into the *Highlander*'s world of work, so Harry tries, and fails, to introduce Redburn into a sexual underworld of mysterious and forbidden pleasures. Harry conducts Redburn to what might be a gambling den, a homosexual brothel, or both, but what in any case represents a "bower" of aristocratic luxury, a paradisiacal world untouched by the curse of labor. The "thick and elastic Persian carpeting" mimics "pastures of tulips, and roses, and jonquils, like a bower in Babylon." But in this paradise, as in the first, evil is present—or rather, omnipresent in the "oriental ottomans whose cunning warp and woof were wrought into plaited serpents, undulating beneath beds of leaves, from which, here and there, they flashed out sudden splendors of green scales and gold" (p. 230). Terrified and appalled, Redburn intuits that Harry is no more likely than his coarse shipmates to offer him "immaculate" friendship. In "spite of the metropolitan magnificence," Redburn confesses, "I was mysteriously alive to a dreadful feeling, which I had never felt before, except when penetrating into the lowest and most squalid haunts of sailor iniquity in Liverpool . . . ; and I thought to myself that, though gilded and golden, the serpent of vice is a serpent still" (p. 234).

The specific form that eros takes is homosexual love, and it is both threatening and attractive. Melville finds it threatening, apparently, not because it "dissipates" or "spends" vital energies which should be directed toward work (Emerson's fear), but because he cannot entirely evade conventional social attitudes, which regard homosexuality as a "vice." Homosexual love has the special attraction, however, of promising to be compatible and co-extensive with work, especially physical work. Men who work together with and through their bodies seem to stand on the threshold of a marvelous possibility—that they might turn from their work together and, without foundering on the culturally constructed divide that separates work from love, grasp and love one another. Heterosexual love seems not to offer this possibility because the sexual division of labor—a division being established and strongly reinforced during the antebellum decades—cuts one sex at work off from the other. Women work at home, men work outside the home. They cannot love each other in and through their work, but only when the man has left his work behind and reenters the home—the site of woman's work and of woman's prerogatives. (As Irving's "Rip Van Winkle," Poe's "The Black Cat," and Hawthorne's "The Birth-mark" all indicate, the antebellum male psyche finds domesticity inimical to erotic life. The male either runs away from home or avenges himself on his wife. This vengeance, I will argue in a later chapter, is directed specifically against the body of the wife—against woman as a representation of, and invitation to, embodied life and corporeal power, which is finally the power to give birth and to create as nature creates, organically rather than through artifice.) Homosexual love, by contrast, seems to offer at least the possibility of accepting the corporeal power of the masculine body at work and of marrying that power to the desire of the masculine body in love. If so, this may be why the three male antebellum writers who most decisively take work as their subject and ponder its relation to the body and to love were homosexual or at least homoerotic: Thoreau, Melville, Whitman.[31]

What Harry represents to Redburn, then, is a complex set of fantasies which cannot (in Redburn's view) be reconciled or realized. He embodies an erotic, artistic, aristocratic sensibility which Redburn would like to be able to integrate with his newly won identity as a worker among other workers—but who stubbornly refuses to join that world and whom Redburn must therefore abandon. He embodies a sexuality

which, "though gilded and golden," might in essence be as corrupt as
the "the most squalid haunts of sailor iniquity in London" (p. 234).
Most importantly, Bolton suggests that for Melville, the bridge that
might link a fully embodied life of rugged physical labor with a writer's
artistic sensibility is not Ripley's combination of "manual" and "mental," nor Channing's mentalization of the manual, but love—the
"abounding, affectionate, friendly, loving feeling" that the "avocation"
of sperm-squeezing, for one, can "beget."[32] But in *Redburn* (and, I
would argue, in *Moby-Dick* also), that bridge never comes out of the
realm of possibility into the broad light of the everyday. Redburn discovers that he cannot preserve the lower-class self of the manual laborer
which he has constructed through his work as a seaman and at the same
time retain Harry as a friend. Harry will not work. When the *Highlander* arrives in New York, Redburn does what he can for Harry (a
wan, helpless, Bartleby in the making) and then, like Bartleby's employer, abandons him. "At last," he confesses, "I was forced to give him
up" (p. 312).

To make authorial work compatible with manual labor by dissolving
both in an alembic of acceptable desire is the primary aim, and the un-
fulfilled hope, of *Redburn*. On the one hand, Wellingborough has been
initiated into the labor of common men, a form of labor that, however
difficult and dangerous, offers the rewards of embodied labor. Through
such labor, Wellingborough the boy has become Redburn the man; perhaps more importantly, he has become the man who will write *Redburn*. Through such labor, he has discovered the power of his body—its
ability to climb the rigging, to weather storms, to subsist on little food
(none of it appetizing), and so on. These powers are now his own; his
labor has allowed him to claim them. At the same time, as the "son of a
gentleman" who has crossed the "spiked barriers" of class, Wellingborough has enjoyed an experience that promises to illustrate the democratization of culture so frequently (if often glibly) called for in the
1840s. Finally, by conjoining the story of a boy who learns how to work
with the story of a man who learns how (and what) to write, the novel
promises to *enact* such a democratization of literature. But these gifts
and promises are fatally compromised by Wellingborough's other lessons. He learns that the self one makes through hard labor is confined
by society to the lowest rank in the social order. He learns also that the
hierarchical and exploitative work manual laborers are called upon to
perform inhibits intellectual growth; he feels, too, that although such
labor promises a union of labor and love, it is instead conducive to
"vice." Sailors become inhabitants of "wooden-walled Gomorrahs of
the deep," haunters of "pestilent lanes and alleys," not the loving com-

rades of Whitman's poems or Mount's genre paintings. It is this degradation of eros that, more than any other factor, seems to Melville to obtrude between such work and the work of writing. At the same time, Melville seems to associate that twisting, or corruption, of a manly "abounding, affectionate, friendly, loving feeling," with the self-repression he has experienced as an author. If there were no conflict between work and desire; if manual labor did not create Jacksons and Blunts instead of men like Mount's farmers; and if writing did not require an author "to refrain from writing the kind of book [he] would wish to,"— then, and only then, could the writer join hands with the laborer in a circle of fellowship through work. But it has been the effect, if not the aim, of *Redburn* to show that these negatives cannot be undone simply by wishing them away. The thrust of Melville's later writings on work, and on the relation between manual work and writing, will be consistently to affirm the pessimistic conclusions of his fourth novel.

4

Naturalized Labor and Natural History in Thoreau's *A Week on the Concord and Merrimack Rivers*

The mastery of the earth is the chief command and trust which the Almighty has committed to mortals here. It is this command which ennobles labor.... Man was made to be an artificer of matter, to gain control of the planet, and to build up civilization, and enlarge his own intellect and nature by that work . . .
 —Thomas Starr King, "The Earth and the Mechanic Arts" (1877)[1]

[Man] needs not only to be spiritualized, but *naturalized,* on the soil of the earth. . . . We have need to be earth-born as well as heaven-born, γηγενεις, as was said of the Titans of old, or in a better sense than they.
 —H. D. Thoreau, *A Week* (1847)[2]

Work is a central concern of both of the books Henry David Thoreau published in his lifetime, *A Week on the Concord and Merrimack Rivers* and *Walden*.[3] Like Melville, Thoreau experiences work as an activity in which the concerns of politics, ethics, and aesthetics converge. But while Melville, as we have seen, represents the value of work as dependent, finally, on its ability to advance rather than impede the worker's erotic requirements, Thoreau complicates matters by questioning the

80

value of these requirements themselves. Thoreau regards work as an activity that is always already imbued with sexual meaning. The problem
he deals with is not how to fuse, but how to distinguish work and desire.
Thus, unlike Marx, who seems to postulate a preindustrial, precapitalist
unity of work and eros, Thoreau would argue that the "progress" of
civilization has tended increasingly and regrettably to conscript the male
worker not as a being but as a sexual being, not as a person but as a man,
or a male. For Thoreau, the challenge is not so much to eroticize labor
as to purify it of sexual desire. To draw another comparison with Marx:
if history is determined ultimately by control of the means of production, then, Thoreau would argue, one must gain personal control of the
means of reproduction—one must attain what he calls "chastity." His
exploration of the erotics of work discovers the body as a sexual "tool"
and nature as the force that wields it.

In his essay on Carlyle, Thoreau writes: "The before impossible precept, 'know thyself,' he translates into the partially possible one, 'know
what thou canst work at.'"[4] In both his river journey and his pond so-
journ, Thoreau's primary concern is to determine who he is by deter-
mining what he can "work at." This quest is more than a problem of
"vocation" (at least as that term is usually employed), for it does not
end when Thoreau chooses to become a writer. On the contrary, he
must still ask, "What kind of work is writing?" and then, "What is the
nature of work itself?" and then, "To what notion of work shall I commit myself in order to minimize the danger of ever laboring under a
mistake?" Indeed, as I hope to make clear, the intensity of Thoreau's
anxiety to find the right calling shatters the conventional meanings of
work and compels him to construct his own.

In the fall of 1845, Thoreau had been at Walden Pond for three
months and was hard at work on three projects: a book that would
eventually become *A Week on the Concord and Merrimack Rivers;* a lecture on Carlyle, which he would deliver at the Concord Lyceum that
winter; and a manuscript, which, many drafts and nine years later,
would in 1854 be published as *Walden.* As Sherman Paul and others
have argued, these first months at Walden saw Thoreau coming to
terms at long last with his vocation and his identity as a writer.
Thoreau's essay on Carlyle, the first of these projects to be completed
and published, is thus his earliest mature formulation of what he hoped
to do and be as a writer himself.[5]

Thoreau's admiration for Carlyle can be summed up in a single word:
"workman." Carlyle *"works"* at his writing. Thoreau describes Carlyle's
writing as a "craft" (p. 205); his books are "solid and workmanlike" and
they "tell of huge labor done." "They are such works of art only as the

plough, and cornmill, and steam-engine—not as pictures and statues"
(p. 228). "There is no more notable working-man in England,"
Thoreau writes, than this author who "toils" for "wages" (p. 243).
Thoreau's purpose in repeatedly characterizing Carlyle as a "strong and
finished workman in his craft" (p. 225) becomes clear when he writes
that:

> Literature has come to mean, to the ears of laboring men, something idle,
> something cunning and pretty merely, because the nine hundred and
> ninety-nine really write for fame or amusement. But as the laborer works,
> and soberly by the sweat of his brow earns bread for his body, so this man
> *works* anxiously and *sadly,* to get bread of life and dispense it. (pp. 243–
> 44)

With these words, Thoreau enlists himself in the project we have seen
being pursued by a number of New England writers—the project of
producing a literary culture more meaningful to, and representative of,
the working class. In the fall of 1843, an article in the *Democratic Review* called "Poetry for the People" warned against a literature that
merely appropriated the concerns of the working class; without men-
tioning Channing or Emerson by name, the anonymous author specifically criticizes "the doctrine of popular improvement and elevation of
the laboring classes" because it may too easily become "a mere party sig-
nal, a stalking-horse for political hypocrisy, and nothing more." What
the people demand instead is "a new species of poetry, expressly designed to represent their condition and utter their aspirations, and at the
same time to encourage and sustain their endeavors."[6]

It is not known whether Thoreau happened to see this article, but he
characteristically offers a more complex account of the relation between
labor and literature. On the one hand, as we have seen, he implies that
for literature to become respectable to the working-man, not "something cunning and pretty merely," the writer must see himself as a
worker, as one who "*works* anxiously and sadly, to get bread of life, and
dispense it." On the other hand, the writer must resolutely avoid writing for money or the market, "for fame or amusement." He must have
higher ends in view. But aren't these principles at cross purposes?
Should not a writer who wishes to emulate the condition and activity of
laborers take pains to submit, just as they must, to the dictates of the
market?

This problem becomes even more tangled when Thoreau offers his
own account of "the spirit of the age" and of the literature appropriate
to such an age. Again, a comparison with "Poetry for the People" is instructive. Echoing Emerson and Carlyle, the author of the *Democratic*

Review article writes that "the poor man, upright, sincere, earnest, with deep enthusiasm and vigorous self-reliance, he is the hero of our time" (p. 267). Thoreau evidently agrees. "The Man of the Age," he declares, "is the working-man" (p. 251). But whereas the author of "Poetry for the People" tends to emphasize *what* such poetry should be about ("the real happiness of domestic love," "the necessity and dignity of labor," "the brotherhood and equality of men" [pp. 267–68]), Thoreau is much more concerned with *how* such a poet should write:

> but above and after all, the Man of the Age, come to be called working-man, it is obvious that none yet speaks to his condition, for the speaker is not yet in his condition. There is poetry and prophecy to cheer him, and advice of the head and heart to the hands; but no very memorable cooperation, it must be confessed, since the Christian era, or rather since Prometheus tried it. It is a note-worthy fact, that a man addresses effectually in another only himself still, and what he himself does and is, alone can prompt the other to do and become. Like speaks to like only; labor to labor, philosophy to philosophy, criticism to criticism, poetry to poetry, &c. (pp. 251–52)

The challenge facing the writer is to labor, to recover the *poesis* or making in poetizing. It is to place oneself "in" rather than merely to "represent" the "condition" of the working man. What the writer writes *about* is, for Thoreau, less important than where he writes *from*. What is needed, in particular, is "cooperation"; writer and worker must be operatives together. Literature must not merely replicate the division of labor by producing "poetry," "prophecy," and "advice" that descend from the writer (as society's "head and heart") to the worker (society's "hands"). Literature must somehow locate itself *in* the hands. "Labor" must speak to "labor."

But in what sense, if any, might literary labor be manual? This is the question Thoreau will pose and try to answer in the opening pages of *A Week,* and in the Carlyle essay he begins to establish the terms of the problem. In alluding to Prometheus, who stole the crafts of artifice from Hephaestus and distributed them among men, Thoreau invokes a model of physical labor that Hannah Arendt was later to call "work"— the making of "durable" tools and goods, the creation of an imperishable human "world" that stands over against the flux of nature.[7] It is the work epitomized first and foremost by the blacksmith, the archetypal artificer who works the earth's ores into enduring metal tools. (Thoreau is by no means the first or the only writer to figure writing as such work. The author of "Poetry for the People" employs the trope when he writes that the poet's "words should ring in every line like the short,

quick blows on the anvil" [p. 277].) It is precisely as such a worker that
Thoreau repeatedly figures Carlyle. When Carlyle writes, says Thoreau,
"Nature is ransacked, and all the resorts and purlieus of humanity are
taxed, to furnish the fittest symbol for his thought." His language is a
"resistless weapon," and his books "tell of huge labor done, well done,
and all the rubbish swept away, like the bright cutlery in shop-windows,
while the coke and ashes, the turnings, filings, dust, and borings, lie far
away at Birmingham, unheard of" (pp. 227–28). But Thoreau figures
Carlyle as a blacksmith enlarged to the proportions of a factory, and he
offers more than a hint of criticism in these images of "nature ransacked" and of writing as a kind of metallurgy or manufacture. Thoreau
makes his criticism explicit when he complains that "Carlyle has not the
simple Homeric health of Wordsworth" and goes on to observe that:

> The smith, though so brawny and tough, I should not call the healthiest
> man. There is too much shop-work, too great extremes of heat and cold,
> and incessant ten-pound-ten and thrashing of the anvil, in his life. But the
> haymaker's is a true sunny perspiration, produced by the extreme of sum-
> mer heat only, and conversant with the blast of the zephyr, not of the
> forge-bellows. (pp. 248–49)

Thoreau's contrast between smith and haymaker adumbrates his decision in *A Week* to reject artifice as a model for the physical labor of writing and to ally himself ever more strongly with cultivation, or what
Arendt calls "labor." For "labor," as Arendt uses the word, does not
stand in opposition to the earth and its rhythms of life and death. Labor
produces nothing durable, nothing that supplements what is already
given to man by nature. Labor produces only things that will be consumed, and the consumption of these gives man the strength to produce more consumables.[8]

Whereas the artificer is usually figured as one who can "gain control
of the planet," who can "subdue" and "master" nature, the farmer who
labors submits himself to the earth's seasonal rhythms of growth and
decay. Whereas the smith works with his hands to make durable goods
like the "cutlery which glitters in shop windows," the haymaker or
farmer labors only in order to feed his family and livestock. The smith
works to produce what Arendt calls a "world" over and against the
earth, while the farmer labors only to ensure his community's survival
among the other species of the earth. In *A Week* it will become increasingly clear that Thoreau was aware of these dimensions of the contrast
between smith and farmer. Even here he reveals a fragmented awareness—as when, wishing to bestow unqualified praise on Carlyle, he figures him for the first time as a kind of cultivator who "feeds" his readers:

He has plucked the finest fruit in the public garden; . . . His works are not to be studied, but read with a swift satisfaction. Their flavor and gust is what poets tell of the froth of wine, which can only be tasted once and hastily . . . These works were designed for such complete success that they serve but for a single occasion. It is the luxury of art, when its own instrument is manufactured for each particular and present use. The knife which slices the bread of Jove ceases to be a knife when this service is rendered. (pp. 241–42)

This passage catches Thoreau negotiating between both models, between "work" and "labor," between artifice and cultivation, trying still to retain the best of each. What he praises in Carlyle's works is precisely their lack of durability, their ready consumability. They are, he writes, "true natural products in this respect." But as if aware of the contradiction between his figuring Carlyle as a kind of smith or manufacturer and this figuring of him as a farmer or cultivator, Thoreau abruptly shifts back to a notion of art as "manufactured." Once again the image of writing as a knife makes its appearance, but this time the knife is not a durable tool but a self-consuming "instrument." The paradoxical trope of the knife which "ceases to be" as soon as it is used epitomizes the contradiction between Thoreau's desire to see writing as cultivation and his lingering inclination to see it as artifice.

The essay on Carlyle, then, written while Thoreau was also beginning to work on *A Week* and *Walden,* sets forth the problems with which both books will have to come to terms. If literature is not to seem "cunning and pretty merely" to the hero or "Man of the Age," that is, to the "working-man," it must be produced by writers who are *in* his condition, not by well-intentioned reformers who are content to stand outside and speak *to* his condition. This means that the writer must be, in a radical sense, a worker himself. It does not mean that he should, like Ripley, Hawthorne, and others at Brook Farm, attempt to be a worker in the mornings and a writer in the afternoons. It means, rather, that his writing itself must be undertaken as a kind of physical labor. But what kind? This question, and others to which it gives rise, constitute the main lines of Thoreau's journey in *A Week on the Concord and Merrimack Rivers.*

*

"Surely the writer is to address a world of laborers," writes Thoreau in *A Week,* "and such therefore must be his own discipline." The writer who wishes to be *in* the condition of "the Man of the Age" must be a laborer who does not "idly dance at his work" but who "has wood to cut and cord before night-fall in the short days of winter"; his "every stroke will be husbanded, and ring soberly through the wood; and so will the strokes of that scholar's pen, . . ." Thoreau's words—a typical expression of Victorian male anxiety to remain "sober" rather than dissipated, and to "husband" scarce psychic and sexual energies—are a reminder that the political project of regarding writing as a kind of manual labor is infused from the start with a psychological motivation: Thoreau appears to want to see writing as work, and especially as virile, outdoor work, at least in part because he wants to compensate for the ways in which writing seems "weak and flimsy," mere idle dancing. "A sentence," he declares, "should read as if its author, had he held a plow instead of a pen, could have drawn a furrow deep and straight to the end" (p. 106).

The psychosexual ramifications of Thoreau's endeavor to be "in" the "condition" of manual laborers become more visible whenever his rhetoric elaborates the two kinds of manual labor he figures here: the farmer's cultivation with his plow, the woodsman's chopping with his axe. For example, when Thoreau invites his readers to join him on his outdoor journey, he promises that they will see:

> greater men than Homer, or Chaucer, or Shakespeare, only they never got time to say so; they never took to the way of writing. Look at their fields, and imagine what they might write, if ever they should put pen to paper. Or what have they not written on the face of the earth already, clearing, and burning, and scratching, and harrowing, and plowing and subsoiling, and in and in, and out and out, and over and over, again and again, erasing what they had already written for want of parchment. (p. 8)

These virile workers are consummate writers; they inscribe themselves directly upon the earth and thus surpass even the greatest of those who write by putting "pen to paper." But this self-punishing suggestion that "the way of writing" is not manly enough gives way to another. As Thoreau yields to the surge of his rhetoric, we see that the clearing of woods and the plowing of fields is ultimately a kind of rape: "clearing and burning, and scratching and harrowing, and plowing and subsoiling, in and in, and out and out, and over and over . . ."

This hint that the psychology of manual labor has a dark side—that sunny labor in the open air has disturbing sexual undertones—becomes fully explicit as Thoreau continues to meditate on farming as an activity on which to pattern his labor as a writer. "We have all had our daydreams," he writes, perhaps with a glance at Brook Farm, "as well as our more prophetic nocturnal visions, but as for farming, I am convinced that my genius dates from an older era than the agricultural. . . . What have I to do with plows?" (p. 54). For Thoreau, the problem with agricultural labor is that it makes one too "familiar" with nature. What he wants to avoid, finally, is an "intercourse" that is "foul" and "vulgar." "The gardener," he writes, "is too much of a familiar" of nature. "There is something vulgar and foul about [his] closeness to his mistress" (p. 56).[9]

Here Arendt's distinction between "work" and "labor" is most useful. "Labor," as she defines it, is an endless cycle of production and consumption undertaken in order to ensure human survival and nothing more. It is labor that produces human life: man's endless labor in the fields is matched by woman's endless labor of childbirth. His labor makes possible hers, hers makes possible his. Thus, the labor of clearing and cultivating the earth is always a sexual labor insofar as it is undertaken in order to reproduce human life. It is sexual also in that men have traditionally figured agriculture as an impregnation of the earth: man has intercourse with the land in order to make her "yield her increase" (p. 55) so that more human mouths can be fed so that more hands can work the fields in order to feed the ever multiplying mouths. For Thoreau, the virtue of the Indian (the male Indian at least) is that he will have none of this. Thoreau's Indian rejects the endless cycle of "scratching and harrowing . . . plowing and subsoiling, in and in, out and out, and over and over, again and again." No human can avoid all sexual relations with nature, but "the Indian's intercourse with Nature is at least such as admits of the greatest independence of each" (p. 56).

Thus, Thoreau ultimately rejects as models for writing not only the blacksmith's work, but also the labor of farmer and woodchopper; the latter, being what Arendt would call "labor," ensnare the male spirit in the coils of reproduction and consumption. Henceforth, he will seek increasingly to model his writing on the life of the Indian, not on the work of the farmer or laborer. Thoreau seems to have taken this figurative project literally. As Hawthorne commented in 1842: "for two or three years back, he [Thoreau] has repudiated all regular modes of getting a living, and seems inclined to live a sort of Indian life as respects the absence of any systematic effort for a livelihood."[10]

The ease (and the seeming unconsciousness) with which Thoreau abandons the political project adumbrated in the Carlyle essay and figured briefly in the opening of A Week at first suggests that he was never deeply committed to "the Man of the Age"—"the working-man." The language Thoreau employs also suggests that what commitment he did have was motivated finally by a sexual orientation—by a desire to escape domestic engulfment and to live the life of a man alone. The degree to which laboring men embody a life of freedom from reproductive obligations and domesticity is precisely the degree to which Thoreau admires and seeks to emulate them. As soon as it becomes clear that, for all their rugged labor in the open air, they are just as tied to domesticity, procreation, and woman as, say, the professional man, Thoreau disdains them and turns instead to the "wild" Indian. As we shall see, however, this move away from the farmer and woodchopper is not the foregoing of political concerns it might at first appear to be. While pursuing his own desires (or fleeing them), Thoreau is nevertheless still tracking down what it means to live and work physically, with the hands and the body. His books will still seek a description of work that does much to collapse the distinction, with all its political ramifications, between manual and mental labor.

The problem confronting him at this point in *A Week,* however, is how to replicate the Indian's relation to nature. How can a white male poet living in the middle of the nineteenth century pattern what he does after the activity of the male Indian? The short answer, of course, is to go to Walden Pond and to see the act of composition as "the striking out of the heart of life at a blow, as the Indian takes off a scalp" (p. 329). But Thoreau will also find it necessary to establish a historical, or rather, a mythological foundation for his way of writing. He cannot simply follow the path of the English literary tradition— after all, it springs from a culture that has exterminated the Indian. Instead, he must go back and rewrite American history (and, indeed, the history of English literature) in order to inscribe a place for himself and the Indian in it.

The dramatic center of *A Week* consists, therefore, of two stories which tell, respectively, the traditional myth of American origins and the alternative myth Thoreau proposes. The first is the tale of "the famous Captain Lovewell," a New England folk hero much celebrated in popular song and verse. Lovewell earned his place in New England history by leading a band of soldiers "into the shaggy forests of Pequaweket," where they surprised and slaughtered many Indians, returning wounded but triumphant "to enjoy the fame of their victory." Thoreau's ironic retelling intertwines lines from popular songs, which are oblivious to the ethical complications of Lovewell's exploit, with passages of his own sardonic narration. The songs tell how "the valiant English," though only thirty-four in all, took on "four score" of the "rebel" Indians and slew almost all of them. Thoreau's account, by contrast, asserts simply that Lovewell's band "exterminated" the enemy and chooses instead to focus on the fact that not all of Lovewell's party returned home safely. In Thoreau's version, the Lovewell expedition *into* the forest becomes a grisly tale of wounded men who spend nearly two weeks trying to get *out* of the woods. Thoreau's imagination is fascinated by the price nature has exacted for these soldiers' "victory."

"Davis had a ball lodged in his body, and his right hand shot off . . ."
The cranberries another survivor had eaten "came out of the wounds he
had received in his body." The dismemberers of the Indians are themselves dismembered; the very food they attempt to pluck from nature is
disgorged through their open wounds (pp. 119–22).

Thoreau follows this unsettling revision with a retelling of the famous story of the capture and escape of Hannah Dustan.[11] Thoreau's
version is at first perfectly consonant with conventional ideological justifications of white conquest and settlement. The settlers seem unag-
gressive, the Indians are brutal, and the specific target of their attack is
a vulnerable woman. Indeed, their assault is a sexual assault, since Dustan is dragged from her bed "half-dressed" and told that she will have
to run the gauntlet "naked."

> On the 15th of March previous, Hannah Dustan had been compelled to
> rise from childbed, and half-dressed, with one foot bare, accompanied by
> her nurse, commence an uncertain march . . . through the snow and the
> wilderness. . . . She had seen her infant's brains dashed out against an ap-
> ple-tree, and had left her own and her neighbors' dwellings in ashes.
> When she reached the wigwam of her captor, . . . she had been told that
> she and her nurse were soon to be taken to a distant Indian settlement,
> and there made to run the gauntlet naked. (p. 321)

From this point forward, however, Thoreau's version of the story subtly
subverts the alignment of womanhood, defenselessness, and civilization
on the one hand against masculinity, aggression, and wilderness on the
other. Dustan is determined not only to escape, but to avenge herself,
and in carrying out her plan, she reveals that the civilized English-
woman is capable of a brutality that matches, and even surpasses, that
of her captors. She asks a young English boy, who is also a prisoner, to
find out from the Indians how best to kill a man. An Indian tells the boy
to strike at the temple and also shows him how to remove a scalp. Rising
before dawn the next morning, Dustan, her nurse, and the boy steal the
Indians' tomahawks and kill them in their sleep—all except one "favorite boy, and one squaw who fled wounded with him into the woods."
Dustan then destroys all the canoes but one, which she launches on the
river to start home. "But after having proceeded a short distance, fear-
ing that her story would not be believed if she should escape to tell it,
they returned to the silent wigwam, and taking off the scalps of the
dead, put them into a bag as proofs of what they had done" (p. 321).

Civilization thus proves to be as "wild" as the wilderness of the Indians. The traditional myth of a war between man and nature, between
civilization and wilderness, is retold as a struggle between woman and

nature. This woman at first seems to be a representative of civilization, with its commitment to domesticity and its devotion to procreation. But the pressure of circumstance uncovers a wildness within Dustan. Protecting a boy (the infantilized male of civilization) and her old nurse (figure of her own foremothers), Dustan reveals that the opposition between civilization and wilderness is only superficial. Both are essentially feminine, generative forces that will brook no opposition. Both are aspects of a single Nature. (This is why the two Indians who escape from her wrath—a squaw and a boy—precisely mirror the two persons who escape with her.) Thoreau thus rewrites the story of the founding of America as a story about nature at war with herself—her civilized against her wild aspect. Males are marginalized in this account: Dustan's husband flees, her captors die. That this event plays a role in history and serves an ideological function is not lost on Dustan herself, who returns to get the scalps so that she will be "believed."

This account helps explain why the closing image in Thoreau's version of the Dustan narrative bizarrely conflates the standard polarities of domesticity and wilderness, violence and pastoral. "The family of Hannah Dustan all assembled alive once more, except the infant whose brains were dashed out against the apple-tree, and there have been many in later times who have lived to say that they had eaten of the fruit of that apple-tree" (pp. 323–24). This tree—Thoreau's most obvious modification of the Dustan story—serves to emphasize that what he is telling is not just any old story, or even any old myth, but a founding myth, a myth of origins. The myth of America's origins is tied to a myth that, deliberately echoing and displacing the book of Genesis, provides a new account of the origin of human knowledge of good and evil. Whereas in Genesis a woman was tempted to that knowledge by Satan, an external tempter, in Thoreau's version that knowledge is immanent in the American landscape. His apple tree stands not at the center of an earthly paradise, but at the boundary between wilderness and civilization. It marks precisely the point at which two forces, two aspects of a single and essentially feminine nature, clash.

What would those Americans who could say "that they had eaten of the fruit of that apple-tree" have learned from it? They would have learned that the knowledge of good and evil, and the distinctively human consciousness that arises as a result of such knowledge, are immanently given rather than supernaturally bestowed. They would have learned that nature is continually engaged in a process of making and unmaking herself, of building civilization and destroying wilderness, of destroying civilization and restoring wilderness. Thus, they would see agriculture not as man's achievement over and against nature, but as an expression of nature's immanent, dialectical struggle with herself. They would see that human history is, finally, natural history, what we would now call ecological history. Thus, when the white man came to the American continent, he came as a force of nature who altered the continent's ecology. He:

> planted orchard seeds brought from the old country, and persuaded the civil apple tree to blossom next to the wild pine and the juniper, shedding its perfume in the wilderness. . . . The white man's mullein soon reigned in Indian cornfields, and sweet scented English grasses clothed the new soil. Where, then, could the Red Man set his foot? (pp. 52–53)

At the same time, crucially, the biblical account of the origin of ethical consciousness is the story also of the origin of human work. According to Genesis, man (Adam) was forced to labor "in the sweat of his face" because he had been tempted and seduced by woman (Eve). That patriarchal account of the origins of labor only half conceals another—one in which woman's labor as mother of the human race gradually forced the male to leave the wilderness and his work as a hunter in order to support an ever-growing human population through agricultural labor.[12] But Thoreau's vision of ecological struggle between the "English flower" and "the wild native ones" suggests that in dropping his bow and taking up the plow, man did not move from an essentially masculine to an essentially feminine world. Both worlds always were feminine: behind the woodland grove of Artemis and the rural shrine to Demeter stands a single deity: *gaia,* earth, mother, nature. The decisive difference lies in the male's relation to that power. In the domain of agriculture, man becomes nature's "familiar," bound to her in coils of "foul" sexual intimacy. In the realm of the "wild," the male preserves his virginity and with it a crucial aspect of his own identity.

Thoreau's version of the Dustan narrative thus provides him with a founding myth that is *not* the story of the founding fathers who came and (like Lovewell) exterminated the Indians, but the story of a founding mother, Hannah Dustan. Her story reveals that she is the representative of both civilization and wilderness, farm and woods. This vision of history as natural history, as an immanent, dialectical struggle between two aspects of nature, has two consequences. First, it means that all men, whether they work (like Lovewell) in the service of civilization or (like the Indians) in the service of wilderness, play a secondary, indeed a subservient role in history. Both work, finally, in and for a feminine Nature. Second, it means that as a white male, Thoreau need not ally himself with the Lovewells of civilization. Recognizing that in either case he works for nature, he can choose, as he does choose, to be an Indian.

Readers familiar with Thoreau's misogynistic tone (and outbursts) in *Walden* might understandably be skeptical of such a reading of *A Week*. But misogyny, as we shall see, is by no means incompatible with a reverence for the feminine or with the desire to model one's artistic activity on natural processes rather than on such human activities as the work of the blacksmith or the labor of the farmer or the woodcutter. And Thoreau in *A Week* makes it very plain that he wishes to replace a patriarchal history composed of conquest and domination with a matriarchal history composed by what I have called immanent struggle. Immediately after finishing the Dustan story he points out that the events recounted "happened since Milton wrote his Paradise Lost"—that is, years after Milton attempted to tell a story that, while recasting Genesis, provided an epic foundation for English history. Thoreau writes that as Americans, however, we need not "regulate our historical time by the English standard." In other words, like all independent people and nations, we are free to improvise our own founding myths, our own points of origin. We can decide, therefore, to place the Dustan story at the beginning of (our) time, to make it "more remote than the dark ages." Mythical time is as long or short as the requirements of the imagination dictate. From a traditional perspective, the "Mosaic account" (that is, the patriarchal account) of history—from "Adam and Eve" to the discovery of "America"—is a "wearisome while." But from a matriarchal perspective it can be revisioned as "the lives of but sixty old women, such as live under the hill, say of a century each, strung together . . ." This vision of history as "gossip" replaces such traditional masculine figures as "Orpheus," "Odin," and "Christ" with sixty old women, sixty witches or hags ("such as live under the hill"), whose primary activity is to "suckle" and "nurse." "Universal" history is in essence the "gossip" of these women because the moving force in history is feminine, not masculine (pp. 324–25).

Thoreau's rejection of the "Mosaic," patriarchal, Genesis-based account of history and labor provides him with entirely new terms in which to understand American history and his own labor as a writer. The Mosaic account explains human labor—the labor of agriculture, the labor of giving birth—as the consequence of woman's weakness and man's disobedience. It places man in a fallen world which stands over and against him as a hostile environment requiring hard labor "in the sweat of his face" in order to survive. The Mosaic account thus gives rise to an opposition between human labor and the natural world. Man

works not in and through, but over and against the world. In the antebellum period especially, these terms powerfully structured the rhetoric
describing the human relationship to nature. As Thomas Starr King de-
clared in a popular lecture:

> The mastery of the earth is the chief command and trust which the Al-
> mighty has committed to mortals here. It is this command which enno-
> bles labor. . . . Man was made to be an artificer of matter, to gain control
> of the planet, and to build up civilization, and enlarge his own intellect
> and nature by that work.[13]

By contrast, Thoreau's myth of American origins allows him to place
human work, including his own work as a writer, within the fold of nature. To work, according to such a vision, is to express the earth, not
subdue or "master" it. But at the same time, Thoreau feels he must be
careful to avoid a "foul" and "vulgar" "closeness to his mistress" and
evade a sexual relation with her. The writer does not marry or cultivate
his mistress; he becomes a part of her, disappears in her—which, paradoxically, allows him more "independence" than a sexual relation because it is not does not enslave him to his own desires. To write in such
a "condition" is certainly to perform a bodily labor; it is to make as nature makes. It is to write sentences that "are verdurous and blooming as
evergreens and flowers, because they are rooted in fact and experience"
(p. 104). Within such a vision of nature and work, true poetry "is a
natural fruit. As naturally as the oak bears an acorn, and the vine bears
a gourd, man bears a poem, either spoken or done" (p. 91).[14]

In the closing pages of *A Week,* Thoreau tries to determine what specific practice follows from this model of human and writerly work based
on natural process. His first step is to review (and rewrite) literary history in order to identify and emphasize those writers who have managed
to enact such a practice. The primary criterion for inclusion in his canon
would be a heroic humility, a willingness to see one's work as an homage to rather than as a supplement or mastery of existence. He finds that
the chief virtue of Goethe, for example, is that he "was satisfied with
giving an exact description of things as they appeared to him. . . . He
speaks as an unconcerned spectator, whose object is faithfully to describe what he sees, and that, for the most part, in the order in which he
sees it. Even his reflections do not, for the most part, interfere with his
descriptions" (p. 326). By describing things "as they are," the writer at
once pays tribute to and mimics nature's mode of making. Instead of
supplementing the world and seeing himself as an alternative source of
creation, the writer like Goethe simply records what is already there. He
accepts the completeness of nature; he does not strive to emulate the

patriarchal creator who creates *ex nihilo*. Similarly Chaucer, "the father of English poetry," had a "genius" that was "feminine, not masculine" (p. 373). At this point, however, Thoreau pulls back from what verges on a total marginalization of masculinity. Chaucer's "was such a femininess . . . as is rarest to find in a woman . . . ; perhaps it is not to be found at all in woman, but is only the feminine in man" (p. 373). Only men, it would seem, are man enough to be feminine.

Thoreau moves, then, toward a radically naturalized (and to that extent feminized) model of human work and artistic creativity. But as *A Week*'s conclusion suggests, this model may require the writer to reduce his ambitions still further—not just from making to recording, but from recording to observing, and finally to observing in silence. Silence is the book's last subject. It is the silence of a natural world so self-sufficient and complete that it does not need to speak or publish itself, to mimic itself in any language; it is also the silence which is man's closest approximation and most fitting tribute to the way the natural world makes and unmakes itself. Drifting home in the twilight, Thoreau reflects that "sometimes a mortal feels in himself Nature, not his Father but his Mother stirs within him, and he becomes immortal with her immortality" (p. 378). To live well and work well is to live and work as nature does. Man "needs not only to be spiritualized, but *naturalized,* on the soil of the earth. . . . We need to be earth-born as well as heaven-born, γηγενεῖς, as was said of the Titans of old or in a better sense than they" (p. 380). As the sun sets and a silence descends upon the earth, Thoreau verges upon a recognition that the destiny of writing patterned upon natural making, the mother's rather than the father's making, is silence. Silence is "the universal refuge, a balm to every chagrin." In "her" presence, "the orator puts off his individuality, and is then most eloquent when most silent." He perfects his art precisely when he no longer practices it, when he "becomes a hearer along with his audience." What he hears is Silence's "infinite din." "She is Truth's speaking trumpet, the true Delphi and Dodona." In the face of such truth, the (male) poet's task is not to advance his own ideas, not to imitate God, the divine artificer, but to acknowledge the power of silence:

> It were vain for me to endeavor to interpret Silence. She cannot be done into English. For six thousand years men have translated her with what fidelity belonged to each, and still she is little better than a sealed book. A man may run on confidently for a while, thinking he has her under his thumb . . . but he too must at last be silent . . . for when at last he dives into her, so vast is the disproportion of the untold to the told, that the former will be but the bubble on the surface where he disappeared. (p. 392)

To write or speak, then, is merely to "translate" silence. To think that one can create a permanent artifice of words or sound is "to run on confidently" but foolishly. The fate that awaits every (male) writer is, finally, engulfment. His words and works are but a "bubble" that mark the spot where he has "disappeared" back into the natural world—the mother—from which he has never fully separated himself. Better to recognize this fate now and come to terms with it, to be "earth-born" and "naturalized," than to think that the male can stand apart from the natural world and create what Sidney called "a golden world," superior to nature's "brazen" one.[15] Thus, while Thoreau's attraction to natural process as a model for his own work promises to deliver him from the vainglory of conventional, masculinized models, it also poses the possibility that he should not write at all—or that he should write only in silence, as a consort to nature and for no human audience. The challenge of this prospect will inspire him to write *Walden;* the logic of it will lead him thereafter to the silence of the *Journal.*[16]

3

Labor's Gendered Body

5

Women Carved of
Oak and Korl

The Female Body as the
Site of Gendered Labor in
Hawthorne and Davis

As we have seen, Thoreau's meditative journey carries him from a desire to be "in" the "condition" of "the working man" who performs manual labor to a realization that embodied artistic practice should be "earth-born," "naturalized," and feminine rather than "heaven-born," "spiritualized," and masculine. Seeking to solve a visible political problem that is structured in terms of class (how to develop a literature of and for the laboring class), he winds up addressing a question about making, or creativity, that is structured in terms of gender (shall I work as a father/man who stands outside his work and fashions it or as a mother/woman who resides within her work, which she spins or births out of her own body?).

That Thoreau's thinking follows this trajectory is no accident. When the body is located as the place where the writer's relation to manual labor is both defined and dramatized, questions of gender identity are bound to arise. Terry Eagleton has observed that "aesthetics is born of a discourse of the body."

> The distinction which the term 'aesthetic' initially enforces in the mid-eighteenth century is not one between 'art' and 'life', but between the material and the immaterial: between things and thoughts, sensations and ideas, that which is bound up with our creaturely life as opposed to that which conducts some shadowy existence in the recesses of the mind. It is as though philosophy suddenly wakes up to the fact that there is a dense,

99

swarming territory beyond its own mental enclave which threatens to fall
utterly outside its sway.[1]

While it is not my purpose here to provide an explanation of why philosophy "suddenly wakes up to the fact" of the body, I have implied
through the order of the foregoing chapters that changes in the nature
of work were instrumental and decisive to this moment. The distinction
between "thoughts" and "things" arises at least in part, I have proposed, out of a distinction between two kinds of knowledge and two
kinds of work—that of the "head" and that of the "hands." When Edward Everett and Timothy Walker seek to exclude the body as a source
of value from the new form of work that emerges within industrialism,
and when John Neal gestures angrily and inadequately toward a
"knowledge of things," the historical genesis of the concerns of aesthetics in the transformation of work becomes manifest.

Yet Thoreau's nervous conclusion that an intimate (as opposed to instrumental) knowledge of things, of the earth, is a feminine knowledge
points toward the possibility of another social genesis of these aesthetic
concerns. Perhaps what Eagleton calls the "territory" of "our sensate
life" is not just the realm of a class regarded as working primarily with
and through its bodies, but of a sex that has been regarded as occupying
that realm through its biological labor as mothers and its social labor as
administrators of what Eagleton calls "the business of affections and
aversions."[2] Perhaps the fact that philosophy "suddenly wakes to the
fact" of the body has as much, or more, to do with a destabilization of
gender relations and gendered work as with industrialism's transformation of work and disruption of class relations.

Our task is not to choose between these explanations but to recognize the ways they converge and entwine, sometimes supporting, at
other times supplanting each other. This chapter explores in particular
the ways two writers—one male and one female—constellate questions
about artistic practice with concerns about gender identity and class
politics. Nathaniel Hawthorne, who wishes to conceive of writing as
both masculine and mental labor, takes pains to distinguish it from
manual labor, which he in turn feminizes and associates with the female
body. At the same time, however, Hawthorne is drawn to the manifest
creative power of the female body, which seems to surpass the potentiality of the disembodied masculine imagination. Rebecca Harding Davis
employs the same terms and works through the same paradigmatic distinctions between mind and body, but with somewhat different results.
As a woman self-consciously writing within and against a patriarchal order that subordinates body to mind, she is concerned with establishing

a linkage between writing and manual labor, with the intent to feminize both. Though the outcomes of their fictions differ, both writers share a predisposition to approach the work they are writing about through the work they are performing; both, in the last analysis, sacrifice class politics to their more immediate concern with the consequences of a gendered authorial identity. The work they represent is subsumed, finally, in the work they perform.

*

"The Artist of the Beautiful" (1843), "The Birth-mark" (1844), and "Drowne's Wooden Image" (1847) have frequently been linked by critics who see them as Hawthorne's most explicit fictional meditations on the nature of art and artistic activity—what I have emphasized is a kind of work. Most readers have focused on the ways the stories either affirm or repudiate some notion, usually dubbed "Romantic," of what art should be.[3] In each story, a man's creativity seeks to achieve an ideal by spiritualizing matter, and in each that achievement is presented with characteristic Hawthorneian ambivalence. In "The Artist of the Beautiful," the young watchmaker Owen Warland attempts "to spiritualize machinery"[4] and in so doing becomes an "artist of the beautiful" but not an artist of actual life. In "The Birth-mark," the scientist Aylmer aims to perfect his wife by eradicating from her body a flaw that, in his eyes, "expressed the indelible gripe in which mortality clutches the highest and purest of earthly mold, degrading them into kindred with lowest, and even with the very brutes, like whom their visible frames return to dust."[5] But by succeeding in erasing the birthmark from her cheek, Aylmer kills Georgiana and becomes himself the agent of the natural mortality he sought to foil. And in "Drowne's Wooden Image," a humble artisan manages once in his life to carve a true work of art out of wood he has somehow "etherealized into a spirit."[6] But his success is more an accident or "dream" (p. 107) than a conscious achievement, and when the model who inspired him goes away, he becomes again a carver of "wooden progeny" in his "own mechanical style" (p. 107).

Hawthorne presents these male artist figures without clearly signaling whether we are to regard them as successes or failures. He applauds Drowne's achievement but denies him any credit for it. He is critical of Aylmer and Warland because in their single-minded pursuit of the spiritual, the beautiful, the immortal, they ignore or repress or destroy what is beautiful in the human condition of mortality and materiality. At the same time, however, Hawthorne's criticism is aimed at the excessiveness, not the substance of their belief that spirit is higher and nobler than matter. Indeed, in all three stories, Hawthorne conveys a traditional preference for the spiritual over the material, for the mental over the bodily, for the imaginary over the merely actual. He celebrates Drowne's achievement, for example, precisely because in etherealizing wood, Drowne attains "the very highest state to which a human *spirit* can attain" (p. 108) [my emphasis].

But while they operate most obviously along the lines of fables about the superiority of spirit to matter in artistic work, Hawthorne's three stories are linked also by two features that have not received notice because so few critics have attempted to historicize the stories.[7] The first of these is the presence of working-class figures, and specifically of men who work with their hands: Robert Danforth, the blacksmith, in "The Artist of the Beautiful"; Aminadab, Aylmer's assistant, in "The Birth-mark"; and Drowne himself—sharply contrasted with the more authentic and more aristocratic artist, the painter John Singleton Copley. This feature is epitomized by the recurrence in these stories of such words as "labor," "laborer," "worker" (or "underworker"), and "mechanical" (having to do not just with machinery, but with "mechanics" or manual laborers).[8]

A second feature, which has received little notice, is the presence in all three stories of a powerful relation between the artist figure and a woman—more specifically, the *body* of a woman. In "The Artist of the Beautiful," the child who has issued from Annie Hovenden's body reaches out and crushes Owen Warland's creation, a beautiful mechanical butterfly. In "The Birth-mark," Georgiana's body is at once the beneficiary, the site, and the victim of Aylmer's experiment. And in "Drowne's Wooden Image," a beautiful young woman inspires Drowne with the love that allows him to create his one work of art—a woman's body carved in wood. In all of these stories, a generalized tension between mind and body, or matter and spirit, is specified as a relation between a man's mind and a woman's body. While the stories work to establish the superiority of the former, they also recognize the power of the latter. They represent the body of woman as capable of creating in a mode not readily available to men—through generation rather than fabrication or artifice (Georgiana's flaw, it should be recalled, is a "*birth-*mark" [my emphasis]). In all three stories, this threatening presence of woman's body and its alternative way of creating is at once marked and resisted by the recurrence of words such as "progeny," "big with," "paternity," "abortion," and "abortive."

The blacksmith Robert Danforth and the watchmaker Owen Warland are both artisans. Both men work with their hands, both are fabricators, makers of things out of metal, and both work in the golden age before independent artisanry had been destroyed or brought under the control of industrial production. But there the similarities between the two men end. Robert Danforth "spends his labor upon a reality" (p. 291), whereas Owen Warland devotes himself increasingly to the impractical scheme of putting "spirit into machinery" (p. 306). On this dichotomy between the useful and the imaginary Hawthorne carefully superimposes another between the material and the spiritual. Robert Danforth is a huge man, all body, and the uniformity of his being delivers him from all confusions and contradictions. Warland, by contrast, is slight, but this does not mean that he is without physicality. On the contrary, his work is motivated in great part by his desire for the lovely Annie Hovenden, daughter of his former master. He is also tied to materiality in another way: as an artist, he works not with such abstractions as words or notes of music, but with metal—precisely the material Robert Danforth hammers out.

But Warland's work entails a systematic repression—then extinction—of the sexual drives that motivated his project at the outset. For Annie eventually marries Robert Danforth, and has children by him, while Warland works increasingly in isolation, motivated by erotic energies that have been detached almost completely from their original object (Annie) and redirected to the project that was supposed to win her. In the story's final scene, Owen brings his completed work to show Annie—ostensibly as a bridal present for her, but in part, no doubt, as a last attempt to win her respect, if not her affections. Over the course of the last scene, he transcends even this last tie to his body and the earth. His beautiful creation, a mechanical butterfly so ingeniously wrought that it has brought metal "alive," is crushed in the hand of Robert and Annie's own creation—their infant son. Is Owen devastated? Not at all. Hawthorne tells us that "he looked placidly at what seemed the ruin of his life's labor, and which was yet no ruin. He had caught a far other butterfly than this. When the artist rose high enough to achieve the Beautiful, the symbol by which he made it perceptible to mortal senses became of little value in his eyes, while his spirit possessed itself in the enjoyment of the Reality" (p. 330).

Hawthorne's tale forces us to make a difficult choice between two kinds of men and two kinds of work. We can be muscular, mindless, but unquestionably alive, like Robert Danforth; or we can be ingenious, imaginative, but pathetically weak, like Owen Warland. We can choose practical, physical labor, or we can choose useless, etherealized tinkering; we can choose the body's generative powers or the imagination's creativity. We can choose a life of the body, the family, and the home, or a life of the mind freed from the constraints of earth, matter, and sexual desire as they are embodied not only in Robert Danforth, but more alluringly in the lovely Annie Hovenden, whom Owen at last no longer needs. Although he poses this difficult choice, Hawthorne himself is hardly neutral. He is surely critical of Warland, but his criticism is indulgent and resigned. Isolation, exhaustion, and asexuality are more the inevitable accompaniments of Warland's kind of work than they are the consequence of his errors. Hawthorne does not fully endorse Warland, but he does not dismiss him as contemptuously as he does his two rivals—old Peter Hovenden and young Robert Danforth. Thus, although his story dramatizes the dangers inherent in Warland's project of spiritualizing matter, Hawthorne still seems to argue for work imbued with mentality and spirituality over labor imbued with practicality and muscular effort.

In "The Birth-mark," where the antagonism between mind and body culminates in the scientist Aylmer's mad attempt to efface a birthmark from his wife Georgiana's cheek, the power of manual labor appears surreptitiously and obliquely—in the odd but compelling figure of Aylmer's "servant" and "under-worker" Aminadab.[9] Aminadab is the archetypal antebellum working man, and Hawthorne attaches to him the epithets so commonly applied to workers by writers of the dominant class. He is of "low stature" and "bulky frame," distinguished by a "great mechanical readiness" represented as a mindless bodily skill; "while incapable of comprehending a single principle" of his "master's" experiments, he executes them ably, just as the factory operative, toiling at complex machinery whose principles he cannot fathom, eventually becomes a mere extension of that machinery and settles ever more deeply into a merely animal or brutish existence. With his "indescribable earthiness," Hawthorne writes, Aminadab "seemed to represent man's physical nature; while Aylmer's slender figure, and pale, intellectual face, were no less apt a type of the spiritual element" (p. 58).

Aminadab is present, however, not just to mark a division of labor within the laboratory; he represents the fact that even Aylmer's most exalted projects have a base, mundane, physical component. When Georgiana reads her husband's personal record of his experiments, she at first sees in them a magnificent spiritualization of matter: "He handled physical details, as if there were nothing beyond them; yet spiritualized them all, and redeemed himself from materialism, by his strong and eager aspiration toward the infinite. In his grasp, the veriest clod of earth assumed a soul" (p. 66). These words recall not only Everett's and Channing's hopes for an intellectualization of manual labor, but more specifically Coverdale's description of the disappointments of Blithedale: "The clods of earth, which we so constantly belabored and turned over and over, were never etherealized into thought. Our thoughts, on the contrary, were fast becoming cloddish. . . . Intellectual activity is incompatible with any large amount of physical exercise."[10] Although Aylmer's experiments at first seem to represent a successful union of mental and manual labor, Hawthorne soon instructs us to read them in another light. Aylmer's book of records "was the sad confession, and continual exemplification, of the short-comings of the composite man—the spirit burthened with clay and working in matter—and of the despair that assails the higher nature, at finding itself so miserably thwarted by the earthy part" (p. 67). In other words, Aminadab represents Aylmer's failed effort to thrust from himself his own physical nature and the physical labor on which his achievements as a scientist have rested. This is why Aminadab gets, quite literally, the last laugh. When Aylmer succeeds in effacing the birthmark only by killing Georgiana, Aminadab (who had earlier remarked, "'If she were my wife, I'd never part with that birthmark'" [p. 58]) lets out a "hoarse, chuckling laugh." It is, says Hawthorne, the triumphant laugh of "the gross Fatality of Earth" (p. 76). But it should now be clear that this metaphysical distinction between "Earth" and "Spirit" is imbued by a political distinction between two kinds of labor. It is no mere coincidence, in sum, that the human embodiment of this "Fatality" is unequivocally a worker, Robert Danforth in another guise.

"Drowne's Wooden Image" offers a third, and more explicit, conflation of metaphysical speculation about mind and body, aesthetic concern with the nature of art, and social anxiety about the relation between manual and mental labor. Drowne is an artisan with a special "knack" for carving the human figure. His productions, says Hawthorne, lack "that deep quality, be it of soul or intellect, which bestows life upon the lifeless and warmth upon the cold" (p. 92). One day Drowne is asked by a sea captain to carve a figure-head for his ship; the captain stipulates that the model for the figure-head remain a secret, known only to himself and Drowne. When the painter John Singleton Copley visits Drowne's studio, he as usual sees around him the stiff, wooden carvings "on the best of which might have been bestowed the questionable praise that it looked as if a living man had been changed to wood" (p. 94). Copley praises what he thinks of as their "mechanical and wooden cleverness," but Drowne will have none of it. He has changed. These "'works of mine,'" he says, "'are no better than abortions.'" Copley is amazed by Drowne's sudden acquisition of taste, "so rare in a merely mechanical character" and then his eye falls on Drowne's new, mysterious project. "'Whose work is this?'" he asks, astounded. "'No man's work,'" replies Drowne. "'The figure lies within

that block of wood and it is my business to find it.'" This declaration
prompts Copley, "the true artist," to seize Drowne by the hand and
proclaim him "'a man of genius'" (p. 95).

The transformed Drowne continues to work on his carving, which
slowly assumes the shape of a woman of great beauty. When he finishes,
Drowne opens his shop and displays his work to a public that gasps with
admiration. At last Hawthorne reveals the mystery: The model for the
figure-head has been a young woman whom the sea captain has taken
under his protection. Carving her, Drowne has fallen deeply in love.
When the figure-head is finished and she departs with the captain (and
the figure-head), Drowne is devastated. He becomes "again the mechanical carver that he had been known to be all his lifetime" (p. 106).
His later productions, like his earlier ones, are all "wooden progeny"
carved in a "mechanical style" (p. 107).

How are we to account for his one work of genius? Hawthorne suggests that "in every human spirit there is imagination, sensibility, creative power, genius, which, according to circumstances, may either be
developed in this world or shrouded in a mask of dulness" (pp. 107–8).
It was "love" that inspired Drowne, "but, quenched in disappointment," love "left him again the mechanical carver in wood" (p. 108).
Although Hawthorne's story may be read as a fable about the necessity
of eros to artistic inspiration, to do so is to overlook Hawthorne's crucial indications that this is also a story about work, class, and the relation
of mental to manual labor. Drowne is specifically a "mechanic" who becomes an artist, a mental worker, and a member of the learned class.
Hawthorne isolates Drowne as the sole working-class figure in a story
otherwise populated only by upper-class personages—the wealthy sea
captain, the prosperous Copley, and the beautiful woman, rumored to
be "a young Portuguese lady of rank." (We are told, significantly, that
she has left home "because of political or domestic disquietude" [p.
108]; thus obliquely does Hawthorne allow the shadow of revolution
to fall across his pages.) Moreover, Hawthorne's proposal that even a
"Yankee mechanic" might have "sensibility, creative power"—that is,
"soul" or "intellect"—at once brings to mind similar formulations by
writers like Channing and Everett. (Recall Everett's assertion that "the
humblest laborer, who works with his hands, possesses a soul.")

What is at stake here once again is the distinction between manual
and mental labor, and behind it, between body and mind, matter and
spirit. Hawthorne's story seems to celebrate the possibility that even a
working-class mechanic can find work that brings out his soul and intellect, but it does so only by damning Drowne in the long run. For
Drowne sees a new "light" and becomes a worker of mind and soul only

when he falls in love with an aristocratic "lady of rank"—who, of course, abandons him. Hawthorne's story thus elevates Drowne only to cast him down again, and in so doing it manages to stage a show of democratic optimism while at the same time affirming the fundamental distinctions between two kinds of work, two kinds of man, two classes, and "true" versus false art.

But here we encounter crosscurrents that do as much to undermine as to uphold this scheme. The first is indicated in Hawthorne's ironic use of birth and generation as a trope for artistic production. At the beginning and end of the story, Hawthorne teasingly refers to Drowne's works as his "progeny" in order to underscore that they are actually anything but organic in nature: they are lifeless, wooden, dead. He "converts" (p. 88) wood into figureheads and his business is a species of "manufacture" (p. 91). This ironic use of the trope darkens toward horror when Drowne refers to his early works as "abortions." What is at play within both these uses of the trope is the notion that true art is not so much manufactured as generated, that the true artist is not so much a fabricator who alters materials as a finder, one who brings to light, or who gives birth to "progeny." When Drowne proclaims that his is "no man's work," the sense cuts two ways: most important, it suggests that art is the outcome not of masculine artifice, but of an unarticulated but distinctly more feminine process.

This figuring of the artist's work as finding or birthing rather than as making is accompanied by rearrangements and complications of gender. For Drowne becomes a true artist himself when, as a man, he prostrates himself before a woman who has seduced him. Whereas earlier he had carved images confirming patriarchal authority—"the monarch himself, or some famous British admiral or general, or the governor of the province, or perchance the favorite daughter of a ship-owner" (p. 91)—the image he now "finds" within the wood is that of a goddess and a witch. When the townspeople of Boston first see the figure, they "reverence" and then "fear" this almost "preternatural" (p. 99) thing. "There was, in truth, an indefinable air and expression that might reasonably induce the query, Who and from what sphere this daughter of oak should be?" (p. 100). She is a "hamadryad," a nymph of the woods, and with "rich flowers of Eden on her head" she evokes not only the world before the Fall, but also a world of prepatriarchal feminine strength, mystery, wildness. No wonder, then, that the "aged" inhabitants of Boston, "whose recollections dated as far back as witch times, shook their heads, and hinted that our forefathers would have thought it a pious deed to burn the daughter of oak with fire" (p. 105).

Thus, Hawthorne's story reinforces a definition of "true art" that rests upon familiar distinctions between mind and body, and between manual or "mechanical" and mental or "intellectual" labor, but at the same time it also introduces complications that threaten this scheme— though from a different point of attack. His story suggests that artistic activity is not at all distinct from the body and the body's labors, but is in fact a supreme bodiliness. The image Drowne finds is, after all, nothing but body and ornamentation that celebrates the body. There is nothing spiritual or transcendental about it. Hawthorne's description of the figure rivets our attention on "the broad gold chain around the neck" and the "curious ring upon her finger," on her "dark eyes" and "voluptuous mouth" (p. 100). Drowne's figure is a "daughter of wood," not a daughter of man; she is not matter infused with spirit, or matter transcended by spirit, but matter *intensified* into art. She resembles a witch precisely because her power calls into question the patriarchal hierarchy of spirit over matter and with it the associated hierarchy of intellectual masculinity over the embodied femininity. The story's blurring of distinctions is epitomized in the confusion of the townspeople, who "knew not whether to suppose the magic wood etherealized into a spirit or warmed and softened into an actual woman" (p. 104).

*

While Hawthorne's three stories combine metaphysical speculation about mind and body, aesthetic concern with the nature of artistic practice, and social anxiety about the relation of mental to manual labor, they also indicate Hawthorne's ambivalent flirtation with the creative powers of the female body. The intersecting of class, gender, and work in Hawthorne's fiction can be explained, in part, by the fact that in this period the opening of new markets and the spread of industrialism were drastically altering the nature of both men's and women's work. To the degree that gender distinctions were based on work distinctions, the movement of women into areas formerly reserved for men clearly threatened to blur traditional markers of gender identity. For example, as increasing numbers of women left home to work in factories, the prevailing notion that women were fitted for work only inside the home and on the farm became increasingly difficult to maintain. As strenuously as the middle class promoted the idea of a separate women's "sphere," it could not entirely allay the excitement and anxiety provoked by women becoming teachers, women becoming writers, women seeking higher education in increasing numbers, and so on. Male writers were hardly immune to these anxieties, which surface not just in

Hawthorne's notorious complaint about "scribbling women," but in the pattern of repeated victimization of strong women—Georgiana in "The Birth-mark," Rappaccini's daughter Beatrice, Hester Prynne in *The Scarlet Letter*, and Zenobia in *The Blithedale Romance*—that we find in Hawthorne's fiction.

Seen from the standpoint of aesthetic thought, Hawthorne's flirtation with the values of materiality and his nervous recognition of the powers of bodily creation have their source in Romantic organicist aesthetics. As Coleridge, the principal advocate in English of the notion of organic form, wrote:

> The form is mechanic when on any given material we impress a predetermined form . . . as when to a mass of wet clay we give whatever shape we wish it to retain when hardened. The organic form, on the other hand, is innate; it shapes as it develops from within, and the fullness of its development is one and the same with the perfection of its outward form.[11]

For Coleridge, the word "mechanic" refers, of course, to a tradition of mechanistic philosophy extending from Bacon to Newton to Locke. It signifies an attitude toward nature and an attitude toward work in which nature is the means to an end (the ever-receding end of "improvement" in the human condition) and work is the process or activity whereby nature is made to serve this end. The word "mechanic" thus points toward a system of ideas on the one hand and, on the other, toward the actual embodiments of those ideas—to the inventor, the artisan, and the factory operative. All were asked to share this appellation and to walk the streets as "mechanics" (though, as we have seen, for the artisan and the operative the term served to conscript them in the instrumentalization of nature and of themselves—their bodies and their sentient knowledge).

In "Signs of the Times," Carlyle explicitly articulates the dangers implicitly recognized by Coleridge's mistrust of mechanism and his rejection of artifice as a model for artistic practice. First, mechanism corrupts the inventor of machines with hubris. Although it raises human ingenuity and artifice to fantastic heights of power and achievement, it at the same time degrades them because it sacrifices the essential human virtue of humility before God. (This is essentially the moral fable told about Aylmer in "The Birth-mark.") "Our true Deity is Mechanism," writes Carlyle. "We are Giants in physical power; in a deeper than metaphorical sense, we are Titans, that strive, by heaping mountain on mountain, to conquer Heaven also."[12] Second, mechanism also degrades those who work with, or rather, for the machinery these men have invented—

the mechanics and operatives of early industrialism. "On every hand," Carlyle complains, "the living artisan is driven from his workshop, to make room for a speedier, inanimate one. . . . Everything has its cunningly devised implements, its preestablished apparatus; it is not done by hand, but by machinery" (pp. 59–61).

These consequences of "mechanism" had the effect of beginning to discredit a tradition of artistic practice that extends back through Shaftesbury to the Greek *poesis:* artifice became stained with the merely artificial. The poet became increasingly uncomfortable with the notion that his work shared essential characteristics with that of the blacksmith or the inventor (trades that are historically and genealogically linked). The poet who wished not to stand outside nature and work upon it required some way of figuring his work as taking place within nature. But as Coleridge's language indicates, such a figuration also entailed feminization. What "develops from within" is the seed, the embryo. The site of artistic creativity is transferred from the impregnating father/penis who remains separate and distinct from his work to the interior of the female body, to the womb, where the maker is organically fused with the thing being made.

Not surprisingly, however, for a *male* artist like Hawthorne, or Thoreau, organicist aesthetics and its emphasis on growth rather than artifice, on development rather than fabrication, poses serious problems. The first is that nature makes nothing durable except herself. Whereas artifice implies the making of an object that stands over and against the natural world with its seasons of growth and decay, generation suggests perishability and ephemerality. When human work is figured as natural generation, it becomes capable only of producing things (like crops) that are to be consumed. It makes nothing durable, lasting, or immortal. For the artist who is invested in creating works that possess such qualities, an organicist aesthetic is as disturbing as it is attractive. What good is a novel if it does not "last?" But, of course, this was precisely the kind of novel, and precisely the kind of aesthetic, against which Hawthorne (and Melville, and Thoreau) felt he had to contend when he lashed out against the "damned mob of scribbling women." The best-selling women novelists of the day not only dominated the marketplace for literature; more threateningly to the male writer, they seemed to have no hesitations whatever about producing literature for consumption. By producing consumable goods for a consumer culture, they were in a crucial (and ironic) way better artists that those male writers who, like Warland and Drowne, clung to antiquated and discredited notions of fabrication, artifice, and imperishability.

Troublesome as this aspect of organicist aesthetics might have been for male artists and writers, it pales beside another. How can a male artist model his activity on the processes of nature without confronting the fact that the labor of giving birth is the most obvious human exemplum of such processes? And how can a male artist figure himself as giving birth to his productions without drastically rethinking some deep and traditional aspects of his gender identity? These questions bring us back to Drowne's "progeny" and "abortions" and to his remark that artistic activity is "no man's work." They bring us back also to "The Birth-mark," able now to see the degree to which this story dramatizes one man's struggle to achieve—indeed to surpass—the power of woman's labor. Georgiana's birth-mark is a *birth* mark—a mark of the power to give birth, which she possesses and which Aylmer, for all his accomplishments, knows he lacks. Aylmer, Hawthorne hints, had "faith in man's ultimate control over nature" (p. 48), and his ambition is one day to "lay his hand on the secret of creative force" (p. 48). Hawthorne goes on to characterize this creative force as "our great creative Mother . . . [who] permits us, indeed, to mar, but seldom to mend, and, like a jealous patentee, on no account to make" (p. 5). In other words, the male maker or artificer of things can never hope to "make" as nature makes—that is, to give birth and thereby to create something, however perishable, out of nothing. It is against both the achievement and the perishability of natural making that Aylmer struggles (futilely) in his attempts to erase Georgiana's birthmark. When she intrudes on the primal scene of this effort, his laboratory, he exclaims: "Would you throw the blight of that fatal birth-mark over my labors?" (p. 69). In the end, as we know, Aylmer succeeds only by failing: he "creates" only by killing; he "makes" only by unmaking the life that is dearest to him.

The project Aylmer and Warland share, then, is not just to "make" as nature makes, but to obliterate what Heidegger would call the "thingly" nature of the thing.[13] Things threaten them; things present them with a radically different order of existence. This order is—as the theory of organic form proposes—one in which design and form are not imposed from without, but work invisibly within an unreachable interior. Both men represent a masculine desire to possess that interior design, to expose it to the light of day. For Warland, the desire takes the form of a need to "spiritualize" inanimate matter—that is, to bring matter over into his own realm, a realm in which the meaning of an object is, paradoxically, inserted into it from without. For Aylmer, the desire takes the form of an obsessive need to destroy the mark that is the sign of his wife's ineluctable materiality and at the same time of her generative power as a woman. To remove the birthmark is to overcome the inner natural law that has made Georgiana's myriad cells constitute her particular body, with its very particular mark. Thus, Aylmer's destructive work is the complement, or obverse, of Warland's ingenious creativity.

Drowne, though he fails in the end, is a relatively successful male maker. He owes his success, in part, to his apprenticeship as a "mechanic" who has performed embodied, manual labor; more important, he succeeds because he is made able to realize that successful making consists not of destroying a thing, or of possessing or altering its thingness, but of "finding" it. In a sense, his work makes the wood's own birthmark visible. However, Hawthorne chooses to represent Drowne's success as temporary and provisional. That success has been made possible by his love for a woman, and as a male maker he is unable to remember what he learns through that love. When she leaves him, he returns to his old self, a mere mechanic once again. Perhaps Hawthorne is suggesting that Drowne fails because he shares Aylmer's and Warland's need to turn nature and matter inside out, to expose and make visible the secrets that are locked in things, the laws that compel them to take one form and not another. As we shall see, this male desire to get at the interior of the thing, and especially of the body, is dramatized in a number of antebellum works of literature—in the sandbank passage of *Walden,* for example. It seems to manifest itself also in Dimmesdale's urge to replicate Hester's embodied guilt (Pearl) by opening wounds in his own body.

Hawthorne's stories suggest that he perceived the self-defeating (for the male imagination) implications of the theory of organic form. He situates the female body at the center of his dramatizations of problems of work because for him, as a male artist, woman's body epitomizes a kind of creativity—labor—which at once attracts and repels him. He is drawn to such labor because it offers such a powerful alternative to "mechanism"—to the "terrible energy of the Iron Laborer," the machine. At the same time, however, he cannot accommodate himself to two implications of this model: first, that the artist's works should be consumable rather than durable; second, that a man should figure his artistic work in terms of the distinctly feminine labor of giving birth to, of generating, something that lives and dies. Hawthorne's trilogy on the nature of artistic work repeatedly rehearses these contradictions: his male artists all fail at the very moment they succeed. Significantly, both Aylmer and Warland, in striving to surpass "our great creative Mother" *(mater)* by spiritualizing matter, are defeated by a hand—the "small hand" of Annie's infant, the "tiny" or "bloody hand" of Georgiana's birthmark. As we have seen, both serve as a synecdoche not only for the "gripe" of "mortality" and matter, but for the *manus* of the manual laborer. Aylmer is Georgiana's husband, but Aminadab is her truest friend and ally.

*

Rebecca Harding Davis's *Life in the Iron Mills,* published in the *Atlantic Monthly* in 1861, explores many of the issues dramatized in Hawthorne's three stories. Like them, it deals with the relation between artistic creativity and manual labor, and like them it chooses the female body as the dramatic locus of its exploration—as the site at which its complications become, so to speak, condensed. Like Drowne, Davis's iron-puddler (Wolfe) astonishes his world by producing a work of art, and like Drowne's his work takes the shape of a woman's body. Like Drowne, Wolfe meets an artist or aesthetician of the upper class and enjoys a brief, though thwarted, comradeship in his cool glance of recognition. And like Drowne, Wolfe finds that although his art affords him a tantalizing glimpse of other worlds and other possibilities, he is unable finally to escape the limited and cruelly limiting realm of manual labor.

More keenly than Hawthorne, though, Davis sees that the body is as much the victim as the agent of manual labor. She writes of "the vast machinery of system by which the bodies of workmen are governed"[14] and repeatedly calls attention to bodies broken and maimed. Like Melville's maids in Tartarus, Deborah (Wolfe's crippled cousin) has been injured sexually. Her "thwarted woman's form," though inwardly still capable of passion and love for Wolfe, "made him loathe the sight of her. . . . his soul sickened with disgust at her deformity, even when his words were kindest" (p. 23). Davis makes clear that it is not women alone who are injured by toil. Wolfe, she writes, "had already lost the strength and instinct vigor of a man, his muscles were thin, his nerves weak, his face (a meek, woman's face) haggard, yellow with consumption." And in this hint that Wolfe is at heart a woman, emphasized a moment later ("In the mill he was known as one of the girl-men: 'Molly Wolfe' was his *sobriquet*"), we have a clear indication of the twist Davis gives to the narrative line developed in Hawthorne's stories. Hawthorne, a male artist, has explored the relation between writing and manual labor by way of male characters who work upon, or through, or against, the female body. Outwardly, Davis appears to do precisely the same thing. However, because he is a man, Wolfe cannot serve completely and appropriately as a vehicle for her imagination and as a representative of her situation in the text. For this reason, Davis subtly feminizes Wolfe and at the same time deflects attention from Wolfe toward Deborah and toward the female figure Wolfe has made. In short, to do justice to this extraordinarily complex story we must read it not just as a representation of manual la-

bor (of life in the iron mills) but as a representation of the work (writing)
of producing that representation and as an exploration of the complicated relation among these subjects and activities.

Davis signals this entwining of subjects and activities at the outset of
her story. The narrator introduces herself in the opening paragraphs as
a spectator who observes, and who therefore must acknowledge, guiltily, her distance from the working men and women who have no opportunity to perceive their own situation. Moreover, the narrator directly
addresses the reader in the opening sentence ("A cloudy day: do you
know what that is in a town of iron-works?") and repeatedly entangles
the reader in her situation as an outsider who both knows and does not
know her subject. "When I was a child, I used to fancy a look of weary,
dumb appeal upon the face of the negro-like river. . . . Something of the
same idle notion comes to me to-day, when from the street window I
look on the slow stream of human life creeping past, night and morning,
to the great mills." Davis emphasizes that as a spectator, the narrator
does not work exactly as the mill-workers do, but instead fancies, in
what appears to be idleness. "My fancy about the river was an idle one."
The reader, too, is made to feel an idler: "There is a curious point for
you to settle, my friend, who study psychology in a lazy, *dilettante* way"
(pp. 12–13).

This implied separation of writer and reader from the subjects of
their fiction becomes explicitly formulated as a problem of silence—the
unwordability of manual labor, the *Pequod*'s carpenter's "deaf and
dumb, spontaneous literal process," Therien's thoughts that "cannot be
reported":

> There is a secret down here, in this nightmare fog, that has lain dumb for
> centuries: I want to make it a real thing to you. You . . . do not see it
> clearly,—this terrible question which men here have gone mad and died
> trying to answer. I dare not put this secret into words. I told you it was
> dumb. These men, going by with drunken faces and brains full of un-
> awakened power, do not ask it of Society or of God. Their lives ask it;
> their deaths ask it. There is no reply. I will tell you plainly that I have a
> great hope; and I bring it to you to be tested. It is this: that this terrible
> dumb question is its own reply; that it is not the sentence of death we
> think it, but, from the very extremity of its darkness, the most solemn
> prophecy which the world has known of the Hope to come. I dare make
> my meaning no clearer, but will only tell my story. (p. 14)

What is this "secret" that takes the form first of a "question," then of a
"reply," then of a "Hope" and finally of a "prophecy"? The "secret" is
what I have called the interiority of manual labor, the "question" is

whether it has value, the "reply" is that the value is self-generated and can be found only through its own terms, and the "hope" and "prophecy" are that one day those terms will cease to be "dumb" and will be allowed to speak for themselves. The narrator's hesitation to make "her meaning clearer," and her decision simply to tell her "story," are indications of her awareness that the secret cannot be told except by those who possess it—and that she, a writer, is not really one of them.

And yet, at the same time, the story is an expression not only of this "Hope," but also of the narrator's desire to be one with her subject, or at least to reside with it. For she does live in the dirty, muddy, smokey mill town, and indeed the site of her writing is the house of labor—"this house is the one where the Wolfes lived" (p. 15). The force of this desire is registered most fully in the fantasy that the iron-puddler Wolfe is at the same time an artist, albeit a thwarted one. Wolfe has "a groping passion for whatever was beautiful and pure"; "God put into this man's soul a fierce thirst for beauty,—to know it, to create it; to *be*—something, he knows not what,—other than what he is." He has a "mad desire, a great blind intellect stumbling through wrong, a loving poet's heart," even though "the man was by habit only a coarse, vulgar laborer, familiar with sights and sounds you would blush to name." A small party of men accompany the son of the mill owner to the mills and there they discover the visible, outward manifestation of this "mad desire" Wolfe has, the "thought" for which he has "no words." It is a statue made of korl, "the white figure of a woman . . . —a woman, white, of gigantic proportions, crouching on the ground, her arms flung out in some wild gesture of warning" (p. 31).

> There was not one line of beauty or grace in it: a nude woman's form, muscular, grown coarse with labor, the powerful limbs instinct with some poignant longing. One idea: there it was in the tense, rigid muscles, the clutching hands, the wild, eager face, like that of a starving wolf's. (p. 32)

This image recalls Melville's Jackson, described as a "wolf, or starved tiger," except, of course, that it is a woman, not a man. Conversely, although she is a woman like Hawthorne's Georgiana and Drowne's statue, this figure is far from beautiful or voluptuous. What Davis has done, in other words, is to retain the female body as an image of the "dumb" and victimized laboring body without investing that body with conventional feminine attributes ("beauty or grace"); instead, the female body has "powerful limbs" and "tense, rigid muscles." Moreover, this figure described as a "wolf" is associated with her male maker ("Wolfe") and at the same time represented as one who makes up for his deficiencies—his muscles are "thin" and he has "lost the strength and instinct vigor of a man."

Wolfe, meanwhile, continues to be feminized, particularly in relation to Mitchell—"the thoroughbred gentleman" with a perfect "white hand," with the "sinewy limbs" of an "amateur gymnast,"—"a Man all-knowing, all-seeing, crowned by Nature, reigning—the keen glance of his eye falling like a sceptre on other men." And on *women,* the text would say, if it could. Mitchell is not just a man, but a "Man," the male, the embodiment here of patriarchy and its power to subdue by the strength of its body and by the reach of its knowing and seeing. The exchange between Wolfe and Mitchell is quintessentially that between the helpless, objectified, silenced woman and the male gaze that defines and degrades her. "Wolfe stammered, glanced appealingly at Mitchell, who saw the soul of the thing, he knew. But the cool, probing eyes were turned on himself now,—mocking, cruel, relentless" (p. 33). Clearly, Mitchell, who alone among the visitors to the mill reads Wolfe correctly, is the textual representative also of the "dilettante" (male) reader who sees into "the soul" of Davis's story, whom she both admires and distrusts, and who accounts for her fears—why she "dare not put this secret into words," why she "dare make [her] meaning no clearer." (Perhaps it is specifically the gaze of the *Atlantic*'s male editors to whom she sent the story, or the gaze of the male critics who would, with some condescension, praise it.) Davis occupies the house of labor with Wolfe precisely insofar as she, a woman, must struggle both for and against the look of recognition that would both applaud and appropriate her.

In a sense, then, Davis provides an opposite, female version of the Pygmalion myth that lies latent in Hawthorne's three stories. Because, as a writer, she is struggling primarily against a patriarchal order that would render her "dumb" like the subjects she represents, not against the implications to male identity of an organicist aesthetic, in her fiction it is the male body that is victimized or destroyed, and it is the objectified female body that endures. Whereas Hawthorne seems to encounter the body of the laboring man (Danforth, Aminadab, Drowne) as a consequence, or byproduct, of his exploration of the relation between the male imagination and the female body, Davis seems to deal with issues of a female aesthetic as a consequence of her attempt to represent the laboring male body of Hugh Wolfe. Having served their purpose, Georgiana and Drowne's models die and disappear, leaving the figure of the male artist alone with, or in, the body of a working man. Similarly, having served his purpose, Wolfe commits suicide. Deborah and the korl woman both live on. Deborah is allowed (thanks to a Quaker woman) to escape into a world of "sunshine, and fresh air" that is denied to Wolfe. The korl woman takes her place on the narrator's writing desk, where she serves as an emblem of the narrator herself, of the narrator's muse or inspiration, and of the manual laborer who has been used up in order to produce her.

To call attention to the ways *Life in the Iron Mills* is self-referential and deals with the work of female authorship is not to deny that the story is also about Wolfe and his manual labor. But we cannot ignore that Wolfe functions in the story as a vehicle, not just as a subject. Indeed, as a subject he falls prey to the conventions and inaccuracies that we have seen marking texts by Melville and Hawthorne. Despite her invocation of "hope" in the story's opening, Davis is not much more ready than Channing or Everett to find value in manual labor itself. Her workers are drunken brutes whose bodies know nothing and who take no craft pride in their work. It is true that one of the upper-class visitors to the mill asks a question whose terms are strikingly similar to those in Melville's meditation on the *Pequod*'s carpenter: "'So many nerves to sting them to pain. What if God had put your brain, with all its agony of touch, into your fingers, and bid you work and strike with that?'" (p. 34). But the question is an expression of horror and functions less to blur the distinction between manual and mental labor than to affirm it. Davis simply does not open the door to the possibility that an iron puddler might possess sentient knowledge and perform skilled work. The omission becomes glaring if we compare her text with the autobiography *(The Iron Puddler)* of James T. Davis, an actual Welsh iron puddler who worked in the Ohio River valley at approximately the time in which her story is set. Allowance must be made for the exaggerated boosterism of James Davis's memoir. Nevertheless, among the florid celebrations of American hard work and enterprise one encounters what at least seem to be authentic moments of self-revelation. James Davis writes that the men in his family "were proud of their skill, and the secrets of the trade were passed from father to son as a legacy of great value." From James Davis, too, one learns more specifically that iron-puddling is a complicated process requiring a bodily knowledge that cannot be obtained in books and stored in the mind. Rather, it is acquired through experience and stored in the muscles:

> This process was handed down from father to son, and in the course of time came to my father and so to me. None of us ever went to school and learned the chemistry of it from books. We learned the trick by doing it, standing with our faces in the scorching heat while our hands puddled the metal in its glaring path. . . . To-day there are books telling just how

many degrees of heat make the water right for scalding hogs, and the metallurgists have written down the chemical formula for puddling iron. But the man who learns it from a book cannot do it. The mental knowledge is not enough; it requires great muscular skill like that of a heavyweight wrestler, besides great physical endurance to withstand the terrific heat. The worker's body is in perfect physical shape and the work does not injure him but only exhilarates him.[15]

Granted that James Davis is to a considerable degree romanticizing this work. (He goes on to say that "No iron worker can be a communist, for communists have inferior bodies.") Nonetheless, his memoir does underscore the license Rebecca Harding Davis takes with her material. Her narrative requires as its central character a man who is brutified, unskilled, and weak, not only because these attributes call attention to industrialism's victimization of the body, but perhaps more importantly because they make possible a dramatic presentation of the self-referential problem Davis's story explores. The woman writer's affiliation with an oppressed working class that labors through the body cannot be dramatized if that body is figured as strong, skilled, and male. The worker's *skill* must be erased because the laboring body should give token of the possibility of its redemption only by leaving its own (degraded) work behind and by undertaking the (exalted) work of an artist instead. The worker's *strength* must be erased both because as a female writer Davis desires his body to serve as a vehicle for her self-representation as a woman enfeebled by patriarchy and because she wishes to displace that strength into the female body (the korl woman) that has been objectified and made passive within patriarchy.

*

Both Hawthorne's and Davis's fictions, like Melville's *Redburn,* appropriate and use the figure of the working man even as they attempt to represent him as a subject. These writers' concern with the nature of their own work encourages them to transform their subject into a vehicle for self-analysis and self-representation. Perhaps these works should be regarded as noble failures in that they challenge, but cannot move beyond, the obstacle that is presented by an ontological distinction between manual and mental labor, body and mind. These dichotomies not only make it impossible for the writer, as a mental laborer, to share the "condition" of the manual laborer, but also make it impossible for him or her to represent a territory that appears to lie beyond words—a territory of matter, sensation, and muscular effort, of sentient knowhow rather than mental knowledge. Thoreau's *Week* is perhaps more conscious of what needs to be done to move beyond this impasse, but it is thwarted by the implications to gender identity of such a move: to speak the body and create as nature creates appears to mean both a feminization of authorial work and a willingness to allow things to speak for themselves. That is, it appears to require the "silence" that follows when one lets go of the need to supplement or surpass through art and artifice what exists already in the world.

Nowhere is that need to supplement and surpass more obviously registered than in the male creation and re-creation of the perfectly beautiful female body. And it is precisely here that Davis's fiction distinguishes itself. Even though *Life in the Iron Mills* in some measure appropriates the figure of the male worker, it also *re*appropriates the female body and transforms what has been made to serve as objectified male desire into subjectified female hunger. I have read Davis's story in the context of antebellum thinking about the relation of manual to mental labor, but its reclamation of the female body could as appropriately be placed within the closely associated discourse about the nature of motherhood and the maternal work of the female body. In that discourse women writers work to subjectify and reclaim the female body, but they do so apprehensively because they have also known and experienced it as a means of their subjugation and as a source of their suffering. It is to these subjects that I turn in the next two chapters.

6

The Labored Discourse
of Domesticity

Early in Susan Warner's best-selling novel *The Wide, Wide World,* her child heroine Ellen Montgomery is sent to live with a distant relative because her own mother is too ill to take care of her. (Eventually Mrs. Montgomery dies; neither Ellen nor we ever see her again.) On the boat that carries Ellen away, a kindly minister sees her sobbing and comforts her. The first in a series of benevolent father figures that culminates in the man she will marry, he tells little Ellen that:

> it is not your mother, but he [God], who has given you every good and pleasant thing you have enjoyed in your whole life. You love your mother because she is so careful to provide for your wants; but who gave her the materials to work with? She has only been, as it were, the hand by which he has supplied you.[1]

In this enormously popular domestic fiction, written at the height of what Mary Ryan has called the age of "the imperial mother,"[2] what is the meaning of this substitution of a disembodied, spiritual male parent (God) for an actual, biological mother? How can we reconcile this suggestion that an actual mother serves merely as God's manual laborer, or "hand," with the familiar notion that antebellum motherhood was constructed as a high spiritual calling?

Indeed, considering how much was made of motherhood by antebellum culture as a whole, one is struck by the *absence* of the mother, or at least of the biological mother, not just from *The Wide, Wide World,* but from many domestic fictions of the antebellum period. Beside this puzzle of the absent and subordinated biological mother must be placed two others, closely related. First, why is it that when the orphaned heroines of so many of these fictions grow to womanhood they choose husbands whose attachment to them is familial, not passionate, and whom they know as a father or older brother, not as a lover? Second, why is it that these heroines are so often figured as owing their deepest obligations to, and learning life's most important lessons from, men not women, from substitute fathers (both divine and human) more than from their own mothers?

These questions point to the presence of a crucial cultural problematic in the period's domestic fiction. Much has been written recently about the techniques and accomplishments of the sentimental domestic novel in antebellum America, emphasizing especially the economy of "power" and the effective "cultural work" the genre performed.[3] Insightful and important as these accounts are, they have paid insufficient attention to the way domestic fictions may have *failed* to work smoothly, to the ways such fiction is complicated and problematic, not just complex and powerful. Their central complication, I will argue, is an ambivalence about the nature and value of the work of mothering. On the one hand, as many historians have noted, motherhood is figured in the discourse of domesticity as a high, spiritual calling, to be undertaken only by women who have learned to master their bodies and passions and who can serve quite literally as angels of the house, as spiritual virtues incarnate for both husband and children.[4] On the other hand, and less-noticed by historians, motherhood is regarded also as significantly and ineluctably embodied labor. Some antebellum writers on domesticity celebrate the physicality of maternal labor; others regret it. Most, however, are undecided and register the indecision of the culture at large. When, therefore, Jane Tompkins writes that *Uncle Tom's Cabin* is "the *summa theologica* of domesticity, a brilliant redaction of the culture's favorite story about itself—the story of salvation through motherly love,"[5] she omits a crucial problem at the heart of this story. Many of these novels, and many of the advice manuals that were produced along with them, do not take the nature of "motherly love" and work for granted. They exist in order to dramatize questions about such love and work, and in particular about whether these are to be regarded as primarily embodied or primarily spiritual in nature.

The nature of middle-class woman's work of motherhood is established and explored, I would suggest, by way of the same categories that structured antebellum thinking about manual and mental labor and the relation between classes. Moreover, in the discourse on domesticity, too, lies the procedural complication that permeates all texts about work: men and women who write about domestic labor in general, and maternal labor in particular, approach these subjects through the medium of their own work of writing. Maternal labor and the literature that takes such labor as its subject entwine with, complicate, and define each other. The language of literary aesthetics is used to construct the meaning of maternal labor, which in its turn offers values and terms that are employed to construct the meaning of the literary labor undertaken by domestic writers. For example, in *The Mother's Book* (1831), Lydia Maria Child writes that: "'In forming human character, we must not proceed as a statuary does in forming a statue, who works sometimes on the face, sometimes on the limbs, and sometimes on the folds of the drapery; but we must proceed . . . as nature does in forming a flower, or any other of her productions; she throws out altogether and at once the whole system of being, and the rudiments of all its parts.'"[6] Does Child's proposal that the work of motherhood should be regarded as organic generation rather than artificial fabrication take these terms (and the trope of statuary) from romanticist aesthetics? Or did aestheticians choose these terms in the first place because they were impressed by the power of woman's biological creativity and maternal nurturing? Child complicates matters by going on to reveal that these words are not in fact her own (note the double quotation marks) but those of a "great writer," thereby at once appealing to and affirming literature's authority in matters domestic and aesthetic. If aestheticians derived these terms from their admiration of natural creativity in general, and childbirth in particular, Child now redeploys them to valorize the realm from which they were drawn in the first place. Whatever their ultimate origins, her use of this trope and her appropriation of these words indicate how readily writers structure the labor that is their subject in terms of the labor that is their work. And, of course, the reverse is also true: like Melville, Thoreau, Hawthorne, and Davis, Child and other writers on domesticity explicitly or implicitly dramatize the problematics of their literary labor through their treatment of the labor they are writing about—namely, maternal labor.

In the remaining pages of this chapter, I will try to show how the ontology of maternal labor is not a given, but a contested issue, in the advice manuals and textbooks of the antebellum period. In the next chapter, I will trace the way uncertainties about maternal labor are dramatized in, and at the same time contribute to the narrative procedures of, two representative domestic fictions, Catharine Maria Sedgwick's *A New England Tale* and Susan Warner's *The Wide, Wide World*. Finally, in chapter 8 I will explore more fully the way a specific construction of maternal labor, one that accents its physicality or corporeality, underwrites Harriet Beecher Stowe's *Uncle Tom's Cabin*.

*

As so many historians have demonstrated, the antebellum cult of domesticity, or "true womanhood," insisted upon the spiritual nature and reach of women and their work. By the mid-1840s, according to Mary Ryan, "Motherhood had been extended beyond the woman's biological role in reproduction and the physical care of the infant; it now gave the female parent responsibility for the whole process of childhood socialization."[7] Especially when the early years of bodily nurturing were over, a woman's principal work was to provide her children with a moral education, primarily by serving as a living exemplar of Christian virtues. New England ministers had begun detailing and emphasizing this new role in the early 1800s, thereby undercutting the older family paradigm, in which the mother was primarily responsible for the care of her children's bodies, while the father took responsibility for their moral and intellectual education. By 1850, the mother's primacy as the domestic custodian of her children's minds and souls was firmly established.[8]

The mother's responsibility for the soul, not just the body, of her child, was regarded as a natural corollary of her very being. Man, one writer observed, "has more body and beard. Woman has more fineness, if less strength. She is more angelic, and he more animal."[9] Recently, historians have persuasively shown that this emphasis on the spirituality of woman's domestic work was actually a consequence of the sexual division of labor that established a "woman's sphere" separate from that of men. "The central convention of domesticity," writes Nancy Cott, "was the contrast between home and world."[10] Whereas the world was marked by a grasping pursuit of material wealth and well-being, the home provided a sanctuary where a man could restore his soul and a woman could inculcate in her children the important spiritual values disregarded in the marketplace. At the same time, as Cott and others have pointed out, the middle-class cult of domesticity encouraged a division of labor that promoted the emerging capitalist order. Soothed by the spiritual refuge their wives provided, men were free the next day to go forth and do battle with their competitors.

The mother's principal means of performing this work was a spiritual "influence" quite distinct from material power, which was usually denied her. As Mary Ryan and more recently Richard Brodhead have pointed out, one way this shift took shape was through a new advocacy of the efficacy of moral persuasion rather than corporeal punishment. Mothers were encouraged to use their naturally sympathetic natures to enter into and control the emotional lives of their children. As one manual advised:

> [The mother] should keep her hold on his [the child's] affections, and encourage him to confide to her, without reserve, his intentions and his hopes, his errors and his enjoyments. Thus maintaining her pre-eminence in the sanctuary of his mind, her image will be as a tutelary seraph, not seeming to bear rule, yet spreading perpetually her wings of purity and peace over its beloved shrine, and keeping guard for God.[11]

The mother works, then, by way of her "image," as a "seraph," in the "mind" of her child, not as an embodied presence taking up space (or a rod) in an actual physical setting.

Examples of this insistence that woman's labor is in essence spiritual—undertaken with spiritual faculties and devoted to improvement of mind and soul—could be multiplied indefinitely. It is not surprising, then, that most recent accounts of the ideology of antebellum domestic labor have stressed its emphasis on the spiritual rather than the corporeal aspects of such work.[12] Nevertheless, it is crucial to be aware that the very passion with which the spirituality of domestic labor is advocated by antebellum writers points also to a consciousness, however repressed, that such labor is also unavoidably corporeal in nature. The bodily character of domestic labor cannot be erased entirely, mainly because woman's body is undeniably the site and means of her labors of childbirth and nursing and also because of what I have called the "rhetorical bias" that favors visible over abstract labor.

Thus, even in the writings of those who emphasize its spirituality, the body invades and undercuts their argument through the channel of their rhetoric. For example, when attempting to describe how the mother's disembodied presence works on the soul of her child, writers frequently make use of the Lockean tropes of "impression" and artifice that Child opposes and that figure most commonly in antebellum accounts of mechanical invention. "You cannot know," writes a contributor to the "Mother's Department" in the *Advocate of Moral Reform*, ". . . how deep is the impression which your earnest and affectionate appeals make upon the minds of your sons and daughters . . . ; and they feel, as every child must, that a mother's affection and soul are bound up in their welfare. A mother's love will accomplish more than anything else except omnipotence."[13] Mrs. Emma C. Embury opines in *The Lady's Companion* that "the infant mind as yet untainted by evil . . ." is "like wax beneath the plastic hand of the mother."[14] While these accounts employ the paradigm of the divine (male) maker who stands outside his work and fashions it, who stamps his ideas on the passive raw material of the natural world, the very language they employ tends to smuggle corporeality ("wax," "plastic," "hand,") into their argument. In a similar rhetorical confusion, a writer in *The Lady's Amaranth* aims to distinguish the brute force of man, who "governs by law," from the spiritual influence of woman, who rules "by persuasion." But this writer, too, represents woman's *means* of persuasion as embodied: "The empire of woman is an empire of softness . . . her commands are caresses, her menaces are tears."[15]

In *Woman in America* (1850), to take another example, the novelist Maria McIntosh repeatedly invokes the familiar paradigm which distinguishes mind and soul from body in order to account for the differences between female and male labor. "The stout heart and strong arm of man," she writes, are the instruments of his toil, while the woman works through her "meek and lowly spirit."[16] By the same token, "all the outward machinery of government, the body, the thews and sinews of society, are man's," while the interior, "working, like nature, in secret, is woman's" (p. 25). Returning to this trope later in her book, she writes that "while man has been endowed with qualities which render him the proper controller of the outward machinery of government, the thews and sinews of society, woman is by nature equally fitted to preside over the inner spirit, over the homes from which the social, as distinct from the political life must be derived" (p. 70). But although McIntosh later specifies this "interior" as an "inner spirit," the force of her imagery, which links this interiority with the "working" of "nature," inadvertently points to the interior of the female *body*, to vagina and womb, not to "spirit." Perhaps the fusion should be seen less as an unintended implication of her rhetoric than as precisely the possibility her book, and many others, rehearses and denies—namely, that in the "interior" of womanhood "body" and "soul" are one and the same.

However, the centrality of woman's body to her work as mother and wife is expressed not just unconsciously and obliquely in such rhetorical confusions but also openly and explicitly in many antebellum texts (including McIntosh's). These recognize the body's value principally in two ways: first, by according respect to the manual labor of housekeeping, emphasizing the benefits to women of physical education and bodily exercise; second, by drawing attention to the purely bodily aspects of motherhood—to the act of conception and the months of pregnancy and lactation.

Manual Labor and Domesticity

Writers of domestic tracts and handbooks often excoriated the idle aristocrat's disdain for work, praised the virtues of manual labor, and explicitly linked woman's mission with the elevation of the laboring classes. Not surprisingly, like their male counterparts writing to fix the value of the labor of the working class, these writers had some trouble articulating the value of manual labor as such and, paradoxically, phrased it in terms of its service to spirit and mind. Maria McIntosh, for example, exhorts the American woman to "show that in her opinion, labor imprints no brand upon the brow" (p. 95). Specifically, she urges women to bring about social "equality of mind" by allowing, or even encouraging, their sons to pursue careers in the manual arts; for many young men, she argued, such labor "is the only way in which undisciplined power may be used successfully" (p. 94). But in her advocacy of manual labor, McIntosh retreats as often as she advances. Anticipating the objections of some of her readers, for example, she writes: "'Not dependent upon hired services! What! would you have a lady cook and wash?' methinks we hear some astonished reader claim. Certainly not, we answer, if she can avoid it" (p. 106). Perhaps her chief reason why women should respect the dignity of manual labor is that such an attitude will make for better domestic servants. "You will always have helpers in every department of labor—for the poor we shall always have with us—and the more intelligent and refined these helpers, the better for us and our children."

In another work titled *Woman in America,* Mrs. A. J. Graves also struggles with her loyalties to these conflicting value systems. She is certain that manual labor is less contemptible than complete idleness— "women who spend their days in idleness and folly, are by far more deserving of contempt that she whose time and thoughts are occupied in the necessary manual labours of her nursery and kitchen . . ."—but she is undecided about the amount of manual labor that is suitable to a woman. Woman, she writes, "was placed in this world to fill a station embracing far higher duties than those of a mere domestic laborer. She has been endowed with intellectual faculties and moral influence, which were designed to be cultivated, not only for her own advancement, . . . but to fit her to be the educator of her children, and the improver of her husband."[17] Thus, both McIntosh and Graves are caught in a dilemma: because they want to praise the bodily labor performed by the middle-class mother in her role as "housekeeper" or "housewife," they make use of the egalitarian Jacksonian rhetoric that ennobles manual labor. But they also fear that any celebration of the embodied aspects of maternal labor risks depriving it of its spiritual aura and elevated status. For here, as in the discourse that tried to make sense of the relation between the "learned professions" and artisanal and factory work, the underlying assumption is that manual labor, being corporeal in nature, is ontologically distinct from and inferior to the work of the mind, or spirit.

Here, I think, we need to pause and ask what this confluence of gender and class concerns means. Certainly it means much more than that Mrs. Graves and Mrs. McIntosh have borrowed an essentially class-generated vocabulary in order to articulate gender differences. Indeed, it seems to point to the opposite possibility: that gender distinctions are actually what structure class distinctions. Yet, tempting as it might be to make an either/or choice with regard to historical causality, I would argue that the crucial fact to grasp here is that work plays a complicated foundational role in the construction of both class *and* gender hierarchies. When we focus our inquiry on work (rather than, say, the marketplace, or gender alone), we see that work's meaning serves not just one or the other order of domination, not just class or gender, but both. More important, we see also that its role is not merely that of a servant. Work is not merely a site onto which meanings are projected by ideological efforts to organize classes and genders. Nor is the meaning assigned to work merely an instrument in the process of articulating class and gender hierarchies. Because ideological efforts are themselves forms of work, because the process of articulating hierarchies is itself work, work plays a constant, active, mediating, and destabilizing role in the construction of ideology. A gender or a class may seek to dominate another class or gender by setting forth various claims. But when that process of claiming takes work as its subject, that process confronts (and both conceals and reveals) its own identity as a kind of work.

Writers like Graves and McIntosh appear to value domestic manual labor but keep trying to articulate that value within the frame of an assumed superiority of mind and spirit. However, other writers on domesticity step closer to valuing the body and its labors in and of themselves when they celebrate the benefits of such labor to the body's health. Just as middle-class men were discovering that moderate exercise made them more manly and more efficient workers, the writers of domestic manuals argued that housework made women healthier and better wives and mothers. Mrs. Graves, for example, argues that "even the minor labors, so distasteful to the indolent, the fastidious, and the fashionable—the daily routine of sweeping, dusting, and cooking, of making and mending apparel, etc.—even these become divested of their apparent insignificance when viewed in relation to the important considerations of health, comfort, and order" (p. 69).

Catharine Beecher was the most famous and the most thorough advocate of embodied domestic labor. American women, she claims, are notoriously frail and unhealthy. Their "delicacy of constitution" has many causes, but the remedy is simple and straightforward: "the physical and domestic education of daughters should occupy the principal attention of mothers, in childhood; and the stimulus of intellect should be very much reduced."[18] Women should teach their daughters how to understand and take care of their bodies; one of the best ways to do the latter is to perform housework. By giving their daughters a "domestic education," mothers will protect their health and prepare them for future responsibilities. Women of the "wealthier classes" especially must lead the way and demonstrate by word and deed that there are benefits, and not disgrace, in performing manual domestic labor. "It is . . . the peculiar duty of ladies who have wealth, to set a proper example in this respect, and make it their first aim to secure a strong and healthful constitution for their daughters, by active domestic employments" (p. 27).

On the one hand, the key point here is that Beecher's logic gives value to domestic manual labor by claiming that it benefits a woman's *body*. Although she will later argue that the health of body and mind are intimately connected, she never suggests that a healthy body is good *only* insofar as it makes for a healthy mind. For her, a healthy body is an absolute good; she verges upon an outright recognition of the body as a source of value independent of the mind and spirit. At the same time, however, Beecher does not explicitly extend this recognition to the body's labors; the corporeal benefits of manual domestic work are never in themselves sufficient to guarantee its worth to an individual. If not to be avoided, domestic embodied labor remains something to be redeemed, and the means of that redemption is, once again, the superiority of mind.

Throughout the *Treatise*, Beecher suggests that in order to maximize its benefits, work should be approached with a particular attitude, with an assumption that one can and should control and direct the work one does. One must master, not be mastered by, one's work. The best method of bringing about such control, for Beecher, is to "systematize" and "order" work. Again and again she urges the housekeeper to bring system and order to the otherwise undifferentiated flow of household work, dividing it into specific tasks, each with its proper worksite, technique, and place in relation to other tasks.

> There is no one thing, more necessary to a housekeeper, in performing her varied duties, than *a habit of system and order*. . . . A wise economy is nowhere more conspicuous, than in the right *apportionment of time* to different pursuits. (pp. 144–45)

> The Writer would urge upon young ladies the importance of forming habits of system, . . . Every young lady can systematize her pursuits, to a certain extent. She can have a particular day for mending her wardrobe, and for arranging her trunks, closets, and drawers. She can keep her

workbasket, her desk at school and her conveniences in proper places, and in regular order. . . . And by following this method in youth, she will form a taste for regularity, and a habit of system, which will prove a blessing to her through life. (p. 155)

Unfortunately, Beecher points out, housework is peculiarly resistant to "system"; in fact, what chiefly distinguishes women's from men's work is its inherent unorderliness: "For a housekeeper's business is not like that of the other sex, limited to a particular department, for which previous preparation is made. It consists of ten thousand little disconnected items, which can never be so systematically arranged, that there is no daily jostling somewhere" (p. 136). Consequently, the wife and mother must balance her rage for order with a willingness to be flexible when necessary, which Beecher calls "good temper." To maintain her composure through the vicissitudes of housekeeping will not be easy, Beecher admits; ". . . there is no class of persons, in the world, who have such incessant trials of temper, and such temptations to be fretful, as American housekeepers" (p. 136). Nevertheless, a woman must vigilantly repress these temptations. Her success as a mother and wife depends entirely upon this mastering of her feelings. "There is nothing," Beecher writes, "which has a more abiding influence on the happiness of a family, than the preservation of equable and cheerful temper and tones in the housekeeper" (p. 134). The specific technique Beecher recommends for achieving such self-mastery is to place complete trust in "superintending Providence" (p. 140). "A woman . . . needs to cultivate the *habitual* feeling, that all events of her nursery and kitchen are brought about by the permission of our Heavenly Father, and that fretfulness and complaint, in regard to these, is, in fact, complaining and disputing at the appointments of God" (p. 141).

In sum, even though she moves much closer than either McIntosh or Graves to an articulation of the body's intrinsic worth, Beecher's celebratory account of housework, like theirs, registers her allegiance to the prevailing values of the mind. On the one hand, she regards a healthy body as the *sine qua non* of a happy life, warning her readers of the dangers of excessive intellectual effort; on the other hand, she recommends that the housewife commit herself to a thorough rationalization of domestic work, employing her mind to bring system and order into the chaotic flow of household chores. Similarly, she recommends that the housewife approach her work as though she could regularize and control it herself, and then warns that such an attitude will certainly lead to "fretfulness" and bad temper. Somehow the housewife must pursue "system" and "order" while at the same time acknowledging that these will always be contravened by "our Heavenly Father"—precisely the parent whom Ellen Montgomery is urged to regard as her mother's superintendent.

The Physiology of Motherhood and Bodily Labor

By the 1850s, the genre of domestic advice books was increasingly taken over by writers claiming to be experts in possession of specialized knowledge. Accompanying this trend was a growing tendency to frame maternal labor as an issue best understood by doctors, physiologists, and men of science generally. As Mary Ryan writes, "The constricted themes that dominated the domestic consciousness of the 1850s were often reduced to narrow physiological and materialistic terms, to questions of the physiology of male and female, or the architecture of homes."[19] As a consequence, woman's body and in particular her sexual organs were apt to be viewed as the ultimate determinant of her being and of her distinctive female labors. "Women's reproductive organs are pre-eminent," wrote John Wiltbank. "They exercise a controlling influence upon her entire system, and entail upon her many painful and dangerous diseases. They are the source of her peculiarities, the centre of her sympathies, and the seat of her diseases. Everything that is peculiar to her, springs from her sexual organization."[20] According to many such "experts," all the decisive actions of maternity were essentially bodily in nature. A child's future well-being, for example, was seen to depend less upon a mother's spiritual "influence" than on her physiological performance during conception, pregnancy, and lactation. By the time a woman stopped breast-feeding her child, her most critical maternal work was already accomplished; for better or worse, her child was in essence already formed.

Henry C. Wright's *Marriage and Parentage* (1855) goes even further in articulating maternal labor as an activity of the woman as body. Wright builds his case on the thesis, shared by all phrenologists and by a number of respectable physiologists, that "the soul is a *substance,* as well as the body, so refined as to be susceptible of thought and feeling, and all the phenomena of mind."[21] Because the soul is a "substance," it "originates with the parents," just as the child's physical characteristics do. Consequently, children inherit from their parents not only certain physical traits, but also their "intellectual, social, and spiritual condition." The Lockean concept of the child's mind as a blank slate was thus replaced by one that saw the child as already inscribed, both physically and mentally, by inherited characteristics. Therefore, the maternal work of educating the child in matters of the intellect, society, and religion were now seen to be accomplished not so much in the home as in the bodies of the parents, and especially in the body of the mother. This logic required women to conduct themselves with extraordinary care during pregnancy. Excitements of all kinds were to be avoided because these would be transmitted directly to the vulnerable fetus. "Excitement of the sexual instincts" (p. 96) was especially to be avoided, so women were urged not only to refrain from sexual intercourse but vigilantly to protect themselves against the stirrings of sexual desire. Orson S. Fowler chased the implications of this thesis into the realm of folklore. "Certain states of maternal mind," he warned, "actually do so change and actually distort even the child's bodily shape as to occasion monstrosities." For example: "A girl is marked on the forehead with a bright-red excrescence resembling a cherry, caused by her mother longing for the last cherry of the season, which she tried in vain to reach."[22]

While the physiologists' emphasis on the importance of the body in maternal labor could thus be used to restrict and subordinate women, it could also be turned to more liberating purposes. One of the more remarkable of the many works that participate in the antebellum revision of the relation between mind and body in maternal labor was *The Laws of Life, with Special Reference to the Physical Education of Girls* (1852) by Elizabeth Blackwell. Blackwell, known today for her criticism of the male-dominated medical profession and its treatment of female disorders, prefaces her plea for female physical education by explicitly challenging traditional Christian denigration of the body. "[A]re we not something more than soul or mind or universal principles?" she asks.

> Are we not also substantial, material, and wonderful *living bodies*—bodies of most strange and complex structure, where all sorts of manufactures are carried on; bodies composed of an infinite number of workmen, governed by their own laws, and full of imperious wants, which must be satisfied, that their work may be carried on well . . .[23]

Blackwell's celebration of the body as "substantial, material, and wonderful" reads like a Whitmanesque refutation of Everett's claim that the "body . . . is material substance, is clay, dust, ashes." (At the same time, her tropes of "manufactures" and "workmen" reveal once again how in this period the subject of work—and class relations—is never far from the subject of the body, and vice versa. Indeed, a rudimentary class analysis pervades Blackwell's account of the body: it is an incarnation of the working class with its mass, or "infinite number," of workmen, with its own way of life and work, or its "own laws," and with its agenda of needs, or "imperious wants," which must be recognized by society's head or mind, the upper class.) Blackwell is radical, too, in her forthright questioning of the traditional view that the body is responsible for man's fall into sin. For her, the body is pristine and perfectly innocent in itself. "We offer our bodies great injustice by attributing to them the low appetites and perverted passions, which really belong to a degraded spiritual nature." Blackwell goes even further than Beecher in criticizing the culture's emphasis on intellectual development at the expense of the body. Not restricting her argument to the education of girls, nor even to the United States, Blackwell views the hyperdevelopment of intellect as an almost inevitable consequence of advanced civilizations. "My object," she writes, "is . . . to dwell upon the sins of this age, in relation to the body; how the later stage in the life of a nation, tending to dwell exclusively in the intellect, neglects the physical frame, thereby producing immense evils, both spiritual and material" (p. 26).

Finally, Blackwell even broaches what we have seen to be, in this connection, the bedrock problem: how to see the body in and for itself, how to recognize the values of the body and develop a vocabulary that voices those values without the prejudicial connotations of conventional language: ". . . the neglect which is so striking in our society is our ignorance of what this physical nature in *itself* demands, what are the laws of its well-being" (p. 29). Nevertheless, like other writers of the period, Blackwell stops short of overturning the conventional hierarchy of mind and soul over body. "[T]he body demands the kingship of soul," she affirms; "it is not intended to lead, and it is not capable alone of unfolding its vast powers" (p. 23).

In her essay "Bodily Religion: A Sermon on Good Health," Harriet Beecher Stowe delivers an even more caustic critique of the culture's "steady contempt for the body" and of "the mind's disdain of the body's needs."[24] Christianity requires a healthy body, she argues: "we are commanded by it to glorify God, not simply in our spirits, but in our bodies and spirits." Jesus himself possessed "a perfectly trained and developed body" (p. 343). Like Blackwell and McIntosh, Stowe goes on to make explicit the wider political implications of a revaluation of the body:

> It is worth remarking that in choosing His disciples He chose plain men from the laboring classes, who had lived the most obediently to the simple, unperverted laws of nature. He chose men of good and pure bodies,—simple, natural, childlike, healthy men . . . (p. 344)

Blackwell's and Stowe's affirmations of the body are not typical, but they are not anomalous in the antebellum period either. As we have seen, while the domestic advice literature of the 1840s and 1850s certainly promoted maternal labor as the activity of a disembodied, spiritually superior woman, this view was powerfully and variously resisted—by the rhetorical figures these writers themselves employed; by the widespread recognition that much domestic work is manual, or physical, in nature; by a parallel discourse that insisted on the nobility of manual labor; and by the rise of self-appointed experts drawing on the materialistic sciences then beginning to exercise their own powerful influence on intellectual life.

Today, it may be difficult to imagine how the female readers of this inconsistent literature on the nature of maternal domestic labor could negotiate the Scylla and Charybdis of body and soul. However, we should not rush to translate our own difficulty into their "contradiction." Our search for illuminating aporias should not blind us to these writers' achievement in synthesizing, or blurring, categories their culture had kept separate. If Graves, McIntosh, Beecher, Blackwell, and Stowe were undecided about the value of the body and its labor, they nevertheless powerfully challenged the dominant paradigm which regarded mental and manual labor as fundamentally distinct and of radically different value. The necessarily embodied nature of much maternal work required them to focus on the health of the female body and the work of the housewife's hands, while at the same time their experience of such work taught them that it was by no means purely or simply bodily. Moreover, in their repeated claim that the housewife must make certain abstract principles ingrained *habits* of behavior, must transform the cognitive into the instinctive, they in practice blur the distinction between mind and body. But as we have seen, no vocabulary was available to them by which they might have expressed the synthetic nature of housework. Beecher and Blackwell could propose a new respect for the body; they could echo the findings of contemporary physiology and write that "there is such an intimate connection between the body and the mind, that the health of one cannot be preserved without a proper care of the other," but they could not take the further step of saying that mind and body are in fact one thing, much less that the body might know things which remain inaccessible to the mind.

This unstable construction of ideal maternal labor seems to challenge not just that period's dichotomy of manual and mental labor, but also models of making and producing that have dominated thinking about work from Marx's *Economic and Philosophical Manuscripts* through Arendt's *The Human Condition* to Elaine Scarry's *The Body in Pain*. For example, Child's contention that the maternal labor of "forming human character" is essentially organic, not artificial, means that it does not conform readily either to Karl Marx's notion of labor as self-realization, or to Elaine Scarry's similar understanding of work as a process of self-objectification.[25] According to Child's view (which was, as I shall show, contested in this period), the mother's aim in raising children is not to express herself or to objectify an inner condition; on the contrary, her work requires that she suppress the promptings of self and submit to a rigid discipline of self-abnegation. Similarly, although she places less emphasis on self-discipline, Margaret Fuller has essentially this distinction between organicism and fabrication in mind when she writes that it is "more native" to woman "to be the living model of the artist than to set apart from herself any one form in objective reality; . . ." Woman's soul "flows," "breathes," and "sings" rather than "deposits soil, or finishes work."[26] Moreover, even those writers who maintained that the mother does in some sense fashion materials (her children) did not figure her as working with "tools" (which, as Scarry has argued, serve as a crucial "axis" of self-projection into the material world). If the mother is in some sense a maker, or artificer, of her children, she works immediately. Indeed, her intentions and means are indistinguishable. She has no "idea" which she seeks to realize concretely in materials, but rather she has living, embodied children in whom there already resides a soul bestowed by God; her job, then, as a fashioner, is to serve as the "hand" of God, to execute the design he has conceived. Thus, even the model of work that most emphasizes the role of mind in conception tended in practice to reduce woman to the status of a "hand" or body in service of God. But while Child's model of maternal labor cannot be subsumed under either Marx's or Scarry's understanding of work, it does not conform readily either to Hannah Arendt's notions of "work" and "labor." Maternal labor does not embody ideas in material that endures, nor does it simply submit to an endless cycle of production and consumption. Rather, it seeks to nurture an imperishable soul in material that decays.

The fact that the antebellum construction of maternal labor resists this diverse array of explanatory theories suggests not only that these have paid insufficient attention to gendered labor but also to a subtler yet more consequential possibility: namely, that these theoreticians often construct the meaning of work over and against, or rather as a hidden denial of, the foundational activity of mothering. Only a moment's reflection is required to see that without the labor of childbirth and childrearing there could be no other kinds of labor. Yet this is a possibility neither Marx, nor Arendt, nor Scarry recognizes, much less explores. All share a predisposition to model work on the pattern of artisanry. To my knowledge, only Charlotte Perkins Gilman pursues and make explicit a foundational status for maternal labor. In antebellum representations, as we shall see, this possibility is repeatedly adumbrated in both fictional and nonfictional texts about women's work—haunting, as it were, the mutually complicating relation between the labors of writing and mothering. For if mothering is our species' original and originating work, then the woman who abandons it in order to write risks losing much more than social approval. She risks losing power.

7

Maternal Labor in the Work of "Literary Domestics"

Catherine Maria Sedgwick and Susan Warner

How do antebellum domestic fictions contribute to or disrupt conventional notions of maternal work? Specifically, where do they stand on the issue of the relation of soul (or spirit) to the body in such work? As I have argued earlier, the answers to these questions must be pursued along two lines—by investigating both the subject and the practice of the writers of these fictions, both their representations of the work of motherhood and the work they perform in producing such representations. In *Woman's Fiction: A Guide to Novels by and about Women in America, 1820–1870,* Nina Baym makes clear that many of these writers "conceptualized authorship as a profession rather than a calling, as work not art." She points out also that this way of seeing themselves and their writing "had an inevitable effect on their work"; perhaps "by dismissing work of traditional literary greatness as outside their scope these women also foreclosed on certain possibilities for themselves and others."[1] Much of what follows builds on Baym's observations, attempting to understand more fully what it might mean to say that something is seen "as work not art." Neither of these terms is stable or transparent; neither can be understood independently of the other. Moreover, although my aim in this study is to investigate the relation between work and art, or at least the particular art of literature, not to make claims about the merit of various works of literature, such an investigation also opens up the meaning of "art." Following the lead of Jane Tompkins, among others, we can look at the ways these writers' conceptions of writing as work made available, rather than simply fore-closed on, certain possibilities.

In the pages that follow, I will focus on two novels, Catharine Maria Sedgwick's *A New England Tale* (1822) and Susan Warner's *The Wide, Wide World* (1850). Of course, no two works alone can be taken to be representative of all women's fiction of the period, or even of women's domestic fiction. But these two works have a special interest because they are, respectively, the first and the most famous of the novels of do-mesticity. Sedgwick's book set a narratival pattern that was followed by many others, and Warner's took that pattern and added elements that made it a stupendous best-seller. As Nina Baym writes: "The genre [of women's fiction] began in America with Catharine Sedgwick's *New England Tale* (1822), manifested itself as the favorite reading matter of the American public in the unprecedented sales of Susan Warner's *Wide, Wide World* (published in late 1850), and remained a dominant fictional type until after 1870."[2]

Both *A New England Tale* and *The Wide, Wide World* begin by kill-ing their heroines' actual, biological mothers, thereby enacting, I would suggest, an erasure of the embodied mother and of embodied maternal work. That is, by killing the biological mother, these fictions detach the essence of maternal labor from specific biological mothers and their bodies, clearing the stage for alternative forms of motherhood, each of which will be tested, then accepted or rejected. In *New England Tale,* a relatively simple narrative, the death of Jane's mother allows her to ex-perience and weigh the mothering of the family servant, Mary Hull, against the mothering of her aunt, Mrs. Wilson. In *The Wide, Wide World,* a more panoramic work, the death of Ellen Montgomery's mother opens the door to a train of surrogate mothers—a society lady, an innkeeper's wife, Aunt Fortune, Mrs. B., her grandmother, and her Scottish aunt. In both novels, however, these surrogates fall into two categories: bad mothers, most of whom (like Mrs. Wilson) are related to the heroine by blood, and thus represent the failings of a diminished but still present possibility of biological, embodied motherhood; and good mothers, who are related to the heroine not biologically, but spiri-tually, and who are thus able to represent the advantages of a purely spiritual form of motherhood.

In *New England Tale,* the house servant Mary is an ideal surrogate mother, devoutly Christian and highly skilled in the spiritual nurturing which is shown to be more important than the mere physical protection offered by Jane's wealthy aunt. Mary advises Jane to place absolute trust in God. "'Make the Bible your counsellor; you will always find some good word there, that will be a light to you in the darkest night; . . .'"[3] Mrs. Wilson by contrast, is in all ways a woman of the world. Sedgwick tells us that "she was sordid and ostentatious; a careful fellow-worker with her husband in the acquisition of property" (p. 35). As a mother, she observes the outward formalities of her role, but she is incapable of rising to the spiritual demands it makes. "As might be expected, her family was regulated according to 'the letter,' but the 'spirit that giveth life' was not there" (p. 40). The crucial difference between Mary and Mrs. Wilson is epitomized in a small incident. Jane's aunt advises her to take away from her parents' house some pieces of silverware and other small things that her father's creditors' inventory would not have noticed. Mary disapproves of this plan and instructs Jane to take only her mother's Bible. Jane obeys, and it is her consistent reliance on Mary's advice that delivers her from the perils of Mrs. Wilson's flawed mothering.

In *The Wide, Wide World,* the contrast between Ellen's Aunt Fortune and her friend Alice Humphreys is drawn with equal boldness and in similar terms. The narrative presents Fortune as a woman constantly at work in the house. Ellen's first view of her is characteristic: "She came in, shutting the door behind her with her foot; and indeed both hands were full, one holding a lamp and a knife, the other a plate of butter" (p. 99). When Ellen comes down to breakfast the next morning, she again finds Fortune in the midst of domestic labor, standing by the fire and "holding the end of a very long iron handle by which she was kept in communication with a flat vessel sitting on the fire" (p. 103). Although her tastes are simple, Fortune is a woman who lives for and through the richly described material world of her house and farm. Like Aunt Ophelia in *Uncle Tom's Cabin,* whom we will meet later, Fortune is a superb housekeeper who carries Catharine Beecher's principles of system and order to precisely the extreme Beecher warns against. Like Ophelia, she indulges in complaint and fretfulness, forgetting that a perfect house does not necessarily make a perfect home.

Fortune soon puts Ellen to work doing manual domestic labor, and when Ellen resists, Fortune makes her values perfectly clear. "There's nothing in this house but goes through my hand, I can tell you, and so must you. I suppose you've lived all your life among people that thought a good deal of wetting their little finger; but I'm not one of 'em, I guess you'll find" (p. 113). Indeed, the novel makes perfectly clear that what is at stake is not just styles of life and class, but styles of motherhood. Fortune, who has a deep but unexpressed desire to be Ellen's mother, is bitterly jealous of Ellen's relationship with Alice. Fortune assumes that Ellen's real mother must have been like Alice, a reader and a thinker rather than a housekeeper:

> "That's the way your mother was brought up I suppose. If she had been trained to use her hands and do something useful instead of thinking herself above it, maybe she wouldn't have had to go to sea for her health just now; it don't do for women to be bookworms."

In a period when health experts were discouraging girls from intellectual effort and urging them to perform housework, *The Wide, Wide World* charts an opposite course. Ellen is by nature a bookworm who is thwarted by Fortune's peevish and unreasonable demands that she perform housework. ("So much yarn as Miss Fortune might think it well she should spin, so much time must be taken daily from her beloved reading and writing, drawing and studying; her very heart sunk within her" [p. 418].) Although in substance and scene, the novel rejoices in the rich, sensual details of domestic labor (particularly in scenes of making quilts and putting up applesauce), its narrative and argument strongly favor the relatively ethereal (and less visually representable) work performed by Alice Humphreys. Alice does nothing, in fact, except pour tea, arrange flowers, and read books, which she calls "her greatest treasure" (p. 164). Alice is a Christian as well as a lady, and her real work, it would seem, is to preach, instruct, and convert others, and to perform small acts of Christian charity.

It might be argued that if we read the novel typologically, and see Aunt Fortune and her demands as part of Ellen's "fortune" or fate, we will see that housework is redeemed because it is one of life's necessary trials. And this is true. Ellen herself reflects that "this wearisome work was one of the many seemingly untoward things which in reality bring out good" (p. 419). But this point simply underscores the fact that Alice Humphreys's more spiritual approach to domesticity in general, and to mothering Ellen in particular, is *not* an "untoward thing" which will "bring out good," but a pleasing thing that is good in itself. Whereas Aunt Fortune's style of mothering and Ellen's manual labor are represented as service to a system of "higher" values, Alice Humphreys's mothering is represented as the actual and essential activity of that system—that is, as the nurturing of spiritual growth.

In both novels, the erasure of the biological mother and the celebration of spiritual motherhood is accompanied by two other features that elevate spiritual, at the cost of embodied, motherhood. First, it is strange but true that the best surrogate parents in both *New England Tale* and *The Wide, Wide World* are men. In the former, Mr. Lloyd becomes both father and mother (and eventually husband) to Jane, offering her some financial support but, more important, giving her Christian counsel. In the latter, Ellen's real mother is shown to be nothing more than a vessel, or channel, for the spirit of God. As the minister on ship tells Ellen, your mother "has only been, as it were, the hand by which he supplied you." Here, once again, the "hand" is a synecdoche for the body, and for material rather than spiritual labor. As God's "hand," Ellen's mother has consummated her divine contract by dying so that Ellen may come to know a higher and more spiritual labor—performed at first by Alice Humphreys, but finally and most purely by a man, John Humphreys. For it is John who, especially after the death of his sister Alice, becomes the mainstay of Ellen's life. She calls him her "brother," but he is actually everything to her—her teacher in all things (biblical study, manners, horseback riding, geography, logic, history), her fatherly counselor, and her source of motherly love. The book underscores John's privileged parental role when, in the last paragraph, Warner writes that Ellen's mind "happily fell again into those hands [that is, Humphreys's] that had *of all been most successful* in its culture" (my emphasis).

Although both *New England Tale* and *The Wide, Wide World* offer for inspection good surrogate mothers unrelated to the heroine by blood (Mary Hull and Alice Humphreys), both eventually award more value to the surrogate parenting provided by men. *The Wide, Wide World* goes so far as to kill off Alice—no doubt as another trial for poor Ellen to overcome, but also as another iteration of what I am arguing is the inner logic of the domestic novel. By this logic, the heroine must be deprived of her mother, and if a capable surrogate mother comes along to take her place, then the heroine must be deprived of that mother as well. To explain this logic by pointing out that the death of a mother is, for the child, the ultimate loss, is to beg the question. On the level of Christian typology—yes, the death of the mother is a first-rate source of redemptive suffering. But on the level of the reader's actual experience of the novel, the death of the mother provides a developed fantasy of motherlessness, especially biological, or embodied, motherlessness. The thousands of women who made *The Wide, Wide World* one of the best-sellers of its time no doubt approved of its affirmation of the power of suffering to bring about conversion. But it is equally true that the novel offered them the opportunity to live for a while without mothers, to test the surrogate mothers the narrative provides, and to experience the fantasy of being brought up by, and eventually marrying, the perfect parent—a (surrogate) father. All three aspects of this experience, or fantasy, suggest that women readers were in flight from the demands of embodied motherhood—a flight more concretely epitomized by the period's rapidly declining fertility rates among middle-class women.[4] Embodied motherhood may have been what these readers wished most to leave behind when they opened the pages of a novel like *The Wide, Wide World*.

Precisely this logic informs a third characteristic, or puzzle, of such novels. When the young heroine eventually grows up, (as, alas, she must—though *The Wide, Wide World* does everything possible to deny and retard her maturity), she faces the specter from which the narrative has repeatedly delivered her. Now she must marry, and in doing so *she* must become a biological mother. Both *New England Tale* and *The Wide, Wide World* attempt to evade, or mitigate, this fate by portraying the heroine's spouse as a relative (brother and/or father) and not a lover. Indeed, the relations between Jane and Mr. Lloyd, and those between Ellen and John Humphreys, are entirely asexual. To imagine these couples engaged in sexual intercourse is to imagine something very close to incest. *A New England Tale,* like many other novels of the genre, offers Jane the temptation of marrying out of passion, and presumably of incurring all the consequences thereof, including motherhood, and then makes the marriage impossible by revealing her lover to be a scoundrel. Moreover, when Jane does finally marry her surrogate parent, Mr. Lloyd, the novel conveniently provides her with a stepdaughter, thereby at once obviating sexual intercourse and allowing her to become a surrogate, rather than a biological, mother herself. The concluding pages of the original edition of *The Wide, Wide World* promise only that Ellen will again fall into Humphreys's "hands" and go "to spend her life with the friends and guardians she best loved" (p. 569). It is true that in the Appendix, which Warner added to the novel, Humphreys and Ellen are reunited and, it is hinted, married. But when the two take a carefully described tour of their home, no mention is made of a bedroom, much less of a nursery.

*

These novels, then, treat the *subject* of maternal work largely by advocating spiritual, at the expense of embodied, maternity. But what about the literary *practice* that produced the novels themselves? Do these novels appear to be the outcome or product of literary practice conceived of as maternal work? And, if so, of what kind of maternal work—spiritual, embodied, or a combination of both?

Mary Kelley has already detailed how a number of the literary domestics attempted to understand their literary labor as a form, or extension of, their work as wives and mothers. "The literary domestics could enter man's world," Kelley argues, "because they had not left behind women's work." Their strategy, accordingly, "was to conceive of the literary habit as no more than a translation of the domestic habit," and they accomplished this aim principally by regarding their books as instruments of moral instruction. "The success of that little book [*Home*]," wrote Catharine Sedgwick, "has been a great pleasure to me, because it strengthens my hope of doing some good to my fellow creatures." "Certainly it is most pleasant to me," Susan Warner wrote, "to know that anything I have written has been of any use and comfort to anyone."[5]

If the writing of fiction is conceived of as moral instruction, and thus made congruent with woman's spiritual work of "influence," it follows also that such writing should be seen as a duty, not a choice. To judge by their own comments in letters and journals, this was precisely how many female writers of fiction viewed their writing—not as a mode of self-expression, but as a social work requiring self-abnegation. Hence these authors' repeated professions that they were not the actual authors of their works, that they were not personally responsible for their books, and that they had no ambitions for literary greatness or success.

While Kelley's observations are drawn almost entirely from biographical and autobiographical sources, from what the literary domestics said and wrote *about* their work, I believe that there is evidence *within* the fictions that when these women wrote, they did so as mothers, guided by some of the same principles that informed the ideal of maternal work. This evidence is found in three features of these narratives. The first is a marked disinterest in narratival originality and self-expression, and a correspondingly deep trust in the narratival conventions of the genre. The second feature is what I call the genre's provisional, or bracketed, representation of material reality. The third is the genre's ambivalent representation of work in general and the work of writing in particular. Each of these features, as I hope to show, has its source in an aspect of the antebellum construction of ideal maternity.

According to Nina Baym, the many novels of the literary domestics "all tell, with variations, a single tale. In essence, it is the story of a young woman who is deprived of the supports she had rightly or wrongly depended on to sustain her throughout life and is faced with the necessity of winning her own way in the world."[6] Jane Tompkins has provided a detailed account of the ways these works structure that drama by repeating again and again a tale of conversion through suffering and of salvation through self-abnegation. That conversion narrative, Tompkins suggests, was drawn from and in turn served the needs of the antebellum revival movement.[7]

However, when this feature of repetitiveness and conventionality is viewed from another perspective—one that situates the work of literary composition in relation to the work of idealized maternity—a complementary explanation emerges. Viewed abstractly, as I have noted, maternal work does not appear to produce a durable thing that exists in the material world outside the maker. The mother's aim is not to express herself or to objectify an inner condition; on the contrary, her work requires that she suppress the promptings of self. It is hardly surprising, then, that women writers of the period denied that they were "authors" in the usual sense of the word, or that they denied that they were producing great works of lasting appeal. The literary domestics would not have tried or hoped to produce self-expressive works that endured (Arendt's "durables," Scarry's "artifacts") because they had quite different intentions: they wished to speak as much as possible *immediately* to an immediate audience of contemporaries. It was not their work that had permanence, but the truth being carried by their work. Thus, having no investment in the illusion of artistic immortality, they did not strive to develop literary techniques that would have enabled them to shape a work in accordance with "eternal" aesthetic principles. Instead, they perfected techniques of reaching the audience of their own time. For the same reason, originality—whether of subject or method—would have had no intrinsic value to them. Since few wrote to express a unique sense of self, few needed to tell a "new" story in a new way. To most, it was not newness that mattered, but need; if there was a social need for their work, they were content. Consequently, they did not hesitate to borrow a story that had already been told, and to retell that story repeatedly. Indeed, conventionality was an auspicious sign of social need, whereas originality pointed suspiciously toward the temptations of self.

A second major feature of these fictions is their practice of exemplification, or illustration, which results in a provisional, or bracketed, representation of the material world. The literary antecedents of this practice are undoubtedly to be found in the Bible, in *Pilgrim's Progress* and other Christian allegories, and in the New England tradition of typological interpretation. But an equally important source of this characteristic of woman's fiction was the antebellum conception of the mother as an exemplification of virtue. Manuals repeatedly urged mothers to bear in mind that for children, personal example was a much more effective mode of instruction than the exposition of principles and rules. Lydia Maria Child, for example, wrote that "the great difficulty in education is that we give *rules* instead of inspiring sentiments."[8] As a consequence of this precept, mothers had to strive ceaselessly for personal perfection. As Susan Huntington described her duty in her diary: "In short nothing but the most persevering industry in the acquisition of necessary knowledge—the most indefatigable application of that knowledge to personal cases—the most decisive adherence to a consequent course of piety—& above all the most unremitted supplications to Him who alone can enable us to resolve & act correctly—can qualify us to discharge properly those duties which devolve upon every Mother."[9] The mother, wrote J. S. C. Abbott, "must learn to control herself; to subdue her own passions; she must set an example of meekness and of equanimity, or she must necessarily expect that all her efforts to control their passions will be ineffectual."[10]

The reader of Sedgwick's novel is never allowed to forget that the illusory material world created by the fiction has no right to exist except as the exemplification of a moral truth. The enduring "reality" of the world created by the novel is not that of commonsense philosophy, a simple pragmatic faith in the world as we experience it through our senses. Reality, for Sedgwick, is an inner truth, known to the heart, and usually made manifest in the word of God. Sedgwick is keenly aware that for the illustration of the truth to be effective, it must be a convincing and compelling illustration; it must *seem* very real. At the same time, she knows that the illustration must never set itself up as something real in itself, for the moment it does so it betrays the truth it is supposed to point toward. Therefore, the writer of fiction whose principal aim is moral instruction must devise techniques that create what we might call a provisional, or bracketed, reality. The narrative presentation of reality must somehow announce at the outset that this reality exists only by license and that when its function has been served, it will disappear.

Sedgwick's technical realization of this imperative is simple, but complete: for the most part, she avoids material description altogether, and when she does provide it, she is careful to make sure that her readers see the material world through the eyes of one of the characters. One senses that her characters do not move through a real world but through their visions of it. For example, as Mr. Lloyd and his wife enter the countryside around the "village of ——" (p. 52), they converse about the landscape around them. For some writers, this would be the time and place to establish the New England locale of the book's title by providing a few details, however conventional—apple orchards heavy with fruit, an old mill by a stream, whatever. But Sedgwick offers this instead:

"Do you know," said she [Mrs. Lloyd] to her husband, "that I prefer the narrow vales of the Housatonic to the broader lands of the Connecticut? It certainly matters little where our dust is laid, if it be consecrated by Him who is the 'resurrection and the life'; but I derive a pleasure I could not have conceived of, from the expectation of having my body repose in this still valley, under the shadow of that beautiful hill."

"I, too, prefer this scenery," said Mr. Lloyd. . . . "I prefer it, because it has a more domestic aspect. There is, too, a more perfect and intimate union of the sublime and beautiful. These mountains that surround us, and are so near to us on every side, seem to me like natural barriers, by which the Father has secured for his children the gardens he has planted for them by the river's side." (p. 52)

The idealism of Sedgwick's fiction is unrelenting, and if it is not matched, it is at least approximated in the work of other literary domestics.

Warner's novel, more typically of the genre, achieves a less perfect union of ends and means. As I have suggested in earlier chapters, the tension between ideality and materiality is nowhere stronger than when work is the subject being represented. For whenever the narrative turns to that subject, it is forced into self-reflexivity. It confronts the question of its own origins (what kind of work, if work it was, brought it into existence) and of its own being (as natural thing or man-made artifact, as an element of the "earth" or a constituent of the "world.") Neither *New England Tale* nor *The Wide, Wide World* knows quite what to make of domestic work in general, and domestic manual labor in particular. In *New England Tale*, as we have seen, the housemaid Mary Hull offers the spiritual sustenance which the proper "lady" who is her official guardian withholds. In *The Wide, Wide World*, Aunt Fortune is far from perfect, but she is certainly better than Ellen's wealthy Scottish relatives. Yet the most telling fact is that neither Jane nor Ellen grows up to be a housekeeper, not even in Beecher's middle-class sense of the word; both have servants who will perform that work for them.

In *The Wide, Wide World*, this deep ambivalence about the value of housekeeping is played out repeatedly. No scenes are more richly and effectively evoked than those in which some kind of work—sweeping, shelling and sorting beans, putting up preserves, laying down hams— takes place. And it is not just the activity of work, but *the home as an objectification* of such work, that figures so memorably in this novel. When Aunt Fortune puts Ellen to work in the buttery, for example, the hitherto mysterious room "which she had never dared to go in . . . before," appears as chaste and solemn as a temple:

It was a long, light closet or pantry, lined on the left side, and at the further end, with wide shelves up to the ceiling. On these shelves stood many capacious pans and basins of tin and earthenware, filled with milk, and most of them coated with superb yellow cream. Midway was the window, before which Miss Fortune was accustomed to skim her milk; and at the side of it was the mouth of a wooden pipe, or covered trough, which conveyed the refuse milk down to an enormous hogshead standing at the lower kitchen door, whence it was drawn as wanted for the use of the pigs. Beyond the window in the buttery, and on the higher shelves, were rows of yellow cheeses; forty or fifty were there at least. On the right hand of the door was the cupboard, and a short range of shelves which held in ordinary all sorts of matters for the table, both dishes and eatables. Floor and shelves were well painted with thick yellow paint, hard and shining, and clean as could be; and there was a faint pleasant smell of dairy things. (p. 141)

This passage is uncompromisingly realistic, expressing an unabashed absorption in the delight of physical things and the material world. The "superb yellow cream," the "wooden pipe," the "rows of yellow cheeses," the "thick yellow paint" are evoked for their own sake, not because they exemplify a moral lesson. The lovingly inventoried abundance—"*many* capacious pans," "*superb* yellow cream," "*forty or fifty* were there at least"—bodies forth the generosity of the natural world. Like Keats's "Autumn" ode, this scene of stored harvest is a reverential tribute to Ceres, to Demeter, to the innate fecundity of nature and to the value of the human labor that cultivates it. Over and against the manifestly etherealistic program of the novel as a whole, it gives expression to *another*, more covert religion of domesticity—one suppressed by Christianity—a religion of immanence rather than transcendence, the natural religion of Aunt Fortune (so aptly named) and, until Ellen converts him to Christianity, of Farmer Van Brunt as well.

This registration of a deep, religious, but non-Christian and hence nonspiritualizing value in the manual labor of domesticity is made repeatedly in the novel. The preparation of preserves, both sausages and apples, to take one other example, is represented as a hilarious harvest festival:

As the party were all gathered it was time to set to work. . . . One party was despatched downstairs into the lower kitchen; the others made a circle round the fire. Every one was furnished with a sharp knife, and a basket of apples was given to each two or three. Now it would be hard to say whether talking or working went on best. Not faster moved the tongues than the fingers; not smoother went the knives than the flow of talk; while there was a constant leaping of quarters of apples from the hands that had prepared them into wooden bowls, trays, or what-not, that stood on the hearth to receive them. Ellen had nothing to do; her aunt had arranged it so, though she would gladly have shared the work that looked so pretty and pleasant in other people's hands. . . . It was a pleasant evening that. Laughing and talking went on merrily; stories were told; anecdotes, gossip, jokes, passed from mouth to mouth; . . ." (p. 253)

Like Melville's famous sperm-squeezing passage in *Moby-Dick*, this scene presents a vision of ideal, unalienating work that binds people together and blends, rather than breaks apart, eros and labor. But the serious little Ellen, for whom such work is usually "a kind of work she had no love for" (p. 141), who regrets "her neglected studies and wasted time" (p. 141), is deliberately excluded from the circle of companionship through labor. She cannot partake in the performance of an activity that is represented as a wonderful harmony of pleasure and purpose, of "talking" and "working." Her fortune, ultimately, is not to live in this world, but in another.

In short, the novel itself seems to be at variance with its own heroine. It is the novel's interest in these scenes of work that brings them to life and makes them so much more memorable than, say, the stylized and repetitive scenes of weeping. But what is the source of this interest? Why does the novel point to an alternative set of values, one that regards materiality and materialism not as things to be despised and ultimately transcended, but as the locus of immanent goodness? Why do these scenes of embodied domestic work associate this alternative set of values with domesticity in the broadest sense of the word—with the world of home and farm, crops and harvest, that the otherwise despised and ridiculed Aunt Fortune presides over? The answer, I suggest, is that the novel lingers in and explores these scenes because it recognizes that therein lie also some of its own values. The work that brought it into being may have more to do with making butter and quartering apples than with disciplining the self and submitting to God's will.

This is precisely the possibility that is raised, or staged, in the final chapter Warner wrote for, but did not include in, the published novel. John has provided Ellen with her own study, next to his own, and in her description of it Warner seems to delight in a fantasy that is full of contradictions. On the one hand, the room will be a place of prayer and study. On the other, it is much more richly furnished and decorated than the rest of the house: "nothing had been spared which wealth could provide or taste delight in." Not surprisingly, however, Warner retreats from, and qualifies, the dangerous and regressive sensuality of Ellen's bower; "though luxuriously comfortable, luxury was not its characteristic; it was the luxury of the mind. *That* had been cared for. For that nothing had been spared" (pp. 574–75). Thus Warner allows Ellen to acquire a sumptuous Victorian room, so crammed with furnishings—"cabinets and tables and bureaus of various material and structure—a little antique book case . . . an old-fashioned but extremely handsome escritoire, . . . easy chairs, footstools and lounges"—that it sounds like a cluttered antique shop, not a study. At the same time, Warner distances Ellen from this rich, densely material space, so pleasing to the eye and comfortable to the body, by claiming that its "luxury" is intended for the "mind" only.

This tension between a longing for the material things of the house and a commitment to the spirituality of the home appears also in the question of what Ellen will *do* in this room. Certainly she will not clean it. (The faithful Margery, whom John has promoted to "housekeeper," will take care of that.) Her first response to the room is fear that it will seduce her into idleness. "You mean to make me a luxurious-liver at my ease," she teasingly accuses Humphreys. He denies the charge, saying "No—we will do the work of life together and help each other to be faithful" (p. 576). But what exactly is this "work of life?" The answer comes when Ellen exclaims, "What a delicious place for reading!" Apparently Ellen's work will consist of reading and, as the escritoire suggests, writing. Of course, Warner cannot explicitly claim that these activities—a replica of her own—actually constitute a woman's proper "work" and "duty." She can only hint at it, by way of a room and the objects in it. Moreover, her clues suggest that Ellen's work as a reader and writer requires a space that is materially rich and stimulating, not austere. Ellen's work, like Warner's, might be undertaken in the service of spiritual truths and moral education (that is, as work analogous to that of spiritual motherhood), but apparently it is best performed in an environment of material luxury, or at least material abundance.

Warner probes further into the relation of a writer's work to the values of body and spirit, "outward" and "inward," "material" and "immaterial," when she has Ellen and John discuss the two paintings he has hung for her in the study. The first one they look at, of Mary Magdalene, they find praiseworthy because it is a beautiful representation of the female body. Ellen especially delights in "the perfect graceful repose of that whole figure," "the natural abandonment of every limb," the body in which "not a muscle is strained." The second picture, depicting a Madonna and child, is a representation of maternal love. "The mother's face in calm beauty bent over that of the infant as if about to give the kiss her lips were already pouting for; the expression of grave maternal dignity and love; but in the child's uplifted deep blue eyes there was a perfect heaven of affection, while the little mouth was parted, it might be either for a kiss or smile, ready for both" (p. 578). While the second painting obviously could be regarded as a celebration of the *incarnation* of spirit—and Warner's description calls attention to "mouth," "lips," and "eyes"—John recognizes only its spirituality. To him, the paintings stand in absolute contrast to each other. The second represents "moral beauty," the first "merely physical." *"There,"* he says, pointing to the first, "'is only the material outside, with all the beauty of delineation, *here* is the immaterial soul.'"

But Ellen objects. The maternity so beautifully rendered in the picture of the Madonna and child seems to her not entirely immaterial. "'I am sure here is a beauty of delineation, too,'" she replies, "her eyes fixed on the picture."

This subtle disagreement between master and pupil prompts a further exchange of views about the relation of mind to body, of (eternal) "truth" to (incarnated) "beauty." Humphreys replies that if the second painting does show a "beauty of delineation," it is a "delineation of something else"—that is, something other than "the material outside." Ellen again disagrees. She is not willing to accept Humphreys's dichotomy. "'I am apt to think there is an eternity of the beautiful as well as of the true,'" she says. Humphreys insists that "'it is the true that makes the beautiful.'"

Ellen, outwardly all submissive, still demurs, and her next question probes the logic of Humphreys's position. If the true is what makes the beautiful what it is, namely beautiful, then everything beautiful must be true. Nothing inwardly mean could possibly appear beautiful and nothing inwardly good could possibly appear ugly. "But surely there is a beauty and a deformity of feature with which the mind has nothing to do?" she asks. Surely, in other words, the body has its own nature—for good or for ill—apart from the mind.

Less sure of himself now, John asserts that "Perfection of mind certainly *tends* to perfection of body"; this is a much more flexible position, and Ellen is now willing to let the matter drop—almost. A moment later she raises the question again, in yet another form. "'I could never make out anything but *humanity* [in the expression of the Madonna and child] when they [others] cried *divinity*.'"

"'It is humanity, I think,' said John smiling, —'but refined from human impurity—pure humanity.'" The painting of Magdalene, he concludes, is "'the beauty that fades—the beauty of earth,'" while the beauty in the painting of the Madonna "'is that which endures.'"

Thus, the familiar dichotomy has been reasserted, but in the process important questions about the nature of art and, consequently, about the nature of the novel we hold in our hands, have been raised. In Ellen's resistance to Humphreys's absolute distinction between mind and matter, truth and beauty, is registered the narrative's uncertainty about its own nature. Is it a painting like that of Magdalene, its beauty "of earth," an "outward" beauty that is destined to "fade?" Or is it a painting like that of the Madonna, one whose truth is "inward," spiritual, and enduring? It should be clear by now that the novel, like Ellen, resists this either/or choice. While it is programmatically committed to the maternal work of moral education, it is also tempted by—or finds its analog in—the maternal work that places body before mind, beauty before truth.

The novel's complicated resistance to the paradigmatic dichotomy of mind and body, spirit and matter, spiritual and embodied motherhood can be understood also as a resistance to Arendt's distinction between "work" and "labor." The novel is "labor" insofar as it is programmatically committed to the view that all artifacts, like materiality itself, are provisional and unreal, in service ultimately to an imperishable spiritual truth. At the same time, the novel is "work" insofar as it becomes interested in its own nature as objectification, as artifact, as "delineation"; it has an impulse to make the "outward" the equal of the "inward," to accord as much value to materiality as spirituality.

*

Antebellum middle-class culture's understanding of work rested squarely, if insecurely, on the distinction between mind and body, spirit and matter. Yet writers who attempted to represent maternal labor were unable to make it conform to either of these categories, and they were especially unable to figure their own work, so apparently mental, as purely so. On the contrary, they repeatedly explored the possibility that literary creation was essentially embodied and material in nature.

While both New England Tale and The Wide, Wide World contain representations of motherhood that accent the spiritual, rather than the embodied, The Wide, Wide World especially reveals that in practice the writing of novels is predicated on an interest in, and dignification of, materiality. Warner's text explicitly suggests that although the activity of writing domestic fiction may be devoted to spiritual ends, it proceeds by material means—material not in the sense that a book consists of paper, ink, cloth, and glue, but in the fact that a novel is woven out of the materials of everyday life. Warner's novel especially moves toward a recognition of the necessity, and hence the value, of materiality—and hence of manual labor and embodied motherhood. While female readers of The Wide, Wide World may have been attracted to its story in part by their desire to escape the demands of embodied motherhood and domestic labor, the book itself recognizes that these are in some ways the appropriate and indispensable social analog of the private work of writing a novel. However spiritual their intentions, both maternal labor and the genre of the novel depend upon and manifest the sensual richness of the material world and the constructive powers of the human body.

8

Literary Composition as Maternal Labor in *Uncle Tom's Cabin*

In one of the many arguments about slavery which Harriet Beecher Stowe stages in *Uncle Tom's Cabin,* two Southern slaveholders discuss the peculiar institution's effect upon white children. Augustine St. Clare, who has grave doubts about the moral ramifications of slavery, points out to his brother Alfred that it has made his son hotheaded and undisciplined. "'Since training children is the staple work of the human race,'" says Augustine, "'I think it something of a consideration that our system does not work well there.'"[1]

Augustine's remark that "training children is the staple work of the human race" is the book's most explicit articulation of a belief that at once jeopardizes and structures Stowe's composition of *Uncle Tom's Cabin.* On the one hand, Stowe's conviction that God has entrusted to woman this most fundamental and important kind of human work discourages her from undertaking any other kind of work, including the work of writing an abolitionist novel. On the other hand, Stowe's effort to make the composition of *Uncle Tom's Cabin* congruent with, and even an extension of, childrearing, produces several of the narrative techniques that give the novel its distinctive narrative power.[2] In other words, perceiving the writing of this novel as a potent threat to her own duties to her children, Stowe compensates by figuring its composition as a form of maternal work, guided by many of the principles that defined the nature and scope of maternal work in the antebellum decades.

Stowe frequently gave voice to her anxiety that writing in general, and the writing of this novel in particular, were taking her away from her principal work—mothering. (She was not alone: Lydia Maria Child had

152

guiltily observed that: "Literary women are not usually domestic; not because they cannot easily be so—but because they early acquire the habit of attending to literary things, and of neglecting others."[3]) In Stowe's case, this work was especially difficult and demanding. Her husband Calvin, a moody hypochondriac, left Harriet alone to look after their three (eventually seven) children while he traveled to raise funds for the Lane Seminary or to take rest cures for his supposed ailments. Harriet, too, was frequently ill, either suffering from "a severe neuralgic complaint" or recuperating from her numerous pregnancies and labors. Calvin was not much of a provider and, strapped for cash, Harriet decided in 1840 to supplement their income by writing articles. Even though the decision could be justified as an extension of her duty to care for her children, she did not find it easy to make. As she wrote to Calvin:

> On the whole, my dear, if I choose to be a literary person, I have, I think, as good a chance of making a profit by it as anyone I know of. But with all this, I have my doubts whether I shall be able to do so.
>
> Our children are just now coming to the age when everything depends on my efforts. They are delicate in health, and nervous and excitable, and need a mother's whole attention. Can I lawfully divide my attentions by literary efforts?[4]

Unless it is read as a disingenuous effort to win Calvin's approval of a *fait accompli*, Stowe's letter suggests how ambivalent she felt toward writing. The work of mothering seemed to her to require her "whole attention"; she doubted whether she could "lawfully divide" her attentions in order to perform the work of writing, even when this was work undertaken not for personal satisfaction but for "profit" that would support her family.

Ten difficult years later, these doubts still troubled her. Considerable evidence suggests that Stowe never could fully admit to herself that she was a writer. She published her first story under her sister Catharine's name and most of her subsequent articles and essays under masculine pseudonyms. Like a number of other women writers of this period, Stowe downplayed and even denied her authorial identity by claiming that *Uncle Tom's Cabin* had in effect written itself, or that God had written it. "I did not write that book," she said to a friend. ". . . I only put down what I saw . . . it all came before me in visions, one after another, and I put them down in words."[5]

Stowe's fear that her writing would deflect her attention from "the staple work of humanity" is registered also in the mutually contradictory accounts she gave of the genesis of *Uncle Tom's Cabin*. According to one account, the vision of Tom's death came to her in church; back at home she quickly wrote it down then read it aloud to her sons. In another account, the scene came to her while she and Calvin were setting up their new home in Andover, Massachusetts; immediately upon writing it down, she read it aloud to Calvin. And according to a third account, *Uncle Tom's Cabin* had its deepest source in her grief over the death of her son Charley: "It was at his dying bed and at his grave that I learned what a poor mother may feel when her baby is torn from her" (*Life,* p. 173). Different as these stories are, they have in common an anxiety to locate the conditions of authorial creativity in the home, among the family; they advance the belief, or fantasy, that a writer's work can harmonize with, as it naturally grows out of, her daily work as a mother and wife. "I wrote what I did," she writes in a preface to *Uncle Tom's Cabin,* "because, as a woman, as a mother, I was oppressed and heartbroken with the sorrows and injustice of what I saw, and because, as a Christian, I felt the dishonor to Christianity."[6]

*

Stowe's need to figure the writing of *Uncle Tom's Cabin* as a form of maternal labor which she undertook "as a woman, as a mother," seeks satisfaction not just in troping and wordplay but in her actual narrative practice. However, in order to give such a narratological account of *Uncle Tom's Cabin,* it is necessary first to have a fuller and more philosophical account of maternal work than I have so far provided. This account can be derived from two sources: Stowe's own writings about domesticity and maternal labor and the writings of her grandniece, Charlotte Perkins Gilman, in *Women and Economics* (1898) and *Human Work* (1904). Gilman, though in several important respects critical of antebellum notions of maternal labor, helpfully articulates their broader implications by situating them at the center of a thesis about human work in general.

Like most of her essays, Stowe's "The Lady Who Does Her Own Work" is written pseudonymously, with a man as its ostensible author. The strategy allows her both to deny (or at least make light of) her identity as a writer and at the same time to distinguish between the means and aims of writing by men and the means and aims of writing by women like herself. Her male narrator assumes a posture that identifies masculinity with idleness, femininity with bustle and work. "Lying back in my study-chair, with my heels luxuriously propped on an ottoman," the narrator reports that he is reading one of his favorite books. This turns out to be a volume of Hawthorne's tales, which, he says, constitutes a "cloud-land" where he loves to "sail away in dreamy quietude, forgetting the war, the price of coal and flour, the rates of exchange, and the rise and fall of gold."[7] The narrator's own natural desire is to persist in such "forgetting." Only the determined intrusion of his more energetic and practical wife yanks him out of this "cloud-land" as she reminds him that he must get to work on his latest essay in order to support his family.

What Stowe subtly implies, then, is that writerly work as it is practiced by men like Hawthorne and the narrator aims to create a separate sphere for the imagination, a sphere as far as possible from the turbulence of "war" and most specifically from the vicissitudes of the market. Although (as its title suggests) Stowe's essay locates itself squarely within the tradition of a separate "woman's sphere," she nonetheless makes clear that when a woman writes from within that sphere she is more likely than a man, or at least than Hawthorne, to remember and transact business with the sphere of politics and economics. Somehow the woman writer's work inside the home makes her more prepared than her male counterpart to think about and contest the realities of the market that appear to lie outside it.

"America," the narrator begins, "is the only country where there is a class of *ladies* who do their own work." That distinction has its historical origin in the hardships of the wilderness that required all of the early settlers, men *and* women of all classes, to labor "side by side." New Englanders could have employed slaves but, "having once felt the thorough neatness and beauty of execution which comes of free, educated, and thoughtful labor," they "would not tolerate the clumsiness of slavery." The colonial work experience not only softened class and gender distinctions, obviated slavery, and married necessity with "beauty," but also "most nearly" solved what the narrator of the essay considers to be the foremost problem facing any culture—the difference between, and hierarchy of, manual and mental labor. "Hence arose, and for many years continued, a state of society more nearly solving than any other ever did the problem of combining the highest culture of the mind with the highest culture of the muscles and physical faculties." It is the early national legitimation of this "combining" of two activities, or faculties, usually kept separate that has made it possible for antebellum middle-class "ladies" to perform physical labor and maintain their self-respect. For, when properly executed, women's domestic work is by nature such a "combining," at once physical and mental, employing the hands and the head. Indeed, the essay goes on to suggest that woman's domestic labor has carried furthest, and with best results, this "combining" of mental and physical culture. The narrator conjures up a matriarchal utopia of "three happy women together" who have perfected their work.

"Long years of practice have made them familiar with the shortest, neatest, most expeditious method of doing every household office, so that really, for the greater part of the time in [their] home, there seems to an onlooker to be nothing to do." This perfect domestic work in effect erases itself. It has always been done; it is never being done.

Thus, like so many other antebellum texts on the subject of work, Stowe's essay approaches its representation of (domestic) work by way of a self-consciousness about the work (writing) of representation. Stowe's preliminary concern in this essay is not with its announced subject, domestic labor, but with literary labor, and with the difference between such labor as *she* performs it and such labor as male writers like Hawthorne perform it. But that difference rests, in turn, upon her notion of a woman's proper work as wife and mother. For this reason, the two kinds of work reflect and help constitute each other. Just as a woman's domestic labor in effect erases itself when it is done in "the shortest, neatest, most expeditious way," so, too, a woman's writerly work will strive to make itself invisible. This invisibility will be achieved partly by way of a masculine pseudonym, but more effectively by managing to replicate domestic labor's "combining" of the mental and the physical, "the highest culture of the mind with the highest culture of the muscles and physical faculties." Moreover, the essay implies, the achievement of that replication will give the female writer an immediate consciousness of and access to the world outside the home—the world from which the male imagination (as represented by the narrator and Hawthorne) seems determined to escape.

How exactly does the domestic labor which her literary labor emulates achieve this "combining" of the mental and physical, and how does this in turn produce invisibility and lead to what I have called "access" to the world outside the home? The answer lies in that characteristic of the antebellum construction of maternal labor which distinguishes it from the parallel discourse about the meaning of manual labor—namely that it is understood not in terms of a rigid dichotomy of "head" and "hands," mind and body, but in terms of a more fluid (though equally problematic) relation among "head," "hands," "soul" and "heart." Woman's noncorporeal essence was described not simply as "intellect" or an abstract "spirit," but as a more human "soul" that was synecdochically identified with an actual organ, the heart. The work of the heart shares characteristics with both the work of the head and the work of the hands. Like the work of the head, it is usually invisible; its operation may be registered by physical symptoms—tears, smiles, kisses—but the work itself consists of an invisible flow of sympathy from one heart to another. Like the work of the hand, however, the work of the heart is in some ways more obviously and ineluctably embodied than mental work. That is, the individual experiences the performance of that work as a bodily experience, as something that happens inside the body. Moreover, insofar as the work of the heart almost always works upon other human beings, it works upon and through their bodies.

Indeed, its manifest corporeality alone would serve to link the "heart" more closely to the "hands" than to the "mind." Margaret Fuller's *Woman in the Nineteenth Century,* for example, contains a staged dialogue that succinctly dramatizes such a linkage. The book's narrator and a typical American husband are in conversation. The husband declares that he "'will never consent'" if his wife tries to "'step beyond the sphere'" of her sex. The narrator replies that "'it is not consent from you that is in question, it is consent from your wife.'" The husband protests:

> "Am I not the head of my house?"
>
> "You are not the head of your wife. God has given her a mind of her own."
>
> "I am the head and she the heart."
>
> "God grant you play true to one another then. I suppose I am to be grateful that you did not say she was only the hand."

Fuller's narrator goes farther in identifying women with embodiment when she says that no problems will arise "'if the head represses no natural pulse of the heart.'" If the embodied woman is permitted actually to live by the laws of her body—that is, her "heart"—then she and her husband "will be of one accord." Unfortunately, it appears to be inevitable that the "head" *will* repress the "heart." The narrator doubts "'whether the heart *does* consent with the head, or only obeys its decrees with a passiveness that precludes the exercise of its natural powers, . . .'" Thus, even while the main thrust of her essay is to argue for women's mentality and possession of mind, Fuller herself lapses into the view that woman is in some respects more embodied and passional, less intellectual and controlling, than man. At the same time, like Melville, she suggests that the core problem of the division of labor is not so much a distinction between physical and mental, execution and design, as a tendency of the head to "repress" the erotic potentialities of the heart. By the same token, however, the embodied nature of female labor suggests that it is more likely than masculine labor to make good these potentialities—at least, if no male mind is there to deny them.[8]

In another of her domestic essays, "What Is a Home?" Stowe writes that "no home is possible without love" and goes on to argue that love,

especially a mother's love for her children, is the source and motive not
only of her own work, but of all human work (since it is only women
who, like the narrator's wife in "The Lady Who Does Her Own Work,"
get their men to work at all).[9] Because woman's maternal work is in essence to love, which is the work of the heart, it can be described as both
"spiritual" and "bodily." (Though, as we saw earlier, for most antebellum writers this doubleness was less a synthesis than an uncertainty to
be resolved, less an achievement than a point to be contested.) In other
words, it is because she loves and works by loving that a woman is more
able than a man to eroticize labor and thereby to experience it as a synthetic operation of all of her faculties, not just of one part of them. Finally, because maternal work is the "staple work" of the human race, the
work that is foundational to all other forms of work, it gives a woman
access not just to the domestic sphere but, when necessary, to any
sphere of human work. That is, because the work of the market, with its
"rates of exchange, and the rise and fall of gold," exists, finally, in order
to nurture the human family, men's prerogative there is always condi-
tional: in a sense, their role is to serve as stand-ins (living pseudonyms)
for the women who perform the most immediately important human
work within the home. In an emergency, men's license to operate there
can be withdrawn—by God, or by women.

Some of these ramifications of the antebellum construction of maternal labor, while only implicit in Stowe's writings, become explicitly articulated in the writings of her grandniece, Charlotte Perkins Gilman.
For Gilman, as for Karl Marx, work is the quintessentially human activity ("Work is human life"),[10] but unlike Marx Gilman locates the urge
to work less in the human species as a whole than in one of its two sexes,
the female. Work, as Gilman sees it, is "mother energy" (p. 207). It is
"primarily an extension of the maternal function" (p. 208), that is, a social elaboration of the mother's bodily labor of gestation, birth, and
nurturing. But while its origins lie in each individual mother, human
work is always social work—work for others. "The need to be supplied
is a social need, the growth to be attained is a social growth, of no more
value to the individual detached, than beating would be to a heart detached. Work is an organic function, incontrovertibly" (p. 184). Perhaps because her model of society is, quite literally, that of a "social
body" (p. 118) or "social organism" (p. 112), work, for Gilman,
emerges from and returns to the body. Just as the energy that comes
spontaneously and naturally out of the mother's body makes another
human body, so what society as an "organism" makes are artifacts that
compose its own "vast body" (p. 161)—"the structure of brick, stone,
and iron, wood, cloth, leather, glass, paper,—all that elaborate com-

pound of materials in which we live" (p. 158) Consequently, Gilman's values are as radically materialistic as Marx's: "In our made things lies that much of our humanness, and as we use them we grow by that much more human; in this reactive process lies the desirability of the thing, and its importance. The power of 'mind over matter' is commonly observed, but the effect of matter upon mind, the reaction of the body upon the spirit, is not so clear to us" (p. 165). Finally, because society is essentially organic, and because it is at once the product and producer of a maternal energy that continually makes its own body, that work is best which subordinates itself to the interests of the whole. "When we accept the organic nature of society, the whole proposition changes, we then see all varieties of work to be social functions, performed in the interests of the whole" (pp. 180–81). To stand apart and take craft pride in one's work is to regress to a more primitive condition, that of the farmer and cattle-keeper whose self-reliance and independence make them "stingy" (p. 136). It is to beat like a "heart detached." (Gilman's choice of organ here is hardly fortuitous.) The ideal worker is one who, like the sailor, unquestioningly subordinates self-interest to the smooth functioning of a large and complex productive system "of specialized, interdependent service, each for all and all for each" (p. 207). The success of human culture lies precisely in the fact that it has persuaded, or rather "forced" (p. 208), its males to perform maternal work, to locate themselves in and work for the benefit of, an organic whole. Less ambivalently than Melville and Thoreau, but nevertheless calling to mind their sentiments, Gilman calls this a "motherising of the male" (p. 208).

Four important features can be identified in this suggestive account of the nature of maternal labor. First, it is in essence a diffusion of love and is by nature *self-sacrificing*. It aims not to create artifacts or durables or commodities, things that stand outside the self in order to objectify and commemorate it. Rather, it subsumes the self in a larger "organic whole"—a whole that is organic precisely because it is the woman's body writ large, an extrapolation of her single identity as a biological producer of new human life—and seeks to maintain and perfect that whole through the diffusion of love and goodwill. Second, maternal labor is *synthetic*. Because it is at bottom the work of the heart, maternal labor manages to combine body and mind, hands and head, which work in harmony as its instruments or lieutenants. Third, maternal labor is so efficient that it verges on self-erasure, or *invisibility*. Because it combines hand and head, and harmonizes them, maternal labor is at once healthful and pleasant, exercising the whole and not just a part of one's being. These qualities make possible, in turn, an extraordinary efficiency—an efficiency that derives not from a division, but from an integration of labor, not from a Tayloresque separation of design and execution, but from the "combining" of these. Fourth, because maternal labor is "the staple work" of the human race, and because all human work is in essence "mother energy," maternal labor is foundational; it undergirds all of civilization and informs all other kinds of human work, even those assigned to men in a sphere of business and politics outside the home. Maternal labor, being the foundation of all labor, gives the woman who properly performs it access to, and moral authority and expertise in, the world outside the home.[11]

These characteristics are repeatedly emphasized in the representations of maternal labor offered within *Uncle Tom's Cabin*. For example, its foundational status is made clear insofar as women are much more likely than men to be found working at all. Like the narrator of Stowe's essays, men tilt back their chairs, put up their feet, and "sprawl" or "lounge." The women sit upright, industriously sewing or knitting. Men like Shelby squander their estates; women like Mrs. Shelby restore them. Ophelia brings order to the St. Clare household. Chloe works long hours to redeem Tom. Cassy contrives a miniature home for herself and Emmaline in Legree's attic and then engineers their escape. In her account of the women of New England, who have "no servants in the house," Stowe underscores also the invisibility, or self-erasure, of domestic work ideally performed. The mistress "sits sewing every afternoon among her daughters, as if nothing had been done, or were to be done—she and her daughters in some long-forgotten fore part of the day, 'did up the work,' and for the rest of the time, probably, at all hours when you would see them, it is *done* up'" (pp. 244–45).

Stowe epitomizes all these characteristics of maternal labor—its synthetic, efficient, foundational, and self-submissive qualities—in the figure of Rachel Halliday. Halliday is likened to the "original mother," Eve, and the morning work she superintends (preparing a large breakfast) is no more arduous than "picking up the rose leaves and trimming the bushes in Paradise." Diffusing Gilman's "mother energy" to all the "hands" that help her, Halliday at once guides, enlivens, and softens the work her assistants perform. "If there was any danger of friction or collision from the ill-regulated zeal of so many young operators, her gentle 'Come! Come!' or 'I wouldn't now' was quite sufficient to allay the difficulty." As Stowe's sly appropriation of the word "operators" from the discourse on factory labor and conditions suggests, Halliday's mode of working is being offered as an alternative to *two* forms of work developed within the patriarchal order of the mid-nineteenth century—slavery and factory labor. Halliday succeeds in realizing the dream (shared in their different ways by Fourier, Emerson, and Melville) of making work "attractive." "Everything went on so sociably, so quietly, so harmoniously,—it seemed so pleasant to do just what they were doing . . . — even the knives and forks had a social clatter . . ." Mother energy has diffused itself even into the tools, "the knives and forks," these workers employ. Amid this enjoyable hustle and bustle, the male titular head of the family is something of an outcast, a tolerated vestige of a displaced order; but Stowe suggests that he can see himself for what he is and might soon take his place in the happy circle: he "stood in his short-sleeves before a little looking-glass in the corner, engaged in the antipatriarchal operation of shaving" (pp. 222–23).

*

How does this construction of ideal maternal labor inform and structure Stowe's composition of *Uncle Tom's Cabin*? Her earliest words about the sources, methods, and intentions of her novel offer the beginning of an answer.

"I am at present occupied upon a story," Stowe wrote her publisher Gamiel Bailey on 4 March 1851, "which will be much longer than any I have ever written, embracing a series of sketches which give the lights and darks of the 'patriarchal institution,' incidents which have occurred in the sphere of my personal knowledge, or in the knowledge of my friends."[12] Stowe's words indicate that from her novel's inception she knew that its subject and target would be a "'patriarchal institution,'" that is, an institution arising as much from gender as from racial hierarchy. Stowe herself, as we shall see, accepts some aspects of both hierarchies, among them the notion that only men may speak publicly about public issues while women devote themselves to the relatively silent, invisible, but so crucial work of maternity. "Up to this year, I have always felt that I had no particular call to meddle with this subject, and I dreaded to expose even my own mind to the full force of its exciting power" (p. 66). Slavery is a "force," a "power," an "exciting" expression of the violent public realm from which women have had to shield themselves, and to be shielded, in order to perform the sacred work of mothering. Only a "particular call" could justify a woman's meddlesome intrusion into the public realm, and this is precisely what Stowe feels she has received. Like the "Cartheginian women who in the last peril of their state cut off their hair for bow-strings to give to the defenders of their country," Stowe will risk symbolically desexualizing, or unfeminizing, herself by speaking out: "I feel that the time has come when even a woman or a child who can speak a word for freedom and humanity is bound to speak" (p. 66).

But when woman speaks, what will she say and how will she say it?

Stowe's letter ponders this question in terms that reveal her deep assumption that the imagination itself is structured by gender distinctions. If, as a woman, she is by nature vulnerable and cautious, as a woman she also has distinctive powers. The rhetoric of Stowe's letter suggests that when the female imagination does risk entering the male sphere, it takes care to do so on its own terms, conscious that the very forces that have shaped slavery have also shaped and defined that sphere. This is why Stowe throughout her letter is so reluctant to describe herself as a writer. The *written* word, what Thoreau in *Walden* calls "the father tongue," belongs to man, to the father. Therefore, she is one who will "speak" (in what Thoreau calls "the almost brutish . . . mother tongue"), not write, her words against slavery.[13] This is why she emphasizes that her story's sources will be personal and oral, not historical and inscribed. Even when she alludes to writing, her language represses it: "every woman who can write will not be *silent*" she proclaims [my emphasis]. And she most piercingly reveals her distrust of the written word, and her reluctance to be a writer, when she tells Bailey that her "vocation is simply that of a painter, and my object will be to hold up in the most lifelike and graphic manner possible Slavery, its reverses, changes, and negro character. . . . There is no arguing with *pictures,* and everyone is impressed by them whether they will or no" (p. 66).

As a woman who should not write, but who must write, Stowe's strategy will be to write as if she were not writing, to write as if she were speaking or painting, because these means are more appropriate to her nature and powers as a woman and mother. As I hope to show in this chapter, from this basic decision arise a number of closely related narrative techniques which, taken together, enormously enhanced her novel's effectiveness. These are: first, a pictorial or scenic presentation of material, with an emphasis on space not time; second, a manipulation of the reader so that she or he experiences a powerlessness that is a precondition of love; third, a representation of slavery (or any other social phenomenon) not as a distinct evil which can be abstracted or surgically removed from an otherwise good social order, but as an organic expression of what is already inherently wrong with that social order. All of these techniques, I believe, have their origin in Stowe's understanding of the nature and power of her work as a mother.

Stowe's reliance on space (not time) as the primary narrative frame of her novel emerges from her concern to model authorial work on maternal labor. For time, as several critics have argued, is a central concern of the masculine imagination (and of any imagination that relies primarily on narrative practices developed by men within a patriarchal order) because fatherhood can be established only through an inferential backward glance through time. "Paternity," writes Mary O'Brien, "is not, like motherhood, an experienced relation to the natural world mediated in labor, but an idea dependent upon . . . the notion of cause and effect." Fatherhood "cannot be confirmed by immediate experience," and must therefore be adduced to be known, whereas motherhood can simply be shown. It is the self-evident, self-demonstrative nature of motherhood, and the mother's "experienced relation to the natural world mediated in labor,"[14] that stands behind Stowe's description of her "vocation" as "simply that of a painter," whose "object is to hold up . . . *pictures* . . ." Whereas paternity is always in doubt (especially within the South's racially ordered system of slavery), there is "no arguing with" the fact of maternity. Moreover, because a woman's labor of giving birth situates her within an entire natural order of making, she can have comparatively little need to grope for such compensations as invention and artifice. Her making is at once inarguably there, in the child she has produced, and at the same time invisible insofar as it has occurred naturally. That is, it need not insist upon its visibility, and in particular it need not make itself visible by attempting to stand over and against the natural world as part of human culture.

Uncle Tom's Cabin begins in one small room, Mr. Shelby's dining parlor, and gradually expands across the length and breadth of "this wide land." As several critics have noted, the novel is organized by two movements through space—Eliza's and George's flight northward to Canada and Tom's descent into the inferno of the deep south. Although these movements at first promise to be symmetrical, Stowe devotes the narrative increasingly to Tom's plight and eventually abandons the other story for some seventeen chapters. As a consequence, the Harris family is left lingering on the threshold of freedom for an indeterminate length of time while Tom meets his Christic destiny at the hands of Simon Legree. But this flaw in the work is insignificant. Since Stowe's narrative is structured by space, not time, the chronological lapse is hardly noticeable, much less bothersome. The spatial imagination concentrates on *locating* characters, events, and readers—that is, on subordinating their differences to the shared condition of being in the same place at the same time. As its title suggests, Stowe's novel is an invitation to occupy a particular space, not a call to follow its characters through a chronologically ordered series of adventures.

The narrative's emphasis on space over time, on demonstration over inference through cause-and-effect, is frequently replicated and represented in the novel itself. Again and again Stowe's text suggests that a "picture" or image has more evidentiary validity and persuasive power than consecutive reasoning, abstract logic, or words. Senator Bird, to take an obvious example, discovers that all of his principles and all of his reasoning, though internally consistent and logically irrefutable, are simply obliterated by the image of a runaway slave in his home. Less obviously, when little Eva reads the Bible she is drawn increasingly to the passages she cannot understand—"parts whose dim and wondrous imagery, and fervent language, impressed her the more that she questioned vainly of their meaning" (p. 380). Although in *Uncle Tom's Cabin* the power of the picture is enlisted most often on the side of justice, it can and does serve evil also. After all, it is the picture of the slave on the posted notices of runaways, and the marks inscribed on the slave's body, that most threaten him or her with capture and return.

Stowe's eagerness to figure the composition of *Uncle Tom's Cabin* as speech, rather than writing, is also replicated in the text. Stowe repeatedly indicates that the disembodied written word is suspect because it lends itself to abstraction and misuse, whereas speech, issuing directly from the speaker's body, is a potent vehicle for the good work of the heart. Again and again Stowe contrasts the "truth" as it is known in human feelings of sympathy and pain with the specious truth that is inscribed in texts—in the circulars for runaway slaves, in Haley's account book, documents, and bills of sale, in the "H" branded on George's hand, in Shelby's certificate for Tom, in Marie's written instructions that Rose be whipped, in the Fugitive Slave Law, and so on. All these form a long chain of false documents that fetter slaves and repress men's better feelings. Even the Bible, Stowe shows, can be appropriated to form a link in this chain (which is another reason why Eva prefers the Bible's meaningless imagery). Most obviously, Stowe scathingly satirizes the ministers who use the Bible's words to justify slavery. More subtly, she occasionally expresses even deeper doubts about the Bible's reliability, as when Chloe responds to Tom's biblically authorized submissiveness by saying "'Wal, any way, thar's wrong about it *somewhar*, . . . I can't jest make out whar 'tis, but thar's wrong somewhar, I'm *clar* o' that'" (p. 164). Similarly, when Lucy jumps overboard with her child, and Prue and Cassy confess to having killed theirs, the reader would hesitate to affirm the Christian orthodoxy that condemns them to eternal perdition. All these written texts take second place to the spoken, or even wordless texts that appear as images, or revelations, of the truth—like the wordless text of Rachel Halliday's brow "on which time had written no inscription, except peace on earth, goodwill to men" (p. 215).

Because this view of maternal labor assumes that human society is an organic whole, within which distinctions and divisions are contingent and provisional rather than essential, Stowe's representation of slavery insists upon its connections with all aspects of national life. The "peculiar institution" is a national, not a Southern problem. Moreover, it is entwined with the other major problems (the relation among classes, the degradation of work, the ascendancy of marketplace over Christian values) that trouble the country. This contextualization of slavery has immediate narrative power: it allows Stowe to appeal to her readers not just by concretizing what for many was an abstract, faraway problem, but by plucking the strings of their own anxieties about class, work, faith, family, and so on.

In the novel's opening scene, for example, Stowe introduces slavery indirectly, as a problem mediated by, or filtered through, her readers' assumed anxieties about class and social status. The narrator presents "two gentlemen . . . sitting alone over their wine, in a well-furnished dining parlor, in the town of P——, in Kentucky." The scene immediately hints at a transgression: the two men have brought business into the home, transforming the dining parlor into a place of business and, as if to emphasize this usurpation, drinking liquor there together. This tremor of tension is amplified when Stowe invokes another instability—the unreliable, or contested, nature of language itself—which in turn gives way to antebellum uncertainty over class status as that was epitomized by uncertainty as to who was, or was not, a "gentleman." "For convenience sake," she writes, "we have said, hitherto, two *gentlemen*. One of the parties, however, when critically examined, did not seem, strictly speaking, to come under the species" (p. 41).

At this point, a knowledge of antebellum literary convention might predispose a reader to suspect that the "real" gentleman in the scene will turn out to be the commoner, not the aristocrat. But Stowe disdains the formula. The man who fails to measure up is the commoner, "a short, thick-set man, with coarse, commonplace features, and that swaggering air of pretension which marks a low man who is trying to elbow his way upward in the world" (p. 41). Here is another appearance of Melville's Jackson, a representative of the Jacksonian "canaille" who, some feared, were about to seize control of the nation. Stowe's more genteel readers would be gratified by her disclosure of another reason to despise Haley: he turns out to be not just a coarse *parvenu*, but a slave-trader.

However, such readers would have just fallen into Stowe's carefully prepared trap. For, after encouraging them to identify with the patrician Shelby, who speaks perfect English and shrinks from Haley's pretensions and crudities, she reveals that the two men are partners in a business "transaction." They are buying and selling slaves. Thus, when "critically examined," Shelby too fails to live up to the standard of a "real gentleman," since no Christian could possibly be engaged in such sordid business. The comedy of the scene reinforces the point: try as he might, Shelby simply can't keep his distance—physical, social, or moral—from Haley. They are implicated together in the evils of slavery. So, too, then, are the readers who have cast their lot with Shelby by identifying with him. Stowe makes her point explicit in Chapter Eight: "If all the broad land between the Mississippi and the Pacific become one great market for bodies and souls, and human property retains the locomotive tendencies of this nineteenth century, the [slave] trader and catcher may yet be among our aristocracy" (p. 132).

Stowe's technique, then, is to entangle her readers in the problem of slavery by compelling them to identify with a character, or point of view, which she later shows to be immoral or untenable. What readers experience as a consequence is less a change of mind than of heart. This goes beyond the technique of the sentimental novel which, as Philip Fisher has described it, "depends upon experimental, even dangerous extensions of self by the reader" into persons from whom selfhood has usually been withheld—like children and slaves.[15] Stowe furthers this extension by inviting, or compelling, her readers to identify not just with the victims, but with the villains of the social order. Not just with the Toms and Harrys, but with the Shelbys and Haleys of the world. When society is an organic whole, no one can stand apart from anyone else or remain untouched by a problem located anywhere within that whole.

Stowe's assumptions about the shape and nature of the social order might at first invite comparison with Emerson's remark in "Man the Reformer" that commerce is "a system of selfishness" in which "every man partakes." But whereas Emerson's response to this notion is to escape, to find a place (call it "solitude" or a call it a dreamy "cloud-land") where the self remains untouched by vice, Stowe's conviction is that escape is neither possible nor desirable. Their difference rests ultimately on very different conceptions of self and work. Emerson's self is profoundly threatened by the incursion of contents—ideas or feeling states—not its own. (When Emerson moves to Concord, he writes: "Henceforth, I design not to utter any speech, poem, or book that is not entirely my own work."[16]) He himself resists any force, including works of art and genius, that might limit his "originality," by which he means primarily an ability to work creatively—to make things (words, essays) that replicate and authenticate his self. For Emerson, therefore, the fundamental paradox of work is that it inevitably obstructs the "crescive" self even as it remains the best way to foster and express (Thoreau would say "publish") it. The self becomes itself in the work it does, in the things it makes; but to be done at all well, work must be taken seriously, and in being taken seriously it becomes something of an end in itself, not just a means. Stowe's sense of self, by contrast, is not threatened but constituted by an awareness (often involuntary) of others. Her work as a writer is constantly to provoke in her readers such awareness and to make an Emersonian solitude impossible for them. Her work is not to empower them but to reveal to them their own powerlessness because powerlessness is an indispensable condition of love and sympathy.

Shortly after Mr. Shelby has agreed to sell Tom and Harry to Haley, Mrs. Shelby confronts him with the immorality of what he has done. But in Kentucky, as elsewhere, the husband's word is final, it is the "law." Shelby has already signed the documents. It is too late to save Harry and Tom. Mrs. Shelby falls silent. By inviting her readers to identify with this woman's powerlessness, even though in this case the woman is also a slaveholder, Stowe enables them to experience powerlessness as the basis of all human sympathy, and of love itself. To love is to relinquish the need to assert one's self, one's desires and one's needs. It is to acknowledge, along with powerlessness, a sense of connection with and obligation to the "organic whole" of human life. To underscore the point, Stowe throughout the novel rings changes on the words "bondage," "bonds," "fetter," "yoke," "slave," and "enslavement": "So much are people the slave of their eye and ear . . . ," she observes. Eva's gaze, by contrast, is "half-loosed from its earthly bonds." Ophelia is "the absolute bond-slave of the *'ought.'*" When Marie St. Clare appears "clasping a diamond bracelet on her slender wrist," we are meant not just to experience an ironic contrast with the manacles on Tom's brawny arms, but to perceive the fact that her bracelet is the fetter placed on her by her vanity.

Even when Stowe's method is obvious, it can have surprising subtleties. When Haley sells Lucy, for example, Stowe comments:

> The trader had arrived at that stage of Christian and political perfection which has been recommended by some preachers and politicians of the north, lately, in which he had completely overcome human weakness and prejudice. His heart was exactly where yours, sir, and mine could be brought with proper effort and cultivation. (p. 208)

Stowe's overt purpose here is to underscore that slavery is not just a Southern, but a national problem, with its defenders in the North as well as the South. But more interestingly, Stowe is willing to satirize the almost iconic words of nineteenth-century New England reform culture. "Perfection," "Christian," "proper effort and cultivation"—all are shown to be capable of carrying the opposite of their intended meaning.

Stowe's target here is a reformist optimism in progress and a reformist faith in rationality. She hints that when it is detached from its roots in human instincts and affections—that is, from the heart—the work of self-cultivation and self-perfection so warmly advocated in so many advice manuals and political addresses may turn out to be the devil's work in a new disguise.

In one of the novel's most subtly manipulative scenes, Stowe offers her readers a difficult choice: to identify with the "poor, ignorant black soul" of a slave or with "certain [white] ministers of Christianity." Tom has been watching a painful "transaction": a young female slave and her baby have been sold downriver without her knowledge. When she protests that her kind master would never have sold her, the trader holds up a bill of sale. The unfortunate woman realizes that it is "no account talking" and lapses into silence—the silence shared by Mrs. Shelby, Mrs. Bird, and numerous other powerless women and men in the novel. Stowe reports that "Tom had watched the whole transaction from first to last, and had a perfect understanding of its results. To him, it looked like something unutterably horrible and cruel, because, poor, ignorant black soul! he had not learned to generalize and take larger views" (p. 209). The transaction effected by Stowe's novel is to compel the reader to identify with Tom and to trade one kind of knowledge for another. The general, abstract, disembodied truth must give way to one that is specific, "graphic," and uncompromisingly located in a black slave—a being doubly embodied by virtue of his status and his race.

I have suggested that key features of Stowe's overall narrative practice—her emphasis on space over time, her scenic presentation of material, her emphasis on the evidentiary and epistemological authority of orality over the written word, her entangling of the reader in problems that might otherwise remain distant and abstract, her manipulation of the reader in order to allow him or her to experience powerlessness as a precondition of empathy—have their source in Stowe's personal concern to make the work of writing congruent with, or an extension of, her work of mothering. I do not mean to imply, however, that Stowe's success in shaping writerly work to conform to maternal work delivered her from the problematics that plagued the other writers I have discussed. If anything, the opposite is true. Stowe's "motherising" (to use Gilman's word) of writerly work in some ways intensifies those problems, especially that of balancing mind and body, discipline and eros. Throughout *Uncle Tom's Cabin* reverberates the deep, unresolved (though ironically enriching) tension between a professed spirituality and an alluring materialism that also informs *The Wide, Wide World*.[17]

It is crucial to bear in mind that it is the antebellum *ideal* of motherhood that manages to combine mental and physical culture, mind and body, and in so doing to make itself attractive (in Fourier's sense) and invisible. In actuality, of course, childrearing tends to go less smoothly. Certainly Stowe herself frequently expressed a pained consciousness of the difficulties of her maternal work and a guilty sense of her inability to do it perfectly. In particular, Stowe seems to have felt that she was temperamentally unsuited to the task of providing her children with an "early education" and "training" in the principles of "system and order" so strongly recommended by her sister Catharine. "For many weeks past," Stowe once wrote in her journal, "my mind has been oppressed with a strong sense of the importance of early education of my children, and with an agonizing sense of my incompetence to undertake it" (*Life,* p. 107). In 1846, she wrote to Calvin: "Oh, that God would give me . . . five years in full possession of body and mind, that I may train my children as they should be trained. I am fully aware of the importance of system and order in a family . . . it is the keystone, the *sine qua non,* and in regard to my children I place it next to piety" (*Life,* p. 113). But if "system and order" rationalize maternal labor and make it wondrously efficient and pleasant, they also require of the mother inordinate self-repression, what Marcuse would later call "surplus repression."[18] The imperative to control one's emotions and to subdue the demands of the body must be internalized and installed as an autonomous disciplinarian of the psyche. Its demands become endless, its word becomes law. "[T]he first rule, and the most important of all . . ." warned Lydia Maria Child, "is, that a mother govern her own feelings . . ."[19]

In other words, the antebellum middle-class mother was required to live a contradiction: she was supposed to be full of feeling, but she was required to control those feelings. She was supposed to preserve a tenderness of spirit and generosity of emotion, especially sympathy, but at the same time she was required to subordinate those feelings to the inflexible principles of good childrearing, or to the commands of her husband, or to the laws of the nation. The ability to negotiate such a contradiction and to "govern one's feelings" would not predispose one to feel "oppressed and heartbroken with the sorrows and injustice of slavery," much less to write a book that gives vent to those feelings even as it distracts one from the immediate duties of motherhood. Even less would such an imperative encourage the dreamy reveries and the unfolding of the self in idleness that were celebrated and cherished as prerequisites of creativity by Emerson, Thoreau, Hawthorne, and Melville. Those moods for Stowe could be regarded only as "physiological infirmities." As she wrote to Calvin, "The absence and wandering of mind that vexes you is a physiological infirmity with me. It is the failing of a mind not calculated to endure great pressure of care" (*Life*, p. 106). The "failure" of "mind" under the "pressure of care" marks precisely the severing of faculties that idealized maternal labor was supposed to avoid. Rather than "combining" mental and physical culture, maternal labor seems at times to annihilate the mind. Moreover, it is significant that Stowe describes her condition not as a sundering of and contest between mind and body, but as a purely bodily failure, as a "physiological infirmity." For Stowe, the accent on the body that is registered in the term "heart" seems to have made the conflict between discipline and desire, self-control and self-expression, especially excruciating. Whereas the masculine imagination might be able to locate itself in a purely mental, or spiritual, realm and complain about yet dissociate itself from the demands of the body, Stowe's felt too identified with the body to be able to will such a disjunction.

Certainly what I have described as an opposition in *Uncle Tom's Cabin* between the spoken word of woman and the written law of man is intensified by the fact that difference between them is, ontologically, blurred: the written word, though abstract, is always physically present as a mark, whereas the voice of woman, though always issuing from and received by human bodies, is at the same time impalpable and invisible. For Stowe, as I have argued, the spoken word is epistemologically more powerful and reliable than the written word. Opposed to the men who "warp and bend language and ethics" and "press nature and the Bible . . . into their service" are the women who speak an original and uncorrupted tongue, which is why "'mother' seem[s] the most natural word in the world" (p. 216). Women can express what even the best men, like St. Clare, have "no language to say"; their speech includes the grim stories of Prue and Cassy and eschews the "dreamy quietude" of a fictional "cloud-land." But although the voice of woman issues from within her body, it may not, in the final analysis, be her own. When Eliza and Harry are on the run from Haley, Harry asks if she is sure that God will take care of them.

> "Yes, *sure!*" said the mother, in a voice that startled herself; for it seemed to her to come from a spirit within, that was no part of her; and the boy dropped his litle [*sic*] weary head on her shoulder, and was soon asleep. (p. 105)

That was no part of her. This moment of supreme maternal achievement—as Eliza, against all odds, soothes Harry to sleep and thereby helps him recover the strength he will need to escape—is figured as the work of a "spirit within" that is not her body, nor even her own spirit.

The epistemological authority of this voice is absolute, but that very authority dispossesses her of it. Though it clearly issues from her body, the invisibility and impalpability of the voice lend themselves to expropriation by the "spirit."

The appropriation of the woman's body by a disembodied "spirit" or "mind" is further underscored in the sentences that follow. So, too, is the contradiction inherent in Stowe's vision of maternity. While the text's description of the mother and child together pays tribute precisely to the ability of the body and its manifold senses to restore and revive the spirit, the author's own disembodied and authoritative narrative voice draws the opposite moral:

> How the touch of those warm arms, the gentle breathings that came in her neck, seemed to add fire and spirit to her movements. It seemed to her as if strength poured into her in electric streams, from every gentle touch and movement of the sleeping, confiding child. Sublime is the dominion of the mind over the body, that, for a time, can make flesh and nerve impregnable, and string the sinews like steel, so that the weak become so mighty. (p. 105)

Clearly the text locates agency in "warm arms" and "gentle breathings," in the especially sensitive skin of the "neck" and in an effluent power ("electric streams") residing in the "gentle touch and movement" of the child's body. Why, then, does Stowe's narrative voice displace this agency elsewhere and interpret the scene as an instance of "the dominion of the mind over the body"? The answer, I think, is only in part that she feels obliged to invoke the conventional Christian hierarchy at a moment when it is most threatened. A complementary explanation is that her own authority as an author resides to some degree in a notion of "mind" distinct from, and superior to, the body. After all, much as she might figure her work as speech she did have to *write* it. By the same token, much as the text might criticize the power of written documents, Stowe herself took pains to base her novel in facts and to collect documents to support her case. As a writer, then, she not only produced a written text but subscribed to the epistemological authority of documented facts. Insofar as written language and documented fact are associated with the mind's desire for an imperishable autonomy from the body—for what Everett called "an earthly immortality" of thought[20] and what Arendt describes as a "durable artifact" liberated from the cyclical mortality of nature—they implicitly advance a hierarchy of mind over the body.

Finally, the appeal to Stowe of this conventional distinction might derive also from her own experience as a mother of eight children, one of whom died. To have been pregnant or nursing for so many of the years of her marriage, and to have toiled meanwhile to hold together the large household while her husband was away for months at a time, might have prompted longings to escape from the body and from embodied maternal labor. Her own "severe neuralgic complaint" and the rest cures she took might have been one expression of this desire. So, too, might have been her decision to write. In the letter to Calvin quoted earlier, Stowe specifies what she will require as a writer: "If I am to write, I must have a room to myself, which shall be my room. . . . All last winter I felt the need of some place where I could go and be quiet and satisfied." This is a need Rachel Halliday seems never to have experienced. It is the need of a person who experiences herself as, in Gilman's words, "an individual detached," a "heart detached" from the social body of the family.

4
Writing the Work of Slaves

9

The Meanings of
Work and Song in
Antebellum Slavery

Harriet Beecher Stowe's commitment to composition undertaken as maternal labor can be viewed also as an indication that the distinctively human capacity to invent and employ symbolic language ("symbolicity" to use Kenneth Burke's term) has its origins not where "mind" becomes something different from "body" (Burke's "animality") but where the body seems to generate a language of its own. I would suggest that the "strength" which "poured into [Eliza] in electric streams, from every gentle touch and movement of the sleeping, confiding child" is an instance of such a language. A parent learns to speak this language with a child long before any other language is available. If writing, as one form of human symbolicity, is seen as having its origin in moments like this, then it can be regarded as actually, not just figuratively, a labor of the body.[1]

This possibility can be approached more conventionally, and perhaps to some more plausibly, if one begins with the premise that what distinguishes literature from other kinds of verbal symbolicity or discourse is its identification with its form. Literature is committed to language that exists for its own sake as opposed to language that, as Paul Valéry has written, goes forth to "perish," language that, in being understood, is "completely replaced by its meaning."[2] While literature, like all language, is "an instantaneous coupling of a *sound* and a *sense* that have no connection with each other," in literature the "sense" cannot be separated from the "sound"—from rhythms and melodies, from voice and eye and ear. This unbreakable "coupling" of sound and sense, form and content, suggests that in a literary work the distinction between idea

175

and thing, mind and body, is not operative. Refusing to relinquish its identity with its sound—that is, with the voice which utters words, the ear which hears them, the eye which sees them—the literary work urges us to recollect that sense is not just attached to these: it has its origins in them. The repetition of the heart beat, the opening and closing of the eye, the give and take of breathing lungs—in these lie also the child's first intuitions of pattern, and hence of order. Without these, without the faith that what has been will be again, there could be no faith in the repeatability of correspondence, and hence no hope for the possibility of "sense" or meaning. Etymologically, the sensual basis of "sense" is always there to be recovered; literature continually makes this recovery possible and actual.

Literature's affinity with its sound is demonstrated also in its affinity to song, and in turn its relation to song helps us recollect literature's relation to physical labor. Poetry is generally believed to originate in song, and insofar as many of the earliest human songs arose from and accompanied the rhythms of the laboring body, to that extent poetry traces its history back to physical labor. This retracing is the subject of a number of poems, including William Wordsworth's "The Solitary Reaper." The poem juxtaposes and contrasts the upright, male "I" of the poet narrator, who is free to come and go as he pleases, with the body of the bent, toiling, female reaper who appears fixed in the landscape, endlessly working and endlessly singing her song. The poet invites the reader to share his status and position with him, to "stop" with him and "behold" and "listen" to the reaper as she works and sings. The meaning of the song at once beckons to and eludes the poet. He poses a series of questions which compare the song to traditional poetic genres and implies that the song is at once none, and all, of these. At the end of the poem, he turns to go, saying that whatever the specific meaning of the reaper's work song might be, he carries it in his heart "long after it was heard no more." The effect of the poem is twofold: it extends the argument of the "Preface" to the *Lyrical Ballads* and suggests that the origin of poetry and the source of the poet's own work is there, in that very different, but rhythmic, embodied, and marvelously self-expressive work of the singing reaper. At the same time, Wordsworth's poem points back to the problematics of embodied labor, to the body as a site of pain and captivity (as Beecher, for example, seems often to have experienced it). The poem painfully calls attention to the void that lies between the poet (and the reader, whom Wordsworth deliberately implicates in the poet's position) and the solitary highland lass, between those who stand and oversee and of course benefit from her work and the worker herself, whose gaze is caught forever in the circle of her own toil and whose voice expresses a mystery that can be heard either as freedom or bondage, contentment or misery.[3]

These deep but puzzling relations among work, song, and literature are precisely the concern also of the famous passage in his *Narrative* (1845), in which Frederick Douglass recalls listening to the songs sung by his fellow slaves as they went for the month's provisions to the "Great House Farm" on Colonel Lloyd's extensive estates. The songs, as he remembers them, were as enigmatic as they were expressive, and in recollection they are as mystifying as they are meaningful. Douglass describes them in terms of mutually contradictory attributes: they revealed "the highest joy and the deepest sadness"; the slaves "would sometimes sing the most pathetic sentiment in the most rapturous tone, and the most rapturous sentiment in the most pathetic tone." One source of these contradictions, Douglass suggests, might have been the incomprehensible but unbreakable bond between the songs' "sound" and their "word," or sense. The songs were spontaneous improvisations, bringing together in apparently random ways verbal articulation and rhythmic, melodic expression. The slaves "would compose and sing as they went along, consulting neither time nor tune." As a consequence of their unrestricted character, the songs could express virtually without mediation the thoughts and feelings of the moment. "The thought that came up, came out—if not in the word, in the sound;—and as frequently in the one as in the other."[4]

But while these songs were undoubtedly and exceptionally expressive, their "meaning" was and is elusive. Douglass distinguishes, as he writes, among several kinds, or locations, of meaning: the meaning of the song to the slaves "themselves"; their meaning to him when he was still a slave; their meaning, or "unmeaning," to those who never have been slaves; and their meaning to him "now," at the time he writes his *Narrative*. These various meanings are by no means consistent with each other. On the one hand, the slaves' songs "were full of meaning to themselves" but probably "unmeaning jargon" to "many" (that is, to whites in the South and the North who have not been slaves); on the other hand, Douglass suggests that he understands the slave songs better "now" that he is no longer a slave. "I did not, when a slave, understand the deep meaning of those rude and apparently incoherent songs. I was myself within the circle; so that I neither saw nor heard as those without might see and hear." Where, then, is one to locate the most authoritative of these meanings—within or without the "circle" of slavery?

The location of an authoritative meaning becomes even more difficult when Douglass goes on to describe the relation between these songs and his own narrative. He suggests that while the songs are wonderfully expressive, their full power remains latent until they are deciphered by the specifically writerly intelligence which recalls them in memory and translates them into narratival form, into a "tale of woe": "They told a tale of woe which was then altogether beyond my feeble comprehension; they were tones loud, long, and deep; they breathed the prayer and complaint of souls boiling over with the bitterest anguish." But if the literary mind of the author of a slave narrative can convert these "unmeaning" songs into a meaningful "tale," that mind is at the same time deeply beholden to them: "The mere recurrence to those songs, even now, afflicts me; and while I am writing these lines, an expression of feeling has already found its way down my cheek. To those songs I trace my first glimmering conception of the dehumanizing character of slavery."[5]

Like Wordsworth, then, Douglass seems to find in the songs of labor an undecipherable and lasting expressive power, a power that appears to originate his own labor as a writer. Indeed, as I hope to show, it is through this meditation on the relation of his narrative to slave song that Douglass explores the larger question of the relation of his writerly work to the work he performed (and his fellow slaves continue to perform) as slaves. That is, just as the other writers we have examined explore the relation between literary and other forms of labor, between the labor of representation and the labor being represented, so Douglass struggles to understand the even more complicated relation between slavery, or slaving, and the writing of slave narratives.

*

But do slaves work? On the one hand, slavery appears to be the very essence of work, what work becomes when it is not relieved or adorned by any mitigating circumstances or conditions. "Ah, poor me!" writes Mary Prince, "—my tasks were never ended. Sick or well, it was work—work—work!"[6] "We didn't know nothin' 'cept to work," recalled one former slave. "We worked from can to can't," recalled another. "Get up at sunrise, go to de field, and stay till dark."[7] Working within the heart of necessity and never ceasing to work, the slave exists as a thing to work and be worked. This unending life of labor which permits no distinction between "life" and "labor" is the oft-repeated complaint of the former slave. "De rule on de place was: 'Wake up de slaves at daylight, begin work when they can see, and quit work when they can't see.'"[8] Perhaps the keenest pain of this unfree labor is that, for the slave, desire (or love, or eros) fails to offer a refuge from, or a balm to, work. Within slavery, and perhaps especially within the form slavery took in the United States,

erotic desire is conscripted to satisfy the lust of the master and to produce more slaves for the plantation. "If there was any one act of my life
while a slave, that I have to lament over," writes Henry Bibb, "it is that
of being a father and a husband of slaves."9 Elizabeth Keckley voices the
same distress: "I could not bear the thought of bringing children into
slavery."10 In sum, when work is regarded primarily as a negative, as the
"curse" of human disobedience, as the toil required by a pitiless necessity, then slavery appears to be the absolute verge toward which all work
tends.

On the other hand, slavery can be regarded as the ontological opposite of work. Work regarded as a blessing is the world-building activity
through which humans most truly are and become themselves. But for
this activity to be itself, for it to be "work," it must be free. This freedom can be defined minimalistically, following Locke, as a person's possession of his body and of the work produced thereby. The freedom can
be described, following Marx, as virtually a biological characteristic
("species behavior") of humanity which certain social formations have
repressed and perverted, but never quite destroyed—since to do so
would be to destroy humanity itself. Regarded as the expression of religious feeling, of reverence, of duty, work makes sense, can be itself,
only when it is freely performed. (The work that is wholly subsumed by
compulsion cannot be offered up as prayer or duty; it is not a supplement; it would have existed anyway.) In all cases, work that contains
within itself no element of freedom is not "work" at all but something
else—slavery or something very close to slavery.

The relation between work and slavery is perhaps equally complex
when viewed as a specific historical problem in the antebellum period.
As we have already seen, work at this time was understood primarily
by way of the distinction between manual and mental labor, which
rested in turn on an assumed dichotomy of body and mind. The dialectical interplay of these two terms constituted the *intrinsic* meaning
of work. That is, the dominant view of work regarded it as valuable
and rewarding to the degree that it was made up of mentality and excluded the effort of the body. At the same time, work was understood
also *extrinsically* as an activity that occupied a middle ground between,
on the one hand, slavery and, on the other, idleness (which was also
figured as leisure, play, or love). Most complaints about the degradation of the work experience, whether voiced by a working-class orator
or a harried professional, a seamstress or a housewife, raised the specter
of work turning into slavery. The author of an article called "White
Slavery" (1842) is representative of widely held beliefs when he writes:
"It [poverty] is the sole inheritance of the *White Slave* of the factory

and of the coal-mine, who in the midst of the most dazzling social improvements and political ameliorations, still continues to trudge on
from morning till night for the bare privilege of living—without even
so much as a prospective termination to the period of his revolting
bondage."[11] Though he deploys them differently, Thoreau uses the
same set of terms when he criticizes excessive devotion to the work
ethic as self-imposed slavery. "It is hard to have a southern overseer;
it is worse to have a northern one; but worst of all when you are the
slave-driver of yourself."[12] Thus, whether degraded from without by
the employer, or from within by a compulsive psyche, work as a meaningful human experience was felt to be constantly in jeopardy of being
transformed into something else, something fundamentally and even
ontologically different—slavery.

But if work is understood and defined as not-slavery, then slavery
cannot be work. What is it then? What does it mean *to slave* rather than
to work?

The nature of the difference between slave labor and free labor was
a puzzle to many antebellum observers of slavery and preoccupied
Frederick Law Olmsted in particular as he traveled through the South
in the years from 1852 through 1853. Olmsted was shocked by his
first glimpse, from a railroad carriage, of slaves toiling in the fields.
"They are very ragged, and the women especially, who work in the
field with the men, with no apparent distinction in their labor, disgust-
ingly dirty. They seem to move very awkwardly, slowly, and undecid-
edly, and almost invariably stop their work while the train is passing."[13]
The more he observes them, the more Olmsted wonders whether the
activity the slaves perform for the benefit of the overseer can be called
work. When a slave owner tells him that he "did not think they even
did half a fair day's work," Olmsted remarks, "This is just what I have
thought when I have seen slaves at work—they seem to go through
the motions of labor without putting strength into them" (I:101). The
longer Olmsted is in the South, the more he comes to realize that a
great many white Southerners do not believe that the slave is by himself capable of work and that for this reason he must be driven to it.
Olmsted quotes with bemusement a Dr. Cartwright's diagnosis and la-
beling of the problem:

> "Dysaesthesia aethiopica, or hebetude of Mind and Obtuse Sensibility of
> Body. *** From the careless movements of the individuals afflicted by
> this complaint, they are apt to do much mischief, which appears as if in-
> tentional, but is mostly owing to the stupidity of mind and insensibility
> of the nerves induced by the disease. . . . When driven to labor by the

compulsive power of the white man, he [the slave] performs the task assigned to him in a headlong, careless manner, treading down with his feet or cutting with his hoe the plants he is put to cultivate—breaking the tools he works with, and spoiling everything he touches that can be injured by careless handling." (I:214)

It may seem incredible that white Southerners could so confusedly mistake cause and effect, refusing to see that it was slavery itself that discouraged work and that the "careless movements" of the toiling slave were very likely the result of intentional resistance or of malnourishment and fatigue. But slave owners were not the only ones to draw the conclusion that black slaves were constitutionally, that is racially, incapable of hard work. Thomas Carlyle advances the argument at great length in "The Nigger Question." "To do competent work," he writes, "to labour honestly for that and no other purpose was each one of us sent into this world; and woe is to every man who, by friend or foe, is prevented from fulfilling this end of his being." In the case of the "Black man," Carlyle continues, it is "his own indolence that prevents and prohibits him"; from these vices he must be rescued, forcibly if necessary. If "your Nigger will not be induced, . . . he must be compelled" to work.[14] Not surprisingly, Carlyle's thesis struck a chord in at least one Southerner; Olmsted reports meeting a man who cites Carlyle's essay and opines that "Every man in the world ought to work for the benefit of mankind at large, as well as himself—the negroes would not do so, unless they were forced to" (II:276).

If white observers, slave owners, and abolitionists alike were undecided about the nature of the slaves' work activity, how did the slaves themselves regard it—as work or as something else? The slave's understanding of his or her activity—as these are represented in various texts available today—appears to have been paradoxical. On the one hand, work for the slave was the focal point of his or her entire experience in slavery. It not only took up the bulk of each and every day, but it was the purpose and justification of his or her captivity. While the first-generation slave had been captured in order to perform work, and could remember (if he or she was not a slave in Africa) a time when life was not co-extensive with work, subsequent generations of slaves were born into an ontologically different situation. For them, "being" was replaced by "working," which would suggest that in a sense the slave never experienced work as such—work as something distinguishable from life. Moreover, this condition of being born to work (not to *be*) was accompanied always by a generalized feeling of inexplicable punishment. (In slavery, as Olmsted observes, "Labor and punishment are almost synonymous" [I:235].) Deprived for the most part of control over his or her labor, and robbed for the most part of labor's product, the slave lived within work as within a state of punishment that had no origin, no termination, no narrative. Work was neither means nor end. It was simply what one was born to do. How, then, could it possibly have meaning, much less redemptive possibilities?

And yet, apparently, it did. A wide variety of documents suggest that work not only could hold meaning for the slave, but could actually serve as a refuge within—or space apart from—slavery itself. Paradoxical as this might seem, it is no more so (and is in a sense the mirror image of) the white slave owner's claim that the slave is incapable of work. While the slave owner claims that the negro is constitutionally incapable of self-motivated work, the slave sometimes finds within self-motivated work an effective escape from the master's control. Although this hypothesis might sound like a reprise of the apologist contention that slaves liked their work and that their songs expressed happiness, nothing could be farther from my point. I suggest only what a number of other historians have argued: that within conditions that threatened constantly to dehumanize them, slaves showed remarkable resourcefulness. For some slaves, one particular resource—albeit a strange one—seems to have been the work they were compelled to perform.

Such a possibility might seem less strange when we recall that, as Elizabeth Fox-Genovese and Eugene Genovese have pointed out, slaves often did have a stake in the economic health of their plantation and thus had a personal incentive to work efficiently and productively. These motives, in turn, may have fostered a degree of pride in their work. Insofar as slaves were proud of their skill at a task, be it cooking or cotton-picking, it is reasonable to infer that their work had self-actualizing meaning to them. That is, they found in their work a way to be themselves, or at least a part of themselves—to be the best cook, to be the best cotton-picker, to be the best gang of loggers, and so on.[15]

But there appears to have been an even more basic way in which work could be meaningful for the slave—even for the field slave who did not work for hire and who had no hope of purchasing his or her freedom. Josiah Henson, in his *Life* (1849), recalls that one of his chief ambitions while a slave was "to be first in the field, whether we were hoeing, mowing, or reaping, . . ."[16] A number of former slaves interviewed in the 1930s were able to recall their work with a measure of pride. "I worked hard always," said Julia Brown. "You can't imagine what a hard time I had. I split rails like a man. I used a huge glut and iron wedge drove into the wood with a maul, and this would split the wood. I helped spin the cotton into thread for our clothes. . . . After the thread was made we used the loom to weave the cloth."[17] The intensity of complaint here is commensurate with the former slave's awareness of the sheer immensity of the work she accomplished, of the physical strength she possessed, of the variety of skilled tasks she was able to perform. Sometimes, the sense of pride in work is expressed more simply and directly. "Mammy de bes' cook in de county and a master hand at weavin'. She made her own dye." "I helped make de baskets for de cotton. . . . Everybody try to see who could make de bes' basket."[18] "When I growed up I was a ploughman," reported Charles Davenport. "I sure could lay off a pretty cotton row, too." When the Union troops pushed south and approached the plantation where he worked, Davenport and other slaves were ordered to burn the cotton crop "so de enemy couldn't get it." The destruction hurt. "Us piled it high in de field like great mountains. It made my innards hurt to see fire attached to somethin' dat had cost us niggers so much labor and honest sweat."[19]

Although convicts are not slaves, the prison-farm system established in the South during reconstruction was modeled on the slave plantation and it seems probable that the experience of the convicts within it resembled that of slaves a generation or two earlier. The Texas convicts whom Bruce Jackson interviews in *Wake Up Dead Man,* his study of African-American prison work songs, are able at times to take pride in their work, though they have very little stake in its outcome. (This pride, moreover, is always closely linked to song—a linkage I will examine shortly.) "I like cutting trees, cutting them down. . . . It just feels like to me I can do that kind of work better on account of when you get to singing good you can do good work." Skill leads to distinction, and a convict sentenced to years of hard, forced labor can nevertheless feel some of the self-esteem of a "pro": "I eventually got to where I could handle an axe with the pros, . . ." The best workers become legends, remembered years later by their fellow convicts. Jesse James Seafus and Johnny Thomas were two of the more famous in the Texas prison farm system. Recalls one convict with awe: "Jesse James Seafus and Johnny Thomas: they'd pick nine hundred, sometimes a thousand pounds of cotton a day. *Apiece.*"[20]

Of course, slaves performing more skilled work would have been considerably more able than field hands to find in their work a kind of refuge from slavery. In some cases, that refuge was a literal one. Sarah Ford, an interviewed ex-slave, recalled the self-protective nature of her father's skills: "Dey knows papa is the best tanner 'round dat part de country, so dey doesn't sell him off de place. I 'lect papa sayin' dere one special place where he hide, some German folks, de name Ebbling, I think. While he hides dere, he tan hides on de sly like and dey feeds him

. . ."[21] In other cases, the protection afforded by work was perhaps more psychological than actual. Linda Brent recalls that as a child she felt "shielded" by the fact that her father, a carpenter, was "considered so intelligent and skilful in his trade. . . . My father, by his nature, as well as by the habit of transacting business as a skilful mechanic, had more the feelings of a freeman than is common among slaves."[22]

Not surprisingly, white Southerners had mixed feelings about slaves with mechanical and artisanal skills. On the one hand, such slaves were clearly of exceptional value to their owners; they could be hired out to others and they could be used to perform many necessary artisanal services on the owner's plantation. At the same time, however, white skilled workers resented having to compete, on such unequal terms, with skilled slaves. They frequently circulated petitions calling for the prohibition of skilled labor by blacks (free or slaves), and in 1845 the Georgia legislature enacted just such a law.[23] Although Georgia was the only state to have passed such a measure, there is considerable evidence to suggest that at about this time throughout the South slave owners were becoming wary of the consequences of training their slaves to perform skilled work. The obvious financial benefits of such work were perhaps outweighed by its emancipatory potential.

In *The Fugitive Blacksmith*, J. W. C. Pennington provides the following account of the way his work was actually objectionable to his master. It is worth quoting at length:

> I was one day shoeing a horse in the shop yard. I had been stooping for some time under the weight of the horse, which was large, and was very tired; meanwhile, my master had taken his position on a little hill just in front of me, and stood leaning back on his cane, with his hat drawn over his eyes. I put down the horse's foot, and straightened myself up to rest a moment, and without knowing that he was there, my eye caught his. This threw him into a panic of rage; he would have it that I was watching him. 'What are you rolling your white eyes at me for, you lazy rascal?' He came down upon me with his cane, and laid on over my shoulders, arms, and legs, about a dozen severe blows, so that my limbs and flesh were sore for several weeks; and then after several other offensive epithets, left me.
>
> This affair my mother saw from her cottage, which was near; I being one of the oldest sons of my parents, our family was now mortified to the lowest degree. I had always aimed to be trustworthy; and feeling a high degree of mechanical pride, I had aimed to do my work with dispatch and skill; my blacksmith's pride was one thing that had reconciled me so long to remain a slave. I sought to distinguish myself in the finer branches of the business by invention and finish; I frequently tried my hand at making

guns and pistols, . . . but after this, I found that my mechanic's pleasure and pride were gone.[24]

What we have here most obviously is an exchange of gazes—concealed, mistaken, unseen; of the powerful, of the powerless; of the owner, of the owned; of the child and of the mother—all intersecting and constituting the complex web of human relations within slavery.

But I want to focus first on the opening sentences: "I was one day shoeing a horse in the shop yard. I had been stooping for some time under the weight of the horse, which was large; and was very tired; meanwhile, my master had taken his position on a little hill just in front of me, and stood leaning back on his cane, with his hat drawn over his eyes." Note the contrast of postures; the stoop versus the slouch. Note the contrast of tools, the farrier's hammer, heavy in the hand, and the light cane used to support an idle, relaxed body. And note also the contrast in activities, a contrast underscored by the fact that Pennington carries the weight of a large horse on his back, while the master supports nothing but himself, and pretends to require a cane in order even to do that. And note, finally, that while the master's gaze is fixed on his workman, that is, his slave, Pennington's eyes are fixed on his work, on the horse's hoof, on his horseshoe, nails, and hammer. Even under the eye of an overseer, work has permitted Pennington a temporary refuge, perhaps an escape from, bondage. The requirements of his work have usurped and replaced the requirements of slavery. He is absorbed into his work, and in turn his work has liberated him. As he says further on, it has given him a realm in which to exercise the scope of his imagination, his inventiveness, his desire, his "blacksmith's pride" and his "mechanic's pleasure." By putting himself into his work, he puts himself out of slavery.

Does the master know this? At some level, yes. His gaze seeks to reclaim the slave. By monitoring his actions, the master seeks to insert himself between the slave and his work, so that the work cannot draw the slave out of his bondage. But the master's effort is futile unless, or until, the slave becomes conscious of his presence and his gaze. The master wants the weight of his ownership to replace the already heavy burden of the horse. Now, when Pennington straightens up "to rest a moment," that humble and perfectly comprehensible action takes on a sudden significance. It signifies that Pennington controls the rhythm of his work, and it is this control, exercised invisibly and beyond the reach of the master, that makes his work somewhat redemptive and not entirely onerous. If Pennington could never straighten himself, or could do so only upon the command of the master, his work would not serve as a conduit out of servitude. It is true that Pennington's "rest" is only a pause, a momentary delay, but the un-selfconsiousness with which he claims it as his due betokens the presence of a vast realm of consciousness inaccessible to, and uncontrolled by, the master. The rest, the pause, is the essential component of rhythm in work, as it is the essential component of rhythm in music.

Nonetheless, the inner freedom implicit in this action would not have been sufficient provocation, probably, to spur the master to reassert his complete ownership of the slave. The catalyst here is an inadvertent glance, when one eye is "caught" by another. Pennington's look at his master is not a look of defiance; indeed, the master could have laughed to scorn such a look. It is simply the look of a human eye, a free eye, an eye made momentarily free by its marginal but immensely important control over its work. Pennington has just come out of his work and glances at his master with the eye of a man who has been somewhere else, who is still enveloped in a feeling, utterly unconscious, of his own freedom. And that is what enrages the master.

His cane now becomes a tool—the only tool of the master and his overseers. It becomes a whip. But the master's actions are self-defeating and self-contradictory on every level. Instead of standing lazily in the enjoyment of his ownership, he is now put to work, the work of whipping his slave and reasserting the nonhumanity of his slave. His rage is a "panic." He is out of control at the very moment he wishes to reassert control over his errant property. His words, in turn, indicate that there is no language to express either the relation he is in or the perversion of meaning that slavery accomplishes. He decries the "white eyes" of his slave—meaning no doubt the proverbial rolling whites of the slave's eyes—but inadvertently calling attention to what he would deny: that through work the slave has become free, has become "white." For the same reason, he is forced to make the patently false claim that his slave is "lazy" because he cannot admit that it is work, not idleness, that has liberated his slave; that the very activity that enriches him as a slave master inevitably challenges the master-slave relation. He should have cried, "You *working* rascal," but to have done so would have been, of course, impossible. Unthinkable. It is unthinkable that the very *activity* that constitutes slavery—an owned person laboring for his owner—could challenge and undo the proprietary *conditions* of that activity—namely, the conditions of owning and being owned.

Pennington's memoir suggests, then, that for the slave and the slave master, at least, slavery and work construct meanings that are mutually exclusive. Ideologically, from the master's perspective, all slaves are regarded as brutes, as animals, as pure bodies. They do not own themselves or their labor precisely because they have no mind capable of possessing that body and that work. Indeed, incapable of possessing their work, they are also incapable of the very activity itself—work—which by definition entails self-possession. The absence of the slave's mind makes possible, and requires, the insertion into that void of the master's mind and will. Since the slave cannot work because he has no mind to own himself, the slave master will provide that mind, own the slave's body, and thereby own the slave's work.

From the master's viewpoint, the slave's activity becomes work only insofar as it is regarded as directed (overseen) and possessed by the master. From the slave's viewpoint, work certainly can be degraded; certainly it can be heaped on a person until he or she has no freedom left within it, not even the bare minimum represented here by the ability to straighten up and rest a moment. But if that increment of freedom is preserved, it becomes an essential condition of, and points toward, a realm of freedom within work, a freedom that may be actualized as concentration, or as daydreaming, or as mere unconsciousness of the surveilling eye of the master, or as countless other states. However, the moment the slave seems to be taking possession of his work—as, for example, when he performs skilled labor—he affirms the existence of his mind and will and his possession of his body and his labor. To transform work-for-the-master into work-for-himself is in this sense to own himself and to become "free."

*

We can return now to the puzzle of the meaning and "unmeaning" of the slave songs Frederick Douglass heard and wrote about. If slave-work could be seen and experienced both as the means and ends of bondage, and yet at the same time as a means of self-emancipation, what was expressed by the songs with which slaves usually accompanied their work? That they did sing while they worked seems to have been, one of the more remarkable facts about their work. "They [Negroes] have magnificent voices and sing without instruction" reported *Dwight's Journal of Music* in 1856. "The maids sing about the house, and the laborer sings in the field."[25] "Wherever negroes may be, if in tolerable spirits, they always sing as the[y] work," wrote plantation owner Henry Watson in 1834. "They then keep time with their song and do not feel their fatigues, and in fact are not fatigued as they otherwise would be. The[y] work more cheerfully."[26] Freed slaves, too, recalled the close connection between song and work. In the fields, "We used to sing and have lots of fun."[27] "I used to pick 150 pounds of cotton a day," an ex-slave recalled, and then, perhaps to explain what made that tedious, grueling task bearable, she added, "We would pick cotton and sing, pick and sing all day."[28]

Historians of antebellum American slavery unanimously confirm this almost ubiquitous association of work with song. "Slaves . . . performed almost every conceivable task to the accompaniment of song with an intensity and style that elicited the comments of whites around them," writes Lawrence Levine. "Throughout slavery black workers contrived to time their work routines to the tempo of their music in much the same manner as their African ancestors."[29] L. H. Owens concurs: "His [the slave's] existence was built around repetitive work and rest rhythms, which, through music, he translated into poignant expressions of life's direction and meaning."[30] Eugene Genovese echoes the refrain: "They willingly sang at work, as well as going to work, coming from work, and at almost any time."[31]

What, then, did song mean to the laboring slave, and in particular what was its relation to his or her labor? Certain meanings are already well known. Slaves sang to express their sorrows in slavery. They sang in order to communicate with one another—to tease one another, to poke fun at the master, to share information. Slaves sang also because their African cultural inheritance, and especially its spiritual dimension, placed song at the very center of life and ritual.

All of these are important characteristics of the slave song, but here I want to speculate more extensively on the particular relation of song to work. What did song mean for the *laboring* slave, for the slave who sang while he or she *worked*? Answers to this question are bound to be speculative. For one thing, we have very little firsthand testimony on the subject by slaves themselves. For another, historians have tended to emphasize the spiritual and religious functions of the slave songs, paying relatively scant attention to their secular functions, and very little to the slave song as a work song. Levine, for example, writes that "the vast preponderance of spirituals over any other sort of slave music rather than merely the result of accident or error is instead an accurate reflection of slave culture during the antebellum period."[32] Yet Levine himself has pointed out that the introduction of Christianity into the slave community in the 1830s led to the prohibition and suppression of many forms of secular song and dance. Presumably, before that time secular songs, and foremost among them the work song, must have played a vital role in slave culture. Moreover, Levine and other historians agree that "spirituals" were as likely to be sung in the fields and around the house as at religious meetings, formal and informal. We must also recall that work songs were likely to have been improvised from day to day, season to season, and thus to have been more perishable than the relatively formal spirituals. In sum, although the work song *per se* was not preserved in significant numbers by the first collectors of slave songs, and although a great body of evidence underscores the importance of song to the slaves' religious beliefs and practices, we should not overlook the important connection between song and work within slavery.

This is the fact to which Imamu Amiri Baraka's *Blues People* points when it locates the roots of the blues in "the Afro-American/American Negro work songs, which had their musical origins in West Africa." Baraka suggests that African work songs were more readily available and useful to the slave than African religious songs partly because white masters suppressed and discouraged religious expressivity and partly because "most of the impetuses that suggested that particular type of singing were still present."[33] That is, the particular rhythmic qualities of many work songs were still appropriate because the kinds of work (hoeing, chopping, hauling, picking, sifting, winnowing) the songs were created to accompany were demanded of the slave in this new environment as well.

What did this transformed, but still in many ways appropriate African work song do for the laboring slave? In the absence of firsthand accounts by slaves themselves, the outlines of an answer might be provided by the accounts of their songs given by Texas convicts to Bruce Jackson. The main purpose of these songs, according to these convicts, was to lighten their work and make it bearable. "You get worked to death or beat to death," relates one convict. "That's why we sang so many of those songs. We would work together and help out our fellow man. Try to keep the officials we was workin' under pacified and we'd make it possible to make a day. Be tired sometimes, be nearly too tired to eat sometimes, but we would make a day like that."[34] Songs lighten physical work in a number of ways. First, their rhythms help the laboring body find and continually adjust to a rhythm of work that can be sustained for long periods of time. "'I can do a whole lot more workin' by time than I can workin' loose'" (p. 18). "'Even picking cotton I likes to sing. When I sing, picking cotton, before I know anything I be three blocks ahead of the squad. Just picking along" (p. 18). The song helps regulate and coordinate the complex physiology of physical labor, assuring that the laborer continue to breathe deeply even when his breath is coming short, that he or she maximize the benefits of the moments of rest within every kind of work activity. "'All you got to do is concentrate on your song and your rhythm and the time goes by'" (p. 26). Particularly when group labor is being performed, the work song helps coordinate the actions of the group, assuring that they work at all times with instead of against each other. "'Actually, we get more work done when there's singing then [*sic*] when we're silent. Because that leads into arguments and confusion if a man hasn't got anything to occupy his mind'" (p. 26).

To make, for the sake of clarity, a false distinction, the work song also seems to provide a number of psychological benefits to the laborer. It continually takes him out of the mute isolation of physical labor and restores him to a community of fellow laborers who share the experience of labor with him. It gives him or her a chance to talk back to the overseer, to complain, to ridicule, and in numerous other ways to reverse the flow of power that descends from the boss astride his horse. Song makes the time pass more quickly, more smoothly. To a laborer burdened not just with the ache of toil, but with the knowledge that this labor is forced labor, and that he must perform it every day for many years to come, the song helps to keep him from dwelling on his sorrows, even as, frequently, it gives voice to them. Finally, the work song makes a world ("a day") that exists parallel to, but independent of, the world controlled by the overseer. That is, song creates a world insofar as the very nature of music instantly enables it to suggest the presence of another order of being, a realm of sound rather than noise, what Valéry in the essay already cited calls the "musical universe":

> We live by ear in a world of noises. . . . The world of music, a world of sounds, is distinct from the world of noises. Whereas a *noise* merely rouses in us some isolated event—a dog, a door, a motor car—*a sound evokes, of itself, the musical universe*. If, in this hall where I am speaking to you, and where you hear the noise of my voice, a tuning fork or a well-tempered instrument began to vibrate, you would at once, as soon as you were affected by this pure and exceptional noise that cannot be confused with others, have the feeling of a beginning, the beginning of a world; a quite different atmosphere would immediately be created, a new order would arise, and you would unconsciously *organize* yourselves to receive it. The musical universe, therefore, was within you, with all its associations and proportions—as in a saturated salt solution a crystalline universe awaits the molecular shock of a minute crystal in order *to declare itself*.[35]

To "make a day," then, is to make this "musical universe." The work song sings a new world into being, and within that world the worker can maintain a degree of autonomy, can possess himself and his labor because he can retrieve his labor back into the world created by his song. As Bruce Jackson writes: "the songs change the nature of work by putting the work into the workers' framework rather than the guards'. By incorporating the work with their song, by, in effect, co-opting something that they are forced to do anyway, they make it *theirs* in a way it otherwise is not" (p. 30). What this world-creating and labor-retrieving power of song suggests, further, is that the transcendental realm so often evoked in slave song—the "oder bright land," the "Paradise," the "new Jerusalem," the "home"[36]—is not so much a place elsewhere as a space immanent within song and labor. Singing his labor, the slave finds his margin of freedom within it.

*

The fact that within antebellum slavery songs were so frequently conjoined with work is suggestive of two possibilities. If the slave experienced his or her labor as absolutely meaningless, as absolute bondage, then it may be that the world-making characteristic of song was *intensified* precisely because it represented a displacement. Hard physical labor is always hard. But when the fruits of that labor are never one's own; when the world one's labor makes is in effect a prison; then perhaps one displaces one's world-making urge into song. Song thus takes the place of work—but only for an instant. For the song itself, "making" a day, creating a world, in turn allows a retrieval of work. Song replaces work only in order to recover it.

At the same time, it is possible also to understand the slaves' work songs as indications that even within work there was a realm of freedom—a realm narrow and rigidly circumscribed, to be sure, but nevertheless a realm where some degree of self-actualization was possible. Perhaps the slave song points to the paradoxical possibility that slave toil, outwardly the very essence of slavery, might have been at times the opposite, a kind of refuge from the institution and even from the surveillant gaze of the overseer. For the slave song and the work song both are formal expressions of the freedom to be found within work. Tuned to the rhythms of the laboring body, the song is in this sense not so much a compensation for as the utterance of work, the exhibition of the interior experience of work.

These two possibilities are not so much alternatives in fact as alternative perspectives. I would argue that within slavery work is experienced as *both* freedom and bondage, and that slave song expresses slave labor's emancipatory *and* its enslaving powers. If this is true, if the slave song emerges from and articulates the felt experience of slave labor as both the most concentrated expression of slavery and yet, at the same time, as a mode of self-emancipation within slavery, Douglass's ambivalence toward the slave song starts to become clearer. That is, the slave song may point to slave labor not as a condition from which Douglass must entirely escape in order to perform his labor as a writer, but rather as the condition to which he must return in imagination in order to locate the first pulse *of* his imagination. For the same reason, the slave song might be at once an inspiration of and an unsettling alternative to his own work as a writer. The slave song may be "unmeaning jargon" requiring translation into a "tale," but in its ability to express without mediation the hopes and sorrows of the slave, it may be the truest and most authentic way of expressing the imaginative power and enduring humanity of the slave. Thus, just as Wordsworth sees in the working and singing body of the solitary highland lass an image of his own work's origin, an origin from which his work now separates him, so Douglass seems to hear in the voices of the singing slaves an origin he wishes both to recover and to repress. Only in Douglass's case, as we shall see, the tension between recovery and repression is doubly intense. Both writers look back at physical labor and the song of labor as indications that their symbol-using urge originated in the realm of necessity, in the laboring body, in an activity where sound and sense are always joined. But whereas for Wordsworth this backward glance recovers a neutral (though, as we have seen, typically feminized body), for Douglass the glance recovers also the much more perilous body of his racial identity. As we shall see, the attitude he takes toward slave labor and slave song conditions not only his construction of authorial labor and slave narrative, but his construction of his identity as a black American.

10

Slavery, Work, and Song in Frederick Douglass's Autobiographies

---

"Oh children of the tropics
Amid our pain and wrong,
Have you no other mission,
Than music, dance, and song?"

—Frances Harper, *Iola LeRoy*[1]

And so before each thought that I have written in this book I have set a phrase, a haunting echo of these weird old songs in which the soul of the black slave spoke to men.

—W. E. B. DuBois, *The Souls of Black Folk*[2]

The framing argument of this book has been that writing must be seen as a form of work and that the work of writing and the work which writing represents are always engaged in a dialectical, mutually constituting relation. That is, a writer's encounter with work as a subject seems to turn the writer back upon himself or herself, to lead the writer into an exploration of the nature of his or her writerly work. That exploration, in turn, returns to the subject of work and informs the way it is represented. At the same time (and this would be my argument to literary historians), the writer's understanding that writing is work, and the writer's engagement in the dialectical relation between representations of work and making those representations, can have the effect of shaping the writer's actual work practice—what and how he or she writes. That is, a considerable part of both the content and the form of some literary works can be understood best as the outcome of a writer's negotiations with the relation between writerly work and other kinds of work. In the antebellum period, I have tried to show, these negotiations were extraordinarily intense and have important consequences for our understanding of certain texts.

This dialectical relation between the work of writing and the work being represented by it occurs also in the writing of slave narratives. The writer of a slave narrative encounters as one of his or her subjects the work performed by slaves; the writer reflects upon and reshapes his or her work of writing a slave narrative; and the writer constructs a representation of slave work that is informed by this understanding of the work of writing a slave narrative. However, difficult as it has been to uncover and describe the ways free, white writers of the antebellum period participated in this process, it is even more difficult to give an account of the way freed, black writers did so. Here all is complicated and intensified by the uncertainty as to whether slave labor is work or the opposite of work; by the uncertainty as to whether slave labor is absolute bondage or a limited means of self-emancipation; by the uncertainty (as we shall see) as to whether the value of the slave's body, and of bodily labor, is jeopardized or augmented by his or her racial identity—an identity the freed slave must decide to accept or reject. Finally, to all these complications we must add that relative to the other kinds of work I have discussed, slave work was accompanied by its own mode of self-expressivity—song. It is to Frederick Douglass's complex sifting of these issues and complications that I now turn.

*

As its title suggests, Frederick Douglass's second version of his autobiography is less a linear account of movement from slavery to emancipation than a self-reflexive and self-circling meditation on a condition in which freedom and bondage are simultaneously present. As William Andrews has shown, whereas the *Narrative* is for the most part the story of how a "thing" rediscovers himself as a "man," *My Bondage, My Freedom* is able to explore more fully what it means to be a man, and specifically a black man in a racist society.[3] To this account I would add that *MBMF* explores also the condition and work of being a writer, specifically an African American writer. Whereas the *Narrative* concentrated on a search for the origins of his decision to regain his humanity, in *MBMF* Douglass goes back to the experience of slavery in order to find the origins of his identity as a writer.

To understand this search, we must understand first the position Douglass finds himself in 1853, as he writes *My Bondage, My Freedom*. He is a man who begins life performing the degraded and exclusively manual labor entailed by slavery. Gradually, though, he is able to achieve a measure of freedom by performing the relatively free and skilled labor of working for hire as a ship caulker; he even experiences a brief period when his master allows him to keep all his surplus wages. After he escapes to the North, Douglass is able to perform labor that is free in the literal sense of the word, but the racism prevalent among working-class whites prevents him from performing the more skilled and relatively profitable labor of caulking. He is forced instead to undertake the most menial kinds of manual labor available—chopping wood, carrying freight, and so on. Then he is discovered by the abolitionists. They allow him to perform the relatively mental labor of lecturing, and then of writing his *Narrative*, but they attempt to restrict the scope of that work's mentality. Eventually, Douglass breaks ranks with the Garrisonians, establishes his own newspaper devoted to the "mental and moral improvement" of his race, and performs work that is at once more free and more mental than any he has done before.[4]

In *MBMF*, Douglass deliberately structures his history as a laborer in terms of an ascent (thwarted at times, to be sure) from manual to mental labor. But one can never be entirely sure whether he is accepting and employing, or mocking, this paradigm. On the one hand, Douglass underscores the miraculousness of his metamorphosis from laborer to abolitionist by invoking the familiar image of the laboring hand as synecdoche for the laboring body: "The three years of my freedom had been spent in the hard school of adversity. My hands had been furnished by nature with something like a solid leather coating, and I had bravely marked out for myself a life of rough labor, suited to the hardness of my hands, as a means of supporting myself and rearing my children" (p. 219). But he seems to distance himself from the distinction between manual and mental labor, mind and body, when he reports that his abolitionist colleagues seemed to treat him purely as a body (just as his masters and overseers had): Mr. Collins, "used to say, when introducing me, . . . that I had graduated from that 'peculiar institution,' . . . '*with my diploma written on my back.*'" Douglass employs the dichotomy again, seeming to have faith in it, when he describes his discovery, in England, that racism is not a universal attitude but a social prejudice peculiar to the United States and to the North in particular. In a letter home, which he quotes, Douglass writes: "'The truth is, the people here know nothing of the republican negro hate prevalent in our glorious land. They measure and esteem men according to their moral and intellectual worth, and not according to the color of their skin'" (p. 227). And the paradigm structures also his understanding of his break from the Garrisonians when he returned from England to the United States.

He was, he writes, hesitant to start his own newspaper lest it should fail and "thus contribute another proof of the mental and moral deficiencies of my race" (p. 240). He felt unprepared for the task because, "In point of mental experience, I was but nine years old" (p. 241). But he perseveres, succeeds, and finds that the "time, money, and labor" bestowed upon his new project are "amply rewarded, in the development of my own mental and moral energies, and in the corresponding development of my deeply injured and oppressed people" (p. 242). He concludes *MBMF* with the familiar reformist rhetoric of "elevation," which rests, as we have seen, on a supposed hierarchy of mind over body, mental over manual labor: "Believing that one of the best means of emancipating the slaves of the south is to improve and elevate the character of the free colored people of the north I shall labor in the future, as I have labored in the past, to promote the moral, social, religious, and intellectual elevation of the free colored people" (p. 248).

Although Douglass's personal labor history is structured in terms of the distinction between manual and mental labor and figured as an ascending movement from the one to the other, this movement is complicated and resisted not just by an occasional note of mockery, but by Douglass's increasing *acceptance* of his racial identity—an identity in which the connection between "self" and "body" is crucial.

Perhaps the most striking indication of this acceptance of his racial identity, and with it of the value of embodied labor, is to be found in the introduction which James M'Cune Smith wrote (and which Douglass must have approved) for *MBMF*. Smith, a black physician, pointedly emphasizes that Douglass's ascent from manual to mental labor does not entail a rejection of the body and the skills it has learned.[5] Smith argues that for his work as an advocate of emancipation Douglass was well prepared by his experience, and specifically his work, as a slave. "And for this special mission, his plantation education was better than any he could have acquired in any lettered school. What he needed, was facts and experiences. . . . His physical being was well trained also, running wild until advanced into boyhood; hard work and light diet thereafter, and a skill in handicraft in youth." Douglass was a born worker and even in slavery found ample opportunity to exercise his energy and even some of his gifts: ". . . he worked, and he worked hard. At his daily labor he went with a will; with keen, well set eye, brawny chest, lithe figure, and fair sweep of arm, he would have been king among calkers, had that been his mission" (p. 12). This is the man, then, who becomes for a while a Garrisonian. Like Douglass, Smith emphasizes the turn Douglass takes at this point from hard manual labor—"sawing wood, rolling casks, or doing what labor he might to support himself and young family" (p. 13)—to the mental labor of abolitionism. And, more explicitly than Douglass, he relates how the Garrisonians both promoted and sought to limit the exercise of his intellectual powers:

> In the society [of Garrisonians], . . . Mr. Douglass enjoyed the high advantage of their assistance and counsel in the labor of self-culture, to which he now addressed himself with wonted energy. Yet, these gentlemen, though proud of Frederick Douglass, failed to fathom and bring out to the light of day, the highest qualities of his mind; the force of their own education stood on their own way; they did not delve into the mind of a colored man for capacities which the pride of race led them to believe to be restricted to their own Saxon blood.

After his experiences in England, however, Douglass "awakened . . . to the consciousness of new powers that lay in him" and "rose to the dignity of a teacher and a thinker" (p. 15).

From this point forward, the bulk of Smith's introduction consists of a description and analysis of Douglass's remarkable intellectual abilities and "mental processes" (p. 18). He praises Douglass's singular clarity of "perception," his "unfailing memory," his "truthful common sense," his "wit," his "descriptive and declamatory powers," and his "logical force" (p. 20). But when he comes to "the most remarkable mental phenomenon in Mr. Douglass," his "style in writing and speaking," he confesses that he is at a loss to explain these, and that Douglass's writing style in particular is "an intellectual puzzle." "The strength, affluence and terseness may easily be accounted for, because the style of the man is the man; but how are we to account for that rare polish in his style of writing, which, most critically examined, seems the result of careful early culture among the best classics of our language" (p. 21). Smith confesses that he was once tempted to attribute Douglass's literary genius to "the Caucasian side of his make-up," but that the "facts narrated in the first part" of *MBMF* "throw a different light on this interesting question." In sum, Smith (like Douglass himself, as we shall see), locates Douglass's literary genius in his "negro blood," and more specifically in the figures of his grandmother ("a woman of power and spirit . . . marvelously straight in figure, elastic and muscular" and possessing great "skill in constructing nets, . . . perseverance in using them, . . . and wide-spread fame in the agricultural way") and his mother ("tall, and finely proportioned; of deep black, glossy complexion"). "These facts show," Smith concludes, "that for his energy, perseverance, eloquence, invective, sagacity, and wide sympathy, he is indebted to his negro blood. The very marvel of his style would seem to be a development of that other marvel,—how his mother learned to read" (pp. 21–22).

Smith here calls attention to a second way in which Douglass's account of his life, and especially of the origins of his work as a writer,
complicates and resists the distinction between (and hierarchy of) mind
and body, mental and manual labor. Indeed, Douglass's account can be
seen as an intensified reproduction of a narrative we have already en-
countered—the narrative of an author's fall from the maternal bower of
childhood into the rough and tumble world of work that is presided
over and controlled by a distant, sometimes dead, father. In outline,
Douglass's representation of his childhood bears a strong resemblance
to Wellingborough's in *Redburn* and to Ellen Montgomery's in *The
Wide, Wide World*. In seeking its origins and the earliest manifestations
of its own powers, the author's imagination does not return to the relatively abstract world of the father, with his command of written language, and of the law, and with his patriarchal ownership of the home
and all its inhabitants. It dwells instead in the densely material world of
the home and seeks to touch once again the body of his or her mother.

At this point it may be useful to recall that Thoreau, in his journey to
discover his own authorial origins and to define the nature of his
authorial work, writes that "We have need to be earth-born as well as
heaven-born," and that "Sometimes a mortal feels in himself Nature,
not his Father but his Mother stirs within him" (*A Week*, pp. 380, 378).
But Thoreau is willing to subordinate the "transitory, almost brutish"
"sound" of "our mother tongue" to the "reserved and select expression" of "written language," which he calls "our father tongue" (*Walden*, p. 101). Similarly, Hawthorne can never decide whether to celebrate "our great Creative Mother" or to shun "the gross fatality of
Earth," while both Ellen Montgomery and Wellingborough Redburn
must come to terms with powerful substitute fathers in order to achieve
identities as writers and to perform authorial work. Douglass, however,
in *MBMF* absolutely rejects *any* paternal contribution to his identity as
a writer. Instead—and here the contrast with the *Narrative*, in which
Douglass writes of his mother but says nothing about her relation to
language, is instructive—Douglass explicitly locates the origin of his
gifts as a writer in the "sable" body of his laboring mother:

> I learned, after my mother's death, that she could read, and that she was
> the *only* one of all the slaves and colored people in Tuckahoe who enjoyed
> that advantage. How she acquired this knowledge, I know not, for
> Tuckahoe is the last place in the world where she would be apt to find
> facilities for learning . . . I can, therefore, fondly and proudly ascribe to
> her an earnest love of knowledge. That a "field hand" should learn to
> read, in any slave state, is remarkable; but the achievement of my mother,
> considering the place, was very extraordinary; and, in view of that fact, I

am quite willing, and even happy, to attribute any love of letters I possess, and for which I have got—despite of prejudice—only too much credit, *not* to my admitted Anglo-Saxon paternity, but to the native genius of my sable, unprotected, and uncultivated *mother*—a woman, who belonged to a race whose mental endowments, it is, at present, fashionable to hold in disparagement and contempt. (p. 42)

This is the most crucial emendation of his 1845 *Narrative*. By referring to the "prejudices" of white racism and its "contempt" for the "mental endowments" of blacks, Douglass indicates that racism, not slavery, is the catalyst that has urged him to retrace the track of his past and to define his authorial identity in terms of race. At one level, Douglass is employing the already familiar vocabulary of the distinction between manual and mental labor and marveling that a mere "field hand" should have been able to acquire knowledge and perform the mental labor entailed by literacy. But Douglass superimposes on this scene a specifically racial dimension, and it is one that calls into question the dichotomy itself. Although the field hand *per se* could theoretically achieve an entirely new identity as a mental laborer, metamorphosing from corporeal to mental worker, this is not true of the *black* or "sable" field hand. This laborer will always remain black, will always labor in and through his or her black body. Douglass thus specifically and unequivocally locates the origin of his "love of letters" and his literary accomplishments in a figure that triply represents the embodied state: in a field hand who is a mother and who is also black; in his "sable . . . *mother.*" By doing so, he expresses a willingness not only to think of himself as an African American writer, but also to acknowledge that this racial identity must have a bodily, a physical origin. For Douglass as an African American writer, "Genius" is not a spiritual chimaera flitting through and attempting to transcend the sinews of the body; it is "native" to and inseparable from that body. To abandon the body would be to renege on his African American identity.

*

But Douglass's affirmation of his racial identity, while crucial to his identity as a writer, also has its costs. To the degree that it requires him to value the body and bodily labor, it also threatens to return him to a condition of bondage and to the kind of identification with the body that Stowe, too, acknowledged and resented. The most concentrated and suggestive expression of Douglass's ambivalence toward the body and toward embodied expressivity is his meditation on the meaning and power of the slaves' songs. As we have already noted, Douglass is drawn to these songs in part because he remains loyal to the slave community and to its mode of expressiveness. More pointedly, he is drawn to them also because, as a mode of expressivity, slave songs are indissolubly associated with the labor of slavery and with the laboring body of the black slave. It is the deep affinity between the slave songs and slave labor that makes them such a powerful and multivalent icon to a freed slave who is discovering and defining his real work as an African American writer. The slave song gives voice to the doubleness of slave labor, to its expropriation of the slave's body and to its potentialities as a refuge from the degradations of slavery. Moreover, behind slave labor stands the slave's body, and as a form of expressivity the slave song never leaves that body behind. ("Stripped of all else," observed Alain Locke, "the Negro's own body became his prime and only artistic instrument, so that dance, pantomime and song became the only gateways for his creative expression.")[6] Whereas the nature of writing is such that it manifests no visible or palpable connection with the writer's body—and even transcends the body, as we have seen Emerson, Everett, and others claim—the nature of song is to be and to remain embodied. In seeking to understand both the origins and nature of his work as a writer, then, Douglass finds the slave song a compelling, but in some ways threatening, forerunner. Not just in theory, but in actual historical experience, the slave song offers the African American an extraordinarily powerful form of expressivity—powerful because its ties to labor call attention to itself at every moment not just as a world-transcending response to sorrow and pain, but as a world-creating force that can work, invisible to the eye of the overseer, within the heart of slavery itself.

Yet Douglass also registers a concern that the slave song is at the same time distinctly inappropriate as a model on which to pattern one's work as an African American writer. In the *Narrative* of 1845, Douglass had voiced three reservations about the songs sung by slaves. First, insofar as he located them only in the slaves' trips to the Great House Farm, he associated them with a slavish sycophancy, with the slaves' self-defeating desire "to please their overseers." Second, the songs worried him because they were so easily misunderstood and misused by white Americans in the North and in the South who found in them evidence of the slaves' "contentment and happiness." Third, he suggested that the spontaneous and improvisational nature of the songs, their conflation of "sound" and "word," helped render them not only "unmeaning jargon" to outsiders but "incoherent" and beyond the "comprehension" even of those who sang them, those within "the circle" of slavery.

In *MBMF,* written ten years later, Douglass still has these reservations about the songs, but in his account of them he makes crucial revisions indicative both of his new concern with his work as a writer and of his wavering loyalty toward an embodied identity. His first major change is to make clear that the songs were sung not only on trips to the Great House Farm but whenever and wherever the slaves worked. "Slaves are generally expected to sing as well as to work. A silent slave is not liked by masters or overseers. *'Make a noise,' 'make a noise,'* and *'bear a hand,'* are the words usually addressed to the slaves when there is silence among them" (p. 64). Douglass accents the songs' association with work again when he describes the outsiders' misunderstanding of the slave songs as, specifically, a misunderstanding of the slaves' attitude toward their work ("The remark is not infrequently made, that slaves are the most contented and happy *laborers* in the world" (p. 66) [my emphasis]). These changes suggest, I would argue, that in *MBMF* Douglass is returning to the slave songs with a new interest in their relation to slave work—an interest that grows out of his own concern to understand his work as a writer.

A second major revision Douglass makes is to explore further the nature and consequences of these songs' spontaneity. The *Narrative*'s implied linkage of improvisation with "incoherence" now becomes explicit: the "words of their own improvising [were] jargon to others but full of meaning to themselves" (p. 65). In this version, moreover, he seems to stress that the songs not only resist full "comprehension" by those who sing them, but that they actually substitute for and thus impede the development of thought and self-consciousness among the slaves: "Once on the road [to the Great House Farm] with an ox team, and seated on the tongue of his cart, with no overseer to look after him, the slave was comparatively free; and, if thoughtful, he had time to think" (p. 64). But it is clear that most slaves were not eager to embrace this opportunity for thought. Instead, they sang.

Why did they sing? Why, when they had opportunity to "think," did the slaves become "*peculiarly* excited and noisy" (p. 65) [my emphasis] and sing with unusual intensity of feeling? Douglass's implicit explanation is that they did so precisely because they could not and did not *want* to think. Their songs offered them an opportunity to express their rage and grief without actually having to think about it. As Douglass makes clear in the *Narrative,* to think about and be conscious of one's "condition"—to stare unblinkingly at what it is to be a slave—is to experience "torment." When Douglass himself becomes aware of his condition he often wishes he were not: "Anything, no matter what, to get rid of thinking! It was this everlasting thinking of my condition that tormented me. There was no getting rid of it." It should come as no surprise that the slaves preferred to sing their condition rather than to think about it.

Yet, crucially, this ability to "view" one's "wretched condition" as a slave is the consequence, for Douglass, of literacy. Thought is the gift, and curse, of reading and writing.

> As I read and contemplated the subject [of slavery], behold! that very dis-contentment which Master Hugh had predicted would follow my learn-ing to read had already come, to torment and sting my soul to unutter-able anguish. As I writhed under it, I would at times feel that learning to read has been a curse rather than a blessing. It had given me a view of my wretched condition, without the remedy. . . . In moments of agony, I en-vied my fellow-slaves for their stupidity. I have often wished myself a beast. (p. 84)

Although he envies his fellow slaves their "stupidity," and wishes him-self "a beast," Douglass nevertheless believes that the thought acquired by reading must be obtained and experienced. It is a necessary precon-dition of emancipation. This is why Douglass has misgivings about the slave songs' conflation of "word" and "sound" and this is why slaves outside the "circle" of slavery have a fuller understanding of the songs' meaning than those locked within it. Literacy, the acquisition of power over the "word," enables one to step outside the circle. Singing, by con-trast, though it powerfully expresses feelings of anguish and sorrow, ob-structs thought insofar as it allows one to vent one's feelings without understanding them.

To point out the ways in which *MBMF* expresses an intensified am-bivalence toward the slave song (and, thereby, to slave labor) is not to propose that *MBMF* ceases to respect these. On the contrary, in the *MBMF* version of the slave-song passage, Douglass writes nothing that qualifies his feeling of obligation toward the slave song. Presumably, as a writer he still feels that he received from the songs his first "glimmer-ing conception of the dehumanizing character of slavery." As a writer, he still locates in the songs the emergence of a consciousness which, while much less developed than that obtained from reading, neverthe-less represents an advance over a condition with no conceptions at all. And to the degree that the slave song itself emerges from and expresses the slave's labor (a connection Douglass emphasizes in *MBMF*), he must still trace his labor as a writer back not only to the songs, but to the labor he performed as a slave.

In *MBMF* he adds an observation about the slave songs that pushes to the breaking point the fundamental dichotomy of mind and body, spirit and matter, on which all these ambivalences and negotiations are predicated. After noting that the songs "represent the sorrows, rather than the joys of [the slave's] heart," Douglass remarks: "Such is the constitution of the human mind, that, when pressed to extremes, it often avails itself of the most opposite methods. Extremes meet in mind as in matter" (p. 66). The "extreme" of slavery combines, or breaks down, the very oppositions by which the institution of slavery is justified. Just as the unending work of slavery might render slavery the opposite of work, and just as the slave might find a paradoxical margin of freedom within the work experience, so, too, the condition of slavery forces individuals to experience syntheses of joy and sorrow, and of mind and matter, which the theory of slavery would consider impossible. More fully even than Susan Warner and Harriet Beecher Stowe, Douglass experiences an "extreme" that enables the falsity, or at least the conditionality, of hierarchical dichotomies to become visible. He may not always see the falsity himself, but his experience makes it legible to others—just as Pennington's experience of his work suddenly made something (his freedom) infuriatingly visible to his master. In both the *Narrative* and *MBMF*, one of the most astonishing instances of such an undoing of categorical distinctions occurs at the close of the passage on reading and thinking cited above. Douglass's new knowledge of his condition, his new way of thinking about slavery, has the unanticipated effect not just of causing pain, but of causing divisions between sentience and insentience, mind and matter, to dissolve. In language that faintly recalls John Neal's knowledge of "things," and Roderick Usher's horrified intuitions of "the sentience of all vegetable things," Douglass writes that thought about his condition "converted every object into an asserter of this right [of freedom]." His enslavement and, simultaneously, his claim to freedom, are spoken to him by and from the world of mere things. "I saw nothing without seeing it, and I heard nothing without hearing it. I do not exaggerate, when I say, that it looked from every star, smiled in every calm, breathed in every wind, and moved in every storm" (p. 101). Paradoxically, the extreme of slavery permits one to see that real thinking does not offer an escape from or transcendence of the material world, but returns thought to matter, both "animate" and "inanimate."

Taken together, Douglass's revisions of the slave-song passage register a misgiving that the *Narrative* version, if left exactly as it was, would have failed to convey the way (in Douglass's view) the slaves' songs restrict their consciousness and become a substitute, not a medium, of thought. His revisions register a misgiving, too, that the *Narrative* version would have suggested that the slave songs were somehow superior to, more effective than, "volumes of philosophy"; so, with a subtle and effective editorial stroke Douglass replaces this phrase with "volumes of mere physical cruelties" (p. 65), thus deflecting an implied criticism away from the more philosophical book he is writing and directing it instead toward the *Narrative,* with its greater emphasis on "physical cruelties." As a freed slave he now feels that he can "take care of" the "philosophy" himself. Performing the work of composing not just a slave narrative, but an autobiography that seeks to account for his origins and development as an African American writer, Douglass at once inherits, but also rejects, the paradigmatic understanding of slave labor as utterly unredemptive and brutifying, as the force of matter against matter. Like many writers of slave narratives, he feels compelled to bear witness that the slave does have a mind; indeed, this *is* the narrator's work, to make the slave's mentality manifest to the reader. Douglass makes it quite plain that this mentality does not come into being when the slave crosses the border into the free states. Nor does it come into existence at the moment the slave becomes literate, though certainly that accomplishment is important. It comes into existence in "glimmerings" that seem to defy representation. How, after all, can emancipatory self-consciousness be located in the labor that is the very cause of the slave's enslavement? How can it be located in the songs the slave sings—songs said by outsiders to reflect the slaves' contentment with their lot and songs which, in Douglass's experience, seem to keep slaves from becoming aware of their situation?

Yet to deny the slaves' ability to appropriate their labor unto themselves, and to reject absolutely the expressivity of the slave song, would be to participate in the process of dehumanizing the slave and to deny one's racial identity as an African American writer. Even as Douglass remains in some sense imprisoned within this dilemma, the "extreme" of slavery implicitly undoes it. Just as slavery promotes miscegenation, which makes racial "purity" impossible, so too it promotes a form of labor that tries to reduce slaves to mere bodies and "things," yet which in doing so inadvertently reveals the self-expressive powers of the body and calls into question the assumed distinction between body and mind, physicality and mentality, manual and mental labor, on which justifications of slavery rest. Douglass himself cannot always perceive and benefit from this undoing, but his texts allow us to do so.

Imagine, if you will, that Wordsworth had been a black poet, and that the Highland lass had been a black woman singing while picking cotton somewhere in Alabama. He, too, would have interrogated her song, and he, too, might have born it in his heart "long after it was heard no more." But alongside the mingled feelings of curiosity, reverence, and pain Wordsworth experienced would lie another complex of feelings. Along with Valéry's observation that literature is an "instanta-neous coupling of sound and sense that have no connection with each other," one would wish to note certain complications. It is one thing for a free white man to emphasize the sensuous origins of literature and to point to its affinities with labor and labor's song. It is quite another for a freed black slave to do so. First, song's apparent conflation of "sound" and "sense" is more troubling when one's work as a slave has been defined as purely embodied and when one's work as a writer is al-ways at the same time part of a project of self-emancipation through self-consciousness. Second, Douglass's recovery in his literary work of a bond between body and mind, manual and mental labor, is also the re-covery of a bondage—the bondage of slavery, of racism, and then of re-sponsibility to race. Third, more than any other form of work, slavery at once carries to an absolute extreme the binary categories of mind and body, and at the same time resists being understood in terms of them—and thus undoes them. Therefore, the antebellum African American writer who approaches the relation of his work to the work of slaves by way of these categories engages in an unraveling and reweaving of the meanings they conventionally construct.

*

Like Douglass, many African American writers of subsequent genera-tions have explored the nature of their work as writers by way of the re-lation between song and writing. One of the opening scenes of Pauline Hopkins's *Contending Forces,* for example, depicts a gang of slaves un-loading a barge and singing as they work. "A band of slaves sang in a musical monotone, and kept time to the music of their song as they un-loaded a barge that had just arrived."[7] The song being sung serves as a kind of choral comment on the immediate, antebellum actions of the novel, but also as an acknowledgment of the seeming futility of such comment. The song carries its singers and auditors in a cycle away from the scene of their work and back to it again. It begins with work, "Turn dat han' spike roun' and roun', . . . Brack man tote de buckra's load," and moves to the possibility of liberation through love, "Allers tinkin' 'bout yer 'ol brack Sue," and of actual escape, "Run 'way wid ol' brack Sue," and then turns back on itself with the recognition that escape is impossible, "Massa ketch yer," and the inevitability of punishment, "Cut yet back and 'ol brack Sue's." The final movement is a bitter ac-knowledgement that while the slave can "cuss massa," that won't change anything because "Massa don' hyar make no differyence," and then a reprise back to the first verse, "Turn dat 'han spike 'roun and' roun', . . . Brack man tote de buckra's load" (pp. 32–33). Here again, liberation is made possible not through desire, or love, from which only recapture and punishment can follow. Rather, self-preservation is maintained through work, and self-expression is achieved through the work song, which at once denies the effectiveness of desire and reaffirms the self-protective aspects of work—work as the place in which slaves are least seen, least heard by their masters, and thus most free to engage in communal comment upon their situation. Work, and the work song, are a site and mode of slave self-consciousness.

When the slaves' work and song appear a second time in this novel, they again appear together. While two white men plan the murder of a white reformer, the slaves occupy a background position, working and singing, their song serving as a choric comment on the foregrounded deliberations of the two men.

> Bill was overseeing the harvesting of a great field of cotton, and the voices of the slaves could be heard droning out their weird and plaintive notes, as they sought by song movement to lighten the monotony of their heavy tasks and bring solace to their sad hearts. Some, in their simple ignorance, may not have known why they were sad, but, like the captive bird, their hearts longed for that which was ever the birthright of man—property in himself. (p. 60)

The account at once brings to mind Douglass's description of slave songs and his observation that those "within the circle" of slavery may not have known of their own songs' "deep meaning." Hopkins represents the songs as having two meanings: first, they alleviate the slaves' suffering, in particular by lightening the "monotony of their heavy tasks." Second, they give voice to the slaves' longing for self-ownership—"property in" themselves. In addition, however, the songs signify something in relation to the deliberations of the white men who are planning an unspeakably evil course of action: the song of the slaves' "sad hearts" delivers comment and judgment on the two white men, both of whom are oblivious to the song, not even hearing it. The slaves are utterly outside the circle in which such actions are planned and executed. But by the same token, the slaves are in a sense left alone. Deprived of free will, and enclosed, as it were, within the protective envelope of their song and labor, they cannot be touched by evil—except as its victim. It is crucial to bear in mind that neither labor nor song would provide this protection if the labor were absolutely monotonous, absolutely controlled by the overseer. Although Hopkins describes the song as "movement" that "lightens" their "heavy tasks," the song has its origins in, and derives its rhythms from, those tasks. In other words, the song can have no movement if there is no movement in the labor; the song cannot "lighten" if there are not relatively light instances in the predominantly monotonous labor.

Just as in the unfolding of its plot the novel represents the present (early twentieth century) as still entangled with the antebellum past, so these scenes suggest that the writing of the novel as a complaint against racism will fare no better than the slave's "cuss" because whites "don' hyar." The novel thus represents itself as a reprise of the slaves' work song, enabling us to infer that, like the song, it rises out of and returns to degraded (but crucially protective and potentially emancipatory) work.

But if the analogy between the slave song and the novel itself reinforces the conjecture that the novel emerges from and returns to the work of the postbellum, post-Reconstruction African American, how does the novel understand and represent this work? It repeatedly insists, first of all, on the fact that Northern racism has striven to deny the African American the opportunity to work. "The masses of the Negro race," writes Hopkins,

> find for their employment only the most laborious work at the scantiest remuneration. A man, though a skilled mechanic, has the door of the shop closed in his face among the descendants of the liberty-loving Puritans. The foreign element who come to the shores of America soon learn that there is a class which is called inferior, and will not work in this or that business if "niggers" are hired and the master or owner, being neither able nor willing to secure enough of the despised class to fill the places of the white laborers, acquiesces in the general demand, and the poor Negro finds himself banned in almost every kind of employment. . . . With about every avenue for business closed against them, it is surprising that so many families of color manage to live as well as they do . . . (pp. 83, 86)

They manage, the novel goes on to show, principally by working for themselves, working within the family, church, and community, within the "circle" drawn now by racism instead of slavery. The enclosed nature of this work is represented literally by enclosure within spaces—within the space of Ma Smith's boarding house, within the space of the first floor of the community's church. Significantly, what both of these work projects (the taking on of boarders, the organizing of a fair) seek to accomplish is the paying off of a mortgage. If the Emancipation Proclamation restored to the slave his ownership in himself, and thereby of his work, a pervasive racism now demands that the freed slave find further protection by devoting labor to the acquisition of real property.

Perhaps the outlines of this complicated relation among slavery, work, song, and writing can be seen most clearly in the very different views of slavery and work advanced on the one hand by Booker T. Washington and on the other by W. E. B. DuBois.[8] Washington can be seen as the inheritor of that side of Douglass which wished to deny the complexity of the slave experience in general, and of slave labor in particular. For Washington, slavery is a painful historical moment that can and should be left behind by the enterprising African American. At the same time, Washington maintains that, in making his way forward, the typical African American should not aspire to perform mental labor, or to become learned, or to cultivate his imaginative powers, but must be willing to undertake and persevere in a regimen of self-disciplined manual labor. That is, the African American should begin at the bottom and solidify his skills as a manual laborer before attempting to push upward into the ranks of the professional classes. The link between Washington's attitude toward slavery and his proscriptions about work is subtle: joining them is the assumption that within slavery the African American did almost nothing of personal value, found no way of cultivating and expressing mental and imaginative abilities, and performed work which, if it was work at all, was exclusively manual and preparatory only for an emancipated life of more manual work.

W. E. B. DuBois, on the other hand, can be seen as the inheritor of that side of Douglass which was drawn back to the slave experience, found some self-affirmative value in slave labor, and felt a writer's indebtedness to slave songs. DuBois does not see the African American emerging *tabula rasa* from slavery, but entering the condition of freedom with "gifts" to offer. Some of these gifts he brought from Africa and preserved, but some—and the most notable of these is the slave song—were produced by the experience of slavery itself. Thus, slavery for DuBois is not just a historical moment, but a historical inheritance of continuing importance. Moreover, his predisposition to find evidence of the African American's ability to develop imaginative and self-expressive powers within slavery also predisposes DuBois to think about, and accord value to, the African American work experience and "work ethic." Although his account of this ethic locates its origins in Africa and the tropics, not in slavery in the southern United States, it nonetheless reflects his recognition that as an African American writer he must establish a relation between his work and the work performed by the black masses within and after slavery. One way to establish that relation is to argue that freed slaves and their children are capable of, and entitled to, education in the fullest sense of the word. They should not restrict themselves to the performance of manual labor, but should develop fully their cognitive, imaginative, and reflective powers. A sec-

ond way to establish that connection is to argue that the work experience of the African American has *always* had within it qualities congen-
ial to imaginative expressivity—that, in some sense, it has always blurred
the distinction between body and mind, senses and spirit, manual and
mental labor.

This is precisely what DuBois suggests in his chapter on "Black Labor" in *The Gift of Black Folk.*

> [T]he black slave brought into common labor certain new spiritual values
> not yet fully realized. As a tropical product with a sensuous receptivity to
> the beauty of the world he was not as easily reduced to the mechanical
> draft-horse which the northern European laborer became. He was not
> easily brought to recognize any ethical sanctions in work as such but
> tended to work as the results pleased him and refused to work or sought
> to refuse when he did not find the spiritual relations adequate; thus he
> was easily accused of laziness and driven as a slave when in truth he
> brought to modern manual labor a renewed valuation of life.[9]

In DuBois's hands, the distinction between spirit and body at once
structures his description of black labor and at the same time seems to
collapse within it. The black slave's "spiritual values" are the product
not of an unworldly, transcendental impulse, but of his "sensuous receptivity to the beauty of the world." The black slave does not labor under the compulsion of an ethic which values work as an end in itself, re-
gardless of what it produces; instead, he or she views work as a means,
and refuses, or seeks to refuse to work, when that work no longer gives
sufficient satisfaction. DuBois goes on to write: "Always physical fact
has its spiritual complement, but in this case the gift is apt to be forgotten or slurred over. The gift is the thing that is usually referred to as
'laziness.' Again and again men speak of the laziness of Negro labor and
some suppose that slavery of Negroes was necessary on that account,
and that even in freedom Negroes must be 'driven.'"[10] But it is precisely
with this attitude, deemed "laziness" by men like Carlyle, that the black
slave retains his humanity; although slavery regards him as a "thing," he
has not himself subscribed to an ethic that reduces "the northern European laborer" to a "mechanical draft-horse."

Although the black slave was required for the most part to perform
manual labor, and unskilled manual labor at that, his labor experience
was by no means devoid of value. On the contrary, insofar as the black
slave brought his "laziness" into his work, that is, insofar as he affirmed
the "beauty of the world" and "the pleasure of life" to be valuable, he
made the work his own. It is this conception of work which DuBois sees
the freed slave bringing with him into freedom. It is a conception of

work which at once contradicts the Northern work ethic to which Washington devoted himself and at the same time disrupts Washington's facile and conventional distinction between manual and mental labor. For DuBois, the black laborer defines bodily labor as something that carries "spiritual values" and "spiritual returns" not insofar as it disregards, but insofar as it promotes, bodily "pleasure." It is the "sensuous receptivity" of the black slave's body that allows him a "spiritual" appreciation of the beauty of the world; this "spiritual value," in turn, leads him to regard work as "a necessary evil ministering to the pleasure of life." Finally, by regarding black labor not as "a great moral duty," but as in essence an *aesthetic* experience, DuBois makes possible a link between the imaginative work of the black writer and the bodily labor performed by most black men and women in his time.

It is fitting, then, that DuBois regards "the Negro folk-song—the rhythmic cry of the slave . . . not simply as the sole American music, but as the most beautiful expression of human experience born this side of the seas."[11] Like Douglass, he is an African American artist who seeks to understand his or her work in relation to the work of other African Americans, including those who were slaves. Like Douglass, he sees the slave song as a powerful affirmation of the slaves' humanity. But he is willing to go further than Douglass and to make very explicit his commitment to maintaining a connection between slave songs and writing, and thus to see in the slaves' work (and work ethic) a fusion of the material and spiritual, the bodily and the mental, that can serve as a model also for the work of the African American literary imagination.

5

Toward an
Ontology of
Labor

11

"By the Labor of My Hands Only"

The Making and Unmaking of *Walden*

When and in what way do things appear as things? They do not appear
by means of human making. But neither do they appear without the vigilance of mortals. The first step toward such vigilance is the step back from
the thinking that represents—that is, explains—to the thinking that responds and recalls.[1]

—Martin Heidegger, "The Thing"

In *Walden*, the concerns I have been discussing—the problematic relation of writerly work to more conventional forms of work, work as an
activity defined by the relation of mind to body, work as constituting
and constituted by gender and class identity—receive their fullest, most
self-conscious, and most philosophically rigorous treatment. However,
while the broadness of Thoreau's treatment of work makes him representative of his period, the fixity of his inward gaze and his willingness
as a writer to abide by what he sees make him unusual. I have already
proposed that because writing is work, it cannot serve as a transparent
medium through which work can be seen, understood, and evaluated.
Thoreau is supremely aware of this fact—and in his hands it cuts two
ways. His consciousness that writing is work allows him to use his writing as both the subject and means of an experiment in redefining the
meaning of work more generally. By the same token, however, his
knowledge that writing is work subjects it to the critique he brings to
bear against all other forms of work. He knows that his writing is not
"privileged," as we would now say, but implicated. Indeed, I would ar-

gue that his most concentrated critical energies are directed not outward—toward the work of his Concord neighbors, or toward the rest-
less ambition of the emerging middle class—but inward, at his own
work as a writer.[2]

Walden, his masterpiece, is a paradox, a book that repeatedly and in-
sistently calls into question the validity of its own existence. "Simplicity,
simplicity, simplicity!" Thoreau urges.[3] Only by stripping life of its su-
perfluities and reducing it to its essentials, can we drive life into a corner
and know it for what it really is. However, because this project of simplification extends to every aspect of life, not even literature is exempt
from its critique. Thoreau tells us that he took only one book with him
to Walden, and that—at least during his first summer—he seldom read
it. What, then, are we supposed to do with *his* book? Take it to our own
Walden, wherever that might be, or leave it behind? Isn't his book a
complication of simplicity, an obdurate cipher standing on the page
Thoreau has spent so much energy trying to make blank?

In other words, although *Walden*'s self-avowed project is critical and
destructive, the very act of writing it (which, as we shall see, Thoreau
both invokes and conceals) is necessarily a constructive act. The challenge he faces is to write a book that disappears rather than endures, a
book that is consumed in the process of being read, just as "the knife
which slices the bread of Jove ceases to be a knife when this service is
rendered."[4]

Walden begins with a sentence which forewarns us that this struggle
with itself will complicate its author's and our own relations to the text:
"When I wrote the following pages, or rather the bulk of them, I lived
alone, in the woods, a mile from any neighbor, in a house which I had
built myself, on the shore of Walden Pond, in Concord, Massachusetts,
and earned my living by the labor of my hands only" (p. 3). Like the
traditional male artificer celebrated by Sidney and Shaftesbury, this "I,"
the author of "the following pages, or rather the bulk of them," now
stands outside his work, which is completed, finished. We cannot read
this sentence without assuming it to be the last sentence Thoreau composed and which he added, as a kind of prefatory postscript, to its beginning. But this distinction between the first sentence and the rest of
the book is blurred by the cunningly inserted, "or rather the bulk of
them." Thoreau's qualification betokens the presence of a fastidiously
accurate reporter (the Thoreau who would insist on revising his galleys
when the commuter fare from Concord to Boston rose fifteen cents).
But, more important, it alerts us to the divided nature of the book that
follows—to the fact that while "the bulk" of the pages were written at
Walden, the first sentence is just one of an unspecified number of others

that were not. Thus, the opening sentence distinguishes between two sites and modes of writing. The "bulk" of the pages were written in one mode, that is, coincidentally and coextensively with the experience of living and earning; the others were written after the fact, not while he lived that experience, but while he occupied some other existence—to which he makes no direct reference and about which we can infer only that in it he writes.

In addition, the first sentence draws distinctions also among the activities (writing, living, earning a living through manual labor) Thoreau performs at Walden. Instead of conflating them, it distinguishes and problematizes the relations among them. Although writing is announced by the book's first three words ("When I wrote"), it is not strongly accented. On the contrary, its position in the subordinate clause of a long and complex sentence encourages us to slip quickly by the activity of writing and to proceed to the sentence's center ("I lived alone.") But this activity, too, is in a sense passed by. The corkscrewing slide of prepositional phrases emphasizes not *what* the living was, but *where* it happened. And even this "where" is problematic: the prepositions draw concentric rings (alone/house/shore/woods/Concord/Massachusetts) around the "I" to emphasize his aloneness, but in so doing they at the same time bind him to a specific human community (Concord, Massachusetts) and obliquely call attention to the unspecificity of the place from which the "I" now writes the sentence.

We emerge from this long but syntactically subordinated part of the sentence to the second part of its main clause ("and earned my living by the labor of my hands only"). This I take to be a claim rather than a mere statement of fact. It carries a ring of defiance, or challenge, as though we were to read, "*and believe it or not* I earned my living by the labor of my hands only." Thoreau is aware that his readers are predisposed to assume the existence of a radical disjunction between the activity with which the sentence begins (writing) and that with which it ends (earning a living by manual labor). Does his sentence implicitly challenge, or does it reinforce that assumption? Are we to see these three activities (writing, living, earning a living by manual labor) as all fused together in his experience at Walden Pond? Or is the lingering emphasis on "hands only" supposed to underscore a distinction between writing with the mind and earning a living with the hands?

Walden's opening sentence is a prefiguration of the divided and dialectical nature of the pages that follow it. As we have already seen in *A Week*, Thoreau's radical skepticism about the value of world-building work has compelled him to question the ideal of the artist as a fabricator who imitates God, the divine artificer, and to search for a mode of making patterned on the immanent, generative power of nature. But, like Hawthorne, he finds that this embrace of organicized or naturalized work leads to complications: the artist who works as nature works must relinquish the "self" that stands outside work and must abandon also the hope that his product will endure forever as part of a human "world" (Arendt's term) created over and against an always decaying "earth." Thoreau cannot bring himself to make these sacrifices and *Walden* is less a solution to the problem of making art without artifice (the problem posed by *A Week*) than a series of restatements, or reformulations, of the problem itself. *Walden* is the enactment of a dialectic precisely between artifice and generation, between the work of the (transcendent) father who stands outside his artifact and the creation of the (immanent) mother who resides within hers. At the same time, it enacts a dialectic between writing conceived of as mental labor and writing conceived of as bodily labor. It is out of the interplay between these two ways of understanding creation that *Walden* will create itself and be created, a fact Thoreau often alludes to—as when he writes that he used to watch "a pair of henhawks circling high in the sky, alternately soaring and descending, approaching and leaving one another, as if they were the embodiment of my own thoughts" (p. 159).

If *Walden* consists of repeated dramatizations of its conflict with itself—a conflict between its constructive and destructive aspects, between artifice and generation, between mental and bodily labor—it must be read as a series of enactments, not as a story or as a narratival unfolding and resolution of the contradiction that generates and constitutes it. (In contrast to *A Week*, *Walden*'s point in occupying a single location is to stress precisely that it goes nowhere.) For this reason, my reading of *Walden* consists of a series of encounters with the book. I come to it at three junctures, each of which is a playing out of what I have called the book's fundamental contradiction. The first of these is the book's representation of work; the second, its representation of the body; the third, its representation of its own creation. Each of these junctures is a reiteration of the others, so that, though we may at times seem to have moved away from the subject of work, we will never have left it.

Work

Walden's critique of work derives much of its power from his being grounded in the two ideologies it would subvert: an ethic that ascribes spiritual value to work and a theory of political economy that values work above all other activities. As a New Englander, Thoreau is the inheritor of a powerful imperative to find a "calling" and then work in it for the glory of God and the good of the human community. Thoreau cannot escape this inheritance. He lives and breathes it. Every now and then he pulls free of it for a moment, but escape is impossible. The very impulse to follow the calling of a writer and to write *Walden* in order to "wake up" his "neighbors" is, as Stanley Cavell has shown, a prophetic impulse. Thoreau willingly inherits the mantle not just of Isaiah and Ezekiel but of Baxter and Cotton and the whole company of "visible saints" whose work is to chastise humans into salvation. But Thoreau turns the force of this tradition against the (in his day dominant) school of political economy that had established work both as the justification of private property (Locke) and as the creator of economic or exchange value (Smith). In other words, Thoreau brings the self-critical anxiety of the search for a calling to his (re)evaluation of work and says, in effect: If labor, or a labor theory of value, is what classical economic theory and bourgeois culture rest on, let us see what labor is. Let us evaluate labor itself. Let us make labor valuable before we affirm that labor creates value.

The more superficial aspects of *Walden*'s critique of labor are too familiar to need much rehearsal. It asserts, first, that the labor most humans perform is endless, so that, as a means to an end (which is precisely the devaluation of work Marx criticized) it fails: there is no getting to the end of it. "The twelve labors of Hercules were trifling in comparison with those which my neighbors have undertaken; for those were only twelve, and had an end; but I never see that these men slew or captured any monster or finished any labor" (p. 4). The second point of Thoreau's critique is that human labor is misdirected: human beings are working for the wrong things. Their aim is only to lay up "treasures which moths and rust will corrupt and thieves break through and steal. It is a fool's life, as they will find when they get to the end of it, if not before" (p. 5). Finally (in what is perhaps only an elaboration of the second point), these mistaken labors prevent humanity from paying attention to what is truly important in life: "Most men, even in this comparatively free country, are so occupied with the factitious cares and superfluously coarse labors of life that its finer fruits cannot be plucked by them" (p. 6).

If humans work far too much, and for the wrong things, then a remedy would require that we determine how little work people can get away with. Here Thoreau's analysis takes a provocative turn. People work, he says, for "Food, Shelter, Clothing, and Fuel," but these necessities can be further reduced. Food is eaten in order to "keep up the internal combustion in the lungs"; clothing and fuel "serve only to retain the *heat* thus generated and absorbed. . . .The grand necessity, then, for our bodies, is to keep warm, to keep the vital heat in us" (pp. 12–13). We work, in short, to keep our bodies warm. And if, as Thoreau seems to be suggesting, the only work we *should* do is the work we *must* do, then the only work we can be perfectly certain is justifiable is the work we devote to maintaining the heat of our bodies. Thus, the body becomes decisive in Thoreau's account of work. While the work ethic is not forsaken, it is grounded now not in the notion of service to humanity and glorification of God, but in the absolute requirements of the physiology of the body. Instead of serving merely as a means, as something we work with, the body becomes both the end and the measure of work's value.

"Economy," then, argues that we can make work bearable only by minimizing the amount of work we have to do. But having applied a Cartesian skepticism to the problem of work, and having arrived at this radically simple formulation—to work is to keep warm—Thoreau goes no further in his critique. His destructive, or simplifying, project comes to a dead end. What more can be written? The work of writing has been rendered just as superfluous (since it doesn't keep the body warm) as all other kinds of wasteful work. Thoreau has written himself into a corner from which there is no escape. But here, characteristically, he reverses course. In order to go on writing, he must find some other grounds for justifying his own and all other forms of superfluous labor. "Some [men]," he writes, "are industrious, and appear to love labor for its own sake, or perhaps to keep them out of worse mischief; to such I have at present nothing to say" (p. 70). This possibility—that labor can be loved "for its own sake," quite apart from what it produces—is what he will have to make real in order to go on generating the book, or mischief, that is *Walden*.

Thoreau works in three ways at Walden: he writes, he builds a house, and he grows beans. All these activities are in large measure superfluous and to that degree undertaken for their "own sake." Of the first, he tells us nothing. (Later we will have to decide whether this omission represents an erasure of that work or a diffusion of it through the other kinds of work and through the book itself.) The second, the work of building a house, is of course fraught with danger, since the house is civilization writ small—it is, to employ Arendt's distinction once again, the highly concentrated essence of the "world" man builds upon the "earth." Therefore, ". . . if one designs to construct a dwelling house, it behooves him to exercise a little Yankee shrewdness, lest after all he find himself in a work-house, a labyrinth without a clew, a museum, an almshouse, a prison, or a splendid mausoleum instead"

(p. 28). Thoreau insists that he would live, if he could, in those "primitive ages" when men "dwelt, as it were, in a tent in this world." But the age of innocence has passed. Humans have degenerated to a state of living in durable houses because they became "the tools of their tools," servants of their sexual, or procreative, drive. This required, in turn, that they commit themselves to an agricultural civilization in order to provide food for an ever-growing human population. They thus became the tools also of their implements, of the plow and the axe and all the other durable instruments with which humanity creates a "world" out of the "earth." "The man who independently plucked the fruits when he was hungry is become a farmer; and he who stood under a tree for shelter, a housekeeper" (p. 37). In short, we are back to the myth Thoreau elaborated in *A Week*: man was once a carefree hunter-gatherer in the woods, but his sexual passion for woman—the excessive heat of his body—has driven him into the coils of civilization and the snares of domesticity.

We must recall that, for Thoreau, this drama is not the outcome of a simple dualism that pits man against nature, masculine against feminine. Rather, in either role, as either hunter or farmer, men (that is, males), work in service to nature. The hunter is the consort of nature-as-wilderness; the farmer is the servant of nature-as-cultivation. The challenge Thoreau sees himself facing is not to choose one side or the other, but to pay homage to nature in both her aspects. If he is to be a writer, he cannot be a hunter pure and simple; as a writer he must contribute to civilization—that is, he *must* build a house. But even as he acknowledges that his whole project is founded on compromise, he commits himself to the task of minimizing that compromise. His house must be as *un*-houselike as possible. Like the knife of Jove, both his house and his book (and the two constructions are implicitly linked) must disappear as soon as they are used.

Thus, his first constructive act—building—is predicated upon a destructive one—cutting: "Near the end of March, 1845, I borrowed an axe and went down to the woods by Walden Pond, nearest to where I intended to build my home, and began to cut down some tall arrowy white pines, still in their youth, for timber" (p. 40). Thoreau acknowledges that his own "experiment" participates in that destruction of the wilderness he so often deplores. But immediately he interjects what he hopes will be redeeming discriminations. The work *he* does is at once relaxed and deliberate. "I made no haste in my work, but rather the most of it"—meaning, I suppose, that he is one of those who "love labor for its own sake." Moreover, his work is satisfactory and justifiable because he can figure it as *natural* work, as an expression of na-

ture working itself out rather than as an instance of man's destruction
of nature. "I never in all my walks came across a man engaged in so
simple and *natural* an occupation as building his house" [emphasis
added]. His building has ample precedent in nature. "There is some
of the same fitness in a man's building his own house that there is in
a bird's building its own nest" (p. 46). This impulse to naturalize human labor—and particularly the labor of house-building—was shared
by Emerson, who writes in "Fate" that "nature makes every creature
do its own work and get its living. . . . Every creature, worm or
dragon, shall make its own lair."[5]

Although by deciding to build a durable house (instead of, say, living
under a tree) Thoreau has departed from his principle of economy, he
nevertheless attempts to minimize his inconsistency by minimizing his
house. His house will have no ornament; it will keep his body warm and
no more. But out of his simplicity comes a new aesthetic, what Raymond Williams I believe has called "the aesthetics of necessity": "What
of architectural beauty I now see, I know has gradually grown from
within outward, out of the necessities and character of the indweller,
who is the only builder,—out of some unconscious truthfulness, and
nobleness, without ever a thought for beauty; and whatever additional
beauty of this kind is destined to be produced will be preceded by a like
unconscious beauty of life" (*Walden*, p. 47).

In other words, there is no essential difference between building
"shrewdly" and living. To build is to grow "from within outward." The
house should express, not contain, what is inside it. The "indweller"
does not so much construct a house to move into as secrete or spin a
house out of his "necessities and character." To build "deliberately,"
then, must be to ensure that the dwelling one builds expresses these necessities and this character. Building is not just co-extensive or compatible with living; it is an outgrowth of living. Thoreau's aim, then, in his
presentation of house-building is in effect to reform or reconceptualize
what Hannah Arendt defines as "work"; he tries to justify his building an
admittedly superfluous house (or book) by dissolving the distinction between building (Arendt's "working") and living. One builds not in order to create a "durable" artifact that stands over and against the cycles
of nature, but precisely in order to "live" naturally and within nature.[6]

Growing beans is Thoreau's other visible productive activity at Walden and through it Thoreau explores the possibility of reforming what
Arendt would later call "labor."[7] Here, too, Thoreau begins by acknowledging that he has departed from the radical "economy" of the absolutely necessary. Although he "learned . . . that if one would only live

simply and eat only the crop which he raised, and raise no more than he ate, and not exchange it for an insufficient crop of more luxurious and expensive things, . . . he could do all his necessary farm work as it were with his left hand at odd hours in the summer" (p. 56), he admits that he did not adhere to this principle himself. He planted more beans than he needed and therefore worked more than was necessary.

Why? "What was the meaning of this so steady and self-respecting, this small Herculean labor, I knew not. I came to love my rows, my beans, though so many more than I wanted" (p. 155). Thoreau writes that his "daily work" was to make "the yellow soil express its summer thought in bean leaves and blossoms rather than in wormwood and piper and millet grass, making the earth say beans instead of grass" (p. 157). Except for the word "make," there is no hint that Thoreau feels he is dominating or subduing nature. His labor has almost nothing in common with that of the farmers in *A Week* who have been "clearing, and burning, and scratching, and harrowing, and plowing, and subsoiling, in and in, and out and out, and over and over, again and again" (p. 8). Both of these accounts figure agricultural labor as verbal action, but whereas the farmers in *A Week* wrote "on the face of the earth," Thoreau feels that he serves as a medium that enables the earth to "express" itself. Both as bean-grower and as writer, he sees his labor not as inscription, impression, or rape, but as attendance upon and redirection of a process that is always underway.

The notion that agricultural labor is an activity that complements, rather than opposes, the natural productivity of the earth serves two purposes. The first is aesthetic: like Thoreau's conception of house-building, or "work," it enables Thoreau to figure his writing as an activity that complements, rather than stands over against, nature. This aesthetic objective originally served, as we have seen, a political purpose. He begins *A Week* by attempting to figure his writing as a kind of manual labor in order to put himself *into* the "condition" of other manual laborers; only by sharing their condition can he effectively and appropriately speak to them. But this vision of writing as a kind of manual labor turns out to be acceptable to Thoreau only if he can envision such labor as an activity that complements rather than opposes nature. The goal of addressing "a world of laborers" can be achieved only if the meaning of labor is suitably revised or reformed.

But now Thoreau's revision of the meaning of agricultural labor comes back to serve a more specific and more powerful political program: a critique of labor as the source of property rights. Again and again, *Walden* attacks the Lockean notion that man's labor creates and justifies private property. "Ancient poetry and mythology suggest," he writes, ". . . that husbandry was once a sacred art;

> but it is pursued with irreverent haste and heedlessness by us, our object being to have large farms and large crops merely. . . . By avarice and self-ishness, and a grovelling habit, from which none of us is free, of regarding the soil as property, or the means of acquiring property chiefly, the land-scape is deformed, husbandry is degraded with us, and the farmer leads the meanest of lives. (p. 165)

As is well known, Locke had argued that whatsoever a man "removes out of the state that nature hath provided and left it in, he hath mixed his labor with, and joined to it something that is his own, and thereby makes it his property."[8] This argument consists of three propositions. First, that "God hath given the world to men in common." Second, that "every man has a property in his own person"—that is, that every man owns his own body. And third, as a corollary of the second, that every man has a natural right to his own labor, which is "the unquestionable property of the labourer" (p. 22). In sum, all men own nature in common, since God has given it to them. Each man exclusively owns his own body, and therefore the labor of his own body also. Therefore, each man owns exclusively whatever is produced by his mixing what he owns exclusively (his labor) with what he owns in common (nature) with all men.

Thoreau's redefinition of labor, in contrast, sees it not as a "mixing" of what one possesses individually with what one owns in common with all men, but simply as a release of nature's potentiality, of its ability to say "beans" instead of "grass." Labor is not mixed with the soil; it facilitates the self-expression of the soil. Indeed, *Walden*'s critique goes further. Locke's second and third propositions—that each man owns his own "person," that is, body, and that he therefore owns the "labor of his body and the work of his hands"—do not at first seem to be put in question here. The book's further undermining of the Lockean position becomes visible, however, when we see that Locke's second and third propositions entail another, namely, that each man is in fact two entities—an owner and a thing ("person," or body) owned. For we cannot make sense of the proposition that a man has a property in his own "person" without distinguishing between the man and the person. Surely it would make no sense to say that the one who owns and the "person" that is owned are one and the same. One can own or possess only what one can exchange or sell; one can own or possess only what one can cease to own or possess. Surely one cannot cease to possess one's self, one's very identity. The "person" Locke refers to must in some way be distinguishable and alienable from the "self" that constitutes each individual's identity.

When Locke uses the term "person," moreover, it is clear that he designates what we would call "the body." He writes that "every man has a property in his own person" and immediately afterward that the "labor of his body and the work of his hands are properly his." He makes no mention of mind or spirit. What a man owns is the work of the "body" and the "hands." Moreover, we can infer a logical reason why Locke must limit what is possessed to the body. The labor Locke envisions being "mixed" with nature simply cannot be mental labor. The mind alone cannot act or operate upon material nature. Only the body can perform the physical actions—picking up acorns, gathering apples, digging ore, and so on—which Locke uses as illustrations of "mixing."

Locke's second and third propositions, therefore, rest on a number of unstated assumptions: that human identity is essentially mental; that this mental identity is ontologically distinct from one's "person," or body; that this mental identity is able to have a property in its "person" or body; and that this essentially mental identity requires the body in order to be able to have a means of mixing what it owns exclusively with what it owns in common with all other men. It is this set of assumptions that Thoreau calls into question throughout *Walden*. As we shall see, his reform of labor is complemented by—or duplicated in—his reform of the body.

Walden's analysis of the meaning of work in general, and of Arendt's "labor" (bean-growing) and "work" (house-building) in particular, is a dramatization of the conflict between *Walden*'s destructive (simplifying) and constructive (visionary) aspects. Thoreau does not, however, contrast agricultural "labor" with constructive "work" (as Arendt uses the terms) and valorize the former because it is simpler and less civilizing. Rather, he uncovers and explores a dialectic *within* each of these kinds of activity: House-building, he acknowledges, must be construed as the most essential and characteristic activity of civilization; it is *par excellence* the activity that builds up a human world over and against the earth or nature. But he goes on to resist as much as he can this characteristic of house-building by building his own house as an impermanent and permeable structure rather than as a durable one, by building a house that serves as an outward expression rather than a kind of container of the living "indweller." He builds a house that can be turned inside-out in a flash rather than one that serves to keep the inside in and nature at bay. ("I did not need to go outdoors to take the air, for the atmosphere within had lost none of its freshness" [p. 85].) Thoreau performs the same operation on "labor." He acknowledges that bean-growing, too, requires human intervention in natural processes, making the earth say "beans" instead of "grass." But again Thoreau does everything he can to soften the impact of this intervention by envisioning agricultural labor not as a domination of nature, but as an activity that facilitates the self-expression of one of nature's aspects.[9]

Most decisively, Thoreau resists the widespread antebellum tendency to romanticize agricultural labor. He sees that although such labor is in many ways closer to nature than the constructive work of fabrication and artifice, it also poses a more profound threat to nature because it is the locus of man's claim to private property. That claim can be resisted by denying that human labor, when "mixed" with nature, can create private property. This second line of resistance has its source, as I have argued, in a revaluation of the body as a constituent of personal identity. It is to *Walden*'s revaluation of the body that I now turn.

The Body

It needs hardly be said that Thoreau himself is ambivalent about the body, and especially about his own body. But through the course of *Walden* this ambivalence becomes a problem he is willing to explore— becomes the second of what I have called *Walden*'s enactments of its conflict with itself: the conflict between its destructive (or simplifying) and its constructive (or visionary) aspects. In his more ascetic moods, Thoreau experiences the body as the ultimate obstacle to his project of simplification; it is the body, after all, with its multitude of needs and appetites, that compels us to live distractedly and to labor mistakenly— indeed, to labor at all. At other moments, Thoreau experiences the irreducibility of the body not as an obstacle, but as the only ground of certainty on which to build a way of being. The body is thus always present both as something to be tested and evaluated and yet—since it is the measure that makes evaluation possible in the first place—as something which resists evaluation itself.

An early example of the dual role the body plays in *Walden* is Thoreau's portrait of the woodchopper whom we know to be Alex Therien. In his depiction of Therien, Thoreau at first seems to employ the conventional distinction between mind and body we have seen operative among so many other antebellum accounts of labor and laborers. "A more simple and natural man it would be hard to find," he writes (p. 145). "Cast in the coarsest mould," Therien consists almost entirely of body, of matter. "In him the animal man was chiefly developed. . . . But the intellectual and what is called the spiritual man in him were slumbering as in an infant" (p. 147). But as I have suggested earlier, Thoreau subtly registers his distance from conventional rhetoric with his careful insertion of the phrase "and what is called."

This is not to say that Thoreau romanticizes Therien. His portrait never quite stabilizes or solidifies because he deliberately keeps his own uncertainties about Therien in play. "To a stranger," Thoreau writes, Therien "appeared to know nothing in general, yet I sometimes saw in him a man whom I had not seen before, and I did not know whether he was as wise as Shakespeare or as ignorant as a child, whether to suspect him of a fine poetic consciousness or of stupidity" (p. 148). On the one hand, "I occasionally observed that he was thinking for himself and expressing his own opinion, a phenomenon so rare that I would any day walk ten miles to observe it . . . " On the other hand, "the highest that he appeared to conceive of was a simple expediency . . . and this, practically, is true of all men" (p. 150). Similarly, although Therien "always had a presentable thought behind" his words, "his thinking was so primitive and immersed in his animal life that, though more promising than a merely learned man's, it rarely ripened into anything which can be reported" (p. 150).

Therien cannot be explained, therefore, by the conventional antebellum categories of "manual" and "mental," "animal" and "spiritual," "body" and "mind." His thought is "immersed in his animal life"—that is, it is bound up with and inseparable from the sensuous life of his body. As I have already argued, because he cannot be explained by these categories, Therien cannot be represented in a discourse that is predicated on them; his mind produces little that "can be reported." Indeed, this "muddy" (opaque) and "bottomless" (unfathomable) worker is resistant even to self-representation in literary texts. "I asked him," Thoreau writes, "if he ever wished to write his thoughts. He said that he had read and written letters for those who could not, but he never tried to write thoughts,—no, he could not, he could not tell what to put first, it would kill him, and then there was spelling to be attended to at the same time" (p. 148). To put himself, or his "thoughts" in writing would be, for Therien, a kind of suicide. His fear suggests that the essence of his identity as a manual laborer is not only resistant to the conventions of writing ("he would not know what to put first") but is actually threatened by writing: "it would kill him." The fully embodied life of this laboring woodsman, so attractive to Thoreau, is apparently unrepresentable, either by the laborer himself or by others.

This unrepresentability has both political and aesthetic consequences. Channing and Everett, with varying degrees of benignity,

sought to appropriate the worker, to "elevate" and bring him into the
fold of a cultured democracy. Thoreau, by contrast, suggests that the
"genius" of such workers might never be comprehensible to the literary
minds of the dominant class. These men "take their own view always"
instead of the view and values espoused by their self-proclaimed advocates. What distinguishes them might be that "they do not pretend to
see at all"—that they choose not to join the learned class in its collec-
tively willed pretence to have seen and understood everything (this is,
after all, what a dominant ideology claims to do). As the "wheels" on
which, as Melville put it, society is "bottomed," they remain apart in
their own world, opaque and unknowable, "dark and muddy" and as
"bottomless" as Walden Pond.[10]

The source of Therien's unknowability and of his resistance to appropriation and representation is his body—his immersion in "his animal
life." The absolute value of this body, however, is not determined. It is
perhaps undeterminable—since all the terms of valuation one might apply to it are embedded in a set of assumptions that devalues the body.
As with the farmers who "write upon the face of the earth," and as with
Thoreau's cultivation which makes the earth say one thing rather than
another, the problem of writing is inscribed in the problem of labor.
Only now it is inscribed also in the problem of the body. How can one
write about something that seems to stand outside language?

Thoreau's most extensive meditation on the body (and bodily labor)
is contained in the two linked chapters "Baker Farm" and "Higher
Laws." "Baker Farm" is an unsettlingly caustic and unsympathetic account of a life literally mired in labor that produces only for consumption. John Field works in order to eat, and what he eats becomes excrement that is indistinguishable from the ground (bog) he works.[11]
"When he had worked hard to eat he had to eat again in order to repair
the waste of his system,—and so it was as broad as it was long, . . . for
he was discontented and wasted his life into the bargain" (p. 205).
Thoreau advises Field to adopt his own principle of economy: to eat
only what he needs and to work only as much is required to obtain that
necessary food. But as he walks away from Baker Farm, Thoreau finds
himself thinking not about the wisdom of bodily frugality, but about
freedom, and sport, and play. He hears his "Good Genius" advising him
to "Go fish and hunt far and wide day by day,—farther and wider,—and
rest thee by many brooks and hearth-sides without misgiving. . . . There
are no larger fields than these, no worthier games. . . . Let not to get a
living be thy trade, but thy sport. Enjoy the land, but own it not" (p.
207).

The complex logic that leads from the futility of Field's labor to the virtues of leisure and sport to the imperative that one should "enjoy" but not "own" the land has its source in Thoreau's ambivalence toward the body. He states this ambivalence openly: "I found in myself, and still find, an instinct toward a higher, or, as it is named, spiritual life, as do most men, and another toward a rank and savage one, and I reverence them both. I love the wild not less than the good" (p. 210). But this explicit acknowledgment of his divided attitude gives way immediately to the development of one side of the dialectic. Having just admitted that he has been "strongly tempted to seize and devour" a woodchuck "raw," he now objects to "animal food" because of its "uncleanness." His rhetoric quickly moves toward an aesthetic of anorexia. "I believe that every man who has ever been earnest to preserve his higher or poetic faculties in the best condition has been particularly inclined to abstain from animal food, and from much food of any kind" (pp. 214–15). Here the project of simplification reaches one of its extreme verges: to live properly, it seems, is to live as a hunger artist. "The wonder is how they, how you and I, can live this slimy beastly life, eating and drinking" (p. 216).

At this point, his argument, or his attitude, has completely reversed itself. Whereas he left Baker Farm disgusted by the way labor mires humans in a cycle of working, eating, shitting, and working, and enraptured with the virtues of idleness, play, and sport, he now sees work as the only guarantor of spiritual purity. "An unclean person is universally a slothful one, one who sits by a stove, whom the sun shines on prostrate, who reposes without being fatigued." In "The Ponds" he had written: "I have spent many an hour, when I was younger, floating over its [Walden's] surface as the zephyr willed, having paddled my boat to the middle, and lying on my back across the seats, in a summer forenoon, dreaming awake, until I was aroused by the boat touching the sand, and I arose to see what shore my fates had propelled me to; days when idleness seemed the most attractive and productive industry" (p. 191). Now he writes that "If you would avoid uncleanness and all the sins, work earnestly, though it be at cleaning a stable" (p. 221).

Yet a consistent logic does inform the bizarre shift from a celebration of play to an exhortation to work (even if it be at "cleaning a stable," that is, working, as John Field does, in excrement). The consistency lies in the fact that Field eats and works and shits as much as he does because he has a family, a wife with "greasy face and bare breast" and a sexual appetite. Sexual appetite, the desire of and for woman, is what tears the virgin male out of his chaste relation with the wilderness into the cycle of production for consumption. Thoreau cannot decide whether labor is (as the book of Genesis suggests) the punishment for carnal knowledge, or whether it is (as Richard Baxter suggests) the best means of subduing carnal desires. Similarly, he cannot decide whether sport is the ideal expression of a pure life in the woods, or whether it is but a prelude to idle fantasies, sexual arousal, and finally enslavement by women like Mrs. Field.

But the force of his rhetoric against the body indicates, of course, the measure of its appeal to him. "The poet," he asserts in his *Journal,* "writes the history of his body,"[12] and to a large degree *Walden* is just such a history. It is the history of a man who is for some time committed to living in and through the senses. Again and again, Thoreau invokes the traditional distinction between body and soul, or body and mind, only to distance himself from it with a qualifying phrase. "I find in myself an instinct toward a higher, *or as it is named* more spiritual life, and another . . . " (p. 210) [my emphasis]. Early one morning Thoreau listens to the "faint hum of a mosquito" and goes on to reflect that after sleep, "a partial cessation of his sensuous life, the soul of man, *or its organs rather,* are reinvigorated each day" (p. 89) [my emphasis]. Sleep has made it possible for him to be in a certain mood, but that mood seems to be one in which he is entirely identified with his body and the natural world, so tuned to it that the faint hum of a mosquito becomes an event of great importance. He starts out to account for this by speaking of an invigorated "soul," but he checks himself, realizing that it is not the soul that hears the faint hum of the mosquito. Nor is it quite "the body" as that term is ordinarily used. Thoreau's solution is to fuse the two by speaking of a soul with "organs." Throughout *Walden,* Thoreau repeatedly strives for such a fusion. It is sometimes subtle, as when he writes that reading well "requires a training such as the athletes underwent" (p. 101), or when he says that he "wanted to live deep and suck out all the marrow of life" (p. 91), or when he writes that he "shall have intelligence with the earth" (p. 138). At other times, the fusion is shocking. "The intellect is a cleaver; it discerns and rifts its way into the heart of things. I do not wish to be any more busy with my hands than is necessary. My head is hands and feet. I feel all my best faculties concentrated in it. My instinct tells me that my head is an organ for burrowing, as some creatures use their snout and forepaws" (p. 98). Here Thoreau's apparent reaffirmation of the distinction between manual and mental labor ("I do not wish to be any more busy with my hands than is necessary") transforms itself into a critique of that distinction. The "mind" is itself "hands and feet" and he uses it not to obey "higher laws" but to burrow down into the ground, "into the heart of things."

No longer an axe that cuts down trees, the "intellect" transforms itself into a "cleaver" that seeks to bury itself in the essence of materiality.[13]

Thus *Walden* repeatedly registers an awareness that work, the body, and the justification of property are conjoined—that in the relation among them each finds its assigned meaning. In the Lockean scheme, the body makes labor possible, and the self's ownership of the body justifies its ownership of the material with which the body's labor has been "mixed." *Walden* disrupts this arrangement whenever it calls into question the distinction between mind and body. If one's mind is "hands and feet," then the body is ontologically indistinct from the self, and one cannot claim to have a "property" in one's body. And if it is not possible to have a property in one's body, then one cannot have a property in one's labor either. Therefore, one cannot have a property in that with which one mixes such labor; one cannot own the land. By this complex logic, labor is disburdened. No longer the means of gaining property, it becomes an end in itself. It becomes a kind of sport, or play. The reformation of the body, of labor, and of the land go together. "Let not to get a living be thy trade, but thy sport. Enjoy the land, but own it not."

Whereas in *Nature* Emerson had alienated his own body, including it in the vast "NOT ME,"[14] which for him constituted nature, Thoreau feels that he is able to see and be with nature only on those occasions in which he fully inhabits his body. When he is his body. These are the occasions "when the whole body is one sense and imbibes delight through every pore. I come and go with a strange liberty in Nature, a part of herself" (p. 129). "The place where they may occur is always the same, and indescribably pleasant *to all our senses*" (p. 112) [my emphasis].[15]

This so fully experienced fusion of self and body gives rise, oddly, to what Thoreau calls a feeling of "doubleness" in one of *Walden*'s more puzzling passages:

> With thinking we may be beside ourselves in a sane sense. By conscious effort of the mind we can stand aloof from all our actions and their consequences; and all things, good and bad, go by us like a torrent. We are not wholly involved in Nature. I may be either the drift-wood in the stream, or Indra in the sky looking down on it. I *may* be affected by a theatrical exhibition; on the other hand, I *may not* be affected by an actual event which appears to concern me much more. I only know myself as a human entity; the scene, so to speak, of certain actions and affections; and am sensible of a certain doubleness by which I can stand as remote from myself as from another. However intense my experience, I am always conscious of the presence and criticism of a part of me, which, as it were, is not a part of me, but spectator, sharing no experience, but taking

note of it; and that is no more I than it is you. When the play, it may be
the tragedy, of life is over, the spectator goes his way. (pp. 134–35)

This passage seems to offer a characteristic Thoreauvian reversal: having reached one pole of his dialectic by becoming "a part of" nature, he
now backpeddles, claiming at first that by "a conscious effort of the
mind" he can become "not wholly involved in Nature"; and then that
"however intense" the experience of such involvement, he is always
conscious of the "spectator" in him. But it is crucial to realize that the
spectator he observes watching him is *not* his innermost self; it is not
what Emerson called the "ME" in distinction to the "NOT ME"; it is
not a sense of a spiritual "I" radically distinct from all materiality, including the body. Thoreau's doubleness is a divided sense of being both
a "scene" and a "spectator." He does not privilege the spectator, however, and imply that that is where his identity primarily resides. The
spectator is not "a part" of him. Indeed, far from echoing Emerson's
disjunction of self and body, mind and nature, Thoreau's formula seems
actually to point in the opposite direction. If anything, he identifies
himself more closely with the scene, the actors, and the drama than with
the spectating "presence."

Thoreau's trope seems to have its source not in the familiar Shake-
spearean notion that life is a stage, but in James Garth Wilkinson's labored effort to recast the relationship between body and mind. Thoreau
read Wilkinson's book, *The Human Body*, in 1851, and he wrote in his
Journal that it "to some extent realizes what I have dreamed of . . ."[16]
Wilkinson's exposition is so highly figurative and so often apparently
self-contradictory that no summary can hope to be entirely accurate.
But one can safely say that, like Thoreau, Wilkinson is at once uphold-
ing the distinction between body and mind and blurring the line between them. For Wilkinson, the mind is an actual physical organ, a material entity. Wilkinson writes: "But for ourselves, we cannot think of
the mind as an *ignus fatuus* in the swamps of the cerebrum, but as a distinct and separate organ, which has the cerebrum and nervous system
between it and the body."[17] Thus, the mind is organic and in some
sense physically in the body, but it is not entirely of the body. When he
tries to describe the ways in which this organic mind communicates with
the body, Wilkinson frequently employs a language of theatricality,
drama, and representation. "The nerves or brain form a representative
system, which does not itself come in contact with objects on the one
hand, or with actions on the other, but deals in the one case with the
images of things, in the other, with the commands of action" (p. 37).
Just as the nerves or brain form a "representative system" midway be-

tween the mind and the world of objects and actions, so the spinal cord serves a similar representative function for the brain or nerves. "This dramatic mechanics, is the marrow of the nervous system, and consequently of the body. . . . The whole system is a . . . mental theatre or drama. The spinal cord moves as though it felt; the medulla oblongata breathes and eats as if it were instinct with appetites; . . . But all is *quasi*, and depends upon a reality somewhere which is in none of the actors, and which reality, proximately, lies in a spiritual organism, or in the human mind" (p. 38).

It is no great distance from Wilkinson's notion of the mind as a "spiritual organism" to Thoreau's of a mind that is "hands and feet" or to Thoreau's soul with "organs." Employing a language of the "theatre" ("scene," "spectator," "play," "dramatic," "actors"), both men desire to revise the relation of mind to body, and both must struggle against a language whose very nature seems to resist such revision: "body," "flesh," "appetite," "sensual" and a host of other words descriptive of the body carry pejorative connotations that seem intrinsic and ineluctable. Thoreau's sense of being beside himself, of experiencing a doubleness of personal identity, seems to have its source in this notion of an inner drama or "system of representations" through which a mind communicates with its other self—the body.[18]

Thoreau is hardly ready to celebrate, with Walt Whitman, a self that is "Disorderly, fleshy sensual . . . eating drinking and breeding."[19] (His horror of the body frequently surpasses Poe's: "Under the nails and between the joints of the fingers of the idle, flourish crops of mildew, algae, and fungi, and other vegetable sloths, though they be invisible,— the lichens where life still exists, the fungi where decomposition has begun to take place."[20]) But Thoreau repeatedly risks experimenting with a re-vision of the body's value. "The forcible writer," he notes in the *Journal*, "stands bodily behind his words with his experience. He does not make books out of books, but he has been *there* in person."[21] Less obviously, but I think more consequentially than Whitman's, Thoreau's revaluation of the body is part of a political project, one that goes far beyond George Ripley's facile attempt to "combine intellectual and manual labor." Thoreau attempts, instead, to dissolve these categories. But because Thoreau's politics are finally an ecological politics, focusing on the human situation in nature rather than the human situation in the polis, his revision of his activity as a writer also compels him to revise the meaning of work in general (and of what Arendt calls "work" and "labor" in particular). Work must be reformed in order to make it express, rather than master, nature. In turn, this project requires him to detach labor from property, since it is through humanity's presumption to own the land that human beings first assert their dominion over the natural order. As I hope I have shown, at each point or turn in this revaluation, Thoreau must confront and re-evaluate the meaning of his body. Perhaps because he has to struggle so hard against, or rather, by means of, a tradition that spurns the body as the province of the devil; or perhaps because he was less at ease with his sexuality than Whitman, Thoreau's achievement in this regard strikes me as more hardwon, and therefore more rich with implications, than Whitman's.

Creation

The third enactment of what I have called *Walden*'s conflict with itself is the least visible and the most pervasive because it takes place in the third of Thoreau's productive activities at Walden Pond, the one he has so cunningly obscured: his writing of *Walden*. Once again, the book's opening sentence forewarns us of complexities, establishing a distinction between having written (at Walden) and speaking now to us. The voice that speaks "When I wrote" is a voice speaking to us in an eternal present it establishes and shares with its auditors; the utterance of "When I wrote" is coeval with the act of reading, which we might express by saying "As I read." If it were strictly delimited (in a preface, for example), the presence of a speaking voice which exists with us in the moment of reading a work that was written some time ago (at Walden Pond) would emphasize the written, created, durable nature of "the bulk of the pages that follow." But in *Walden* the presence of voice is not delimited, not enclosed in a preface, or marked with space breaks or italics. The voice flows so smoothly into the sentences that follow that we cannot discern where it leaves off and where "the bulk of the following pages" begins. The presence of the voice thus destabilizes *Walden* as a written text and requires us to be uncertain, at any given moment, whether we are reading or listening, whether we are leafing through pages written at Walden Pond or sharing the moment in which Thoreau orally presents those pages to us.

If the first sentence at once draws and then blurs a distinction between written text and spoken word, the rest of *Walden* is committed to keeping this instability in play. Scholarship informs us that much of "Economy" was first delivered as a lecture to the Concord Lyceum, but it has not yet explained why Thoreau takes such pains to preserve the air of speech in the artifice of the book he makes. When he says (writes), "I will therefore ask those of my readers who feel no particular interest in me to pardon me if I undertake to answer some of those questions [about his life at Walden Pond] in this book" (p. 3), he again points in two directions at once. By telling us that we are about to get to the book that answers the questions, the sentence effectively suggests that we are not yet *in* the book—even though we are holding the book *Walden* in our hands and reading it. The very next sentence repeats this gesture of pointing to the book, as a written entity, and then telling us that we are listening to a voice, not reading words. "In most books, the *I*, or first person, is omitted; in this book it will be retained; that, in respect to egotism, is the main difference. We commonly do not remember that it is, after all, always the first person that is speaking." The *I* "will be" not "is" retained; it is the first person that "is speaking," not that "has written." Thus, Thoreau places his book among other books, and then hints that it hasn't quite started yet: it remains unwritten.

The dialogue, as it were, between the spoken and the written becomes an explicit subject of *Walden* in the chapter called "Reading." Not surprisingly, given the topic of the chapter, reading and writing are here given precedence over listening and speaking. And these alignments are shown to be entangled with others.

> Books must be read as deliberately and reservedly as they were written. It is not enough even to be able to speak the language of that nation by which they are written, for there is a memorable interval between the spoken and the written language, the language heard and the language read. The one is commonly transitory, a sound, a tongue, a dialect merely, almost brutish, and we learn it unconsciously, like the brutes, of our mothers. The other is the maturity and experience of that; if that is our mother tongue, this is our father tongue, a reserved and select expression, too significant to be heard by the ear, which we must be born again in order to speak. (p. 101)

Readers, writers, and fathers take sides against listeners, speakers, and mothers. Writing is "reserved and select," not "brutish"; it is durable and lasting, not "transitory." Writing thus takes its place in the service of civilization, of man's efforts to make or build a world over and against the earth. That effort is explicitly a masculine, or patriarchal, effort, the work of fathers and sons. Its realm, by implication, is also that of mental not manual labor, and of intellectuals not manual laborers.

The creation of *Walden* as a written work is therefore fundamentally at odds with the existence of *Walden* as a spoken work. The writer as masculine artificer works directly against the feminine speaker. But—consistent with the book's ongoing dialectic—speech gets "her" say in the very next chapter, "Sounds":

But while we are confined to books, though the most select and classic, and read only particular written languages, which are themselves but dialects and provincial, we are in danger of forgetting the language which all things and events speak without metaphor, which alone is copious and standard. . . . What is a course of history, or philosophy, or poetry, no matter how well selected, or the best society, or the most admirable routine of life, compared with the discipline of looking always at what is to be seen? (p. 111)

It is better to see and hear than to read. To be a "seer," for Thoreau, is to be one who lives in and through the senses, whose purified senses permit him to "*see* God" (*A Week*, p. 382). It is to hear in the faint hum of a mosquito "an Iliad and an Odyssey in the air, singing its own wrath and wanderings" (p. 89). To live through the senses is to be able to hear the language which speaks "without metaphor" because it is not representative language—words standing for things—but self-expressive language. Thus, in a classic rehearsal of nostalgia for presence, Thoreau tries to evade the ineluctably representative nature of language and literature by presenting his creation as speech, not text, by eliding the speech action of *Walden* with the "language which all things and events speak."

But if in "Reading" and "Sounds" the notion of literary creation as listening and speaking is given the last word over the more traditional notion of literary creation as the making of a durable and more perfect world, the opposite is true in the ordering of *Walden*'s most extensive and familiar tropes of creativity: the thawing sandbank and the artist of Kouroo. The extraordinary meditation Thoreau offers on natural labor and creativity at the sandbank is, to a large degree, displaced by, and subordinated to, the book's concluding image of the divine male artificer.

Thoreau's description of "the forms which thawing sand and clay assume in flowing down the sides of a deep cut on the railroad" is more than a celebration of natural creativity. It is an attempt to uncover the ontology of what I have been calling "naturalized labor." The passage makes clear that more is at stake in Thoreau's reform of labor than our assumptions about the relation of civilization to nature. What his ontology calls into question, ultimately, is a way of ordering the world in terms of an exterior that can be seen and manipulated and an inside that can be inferred but that remains unreachable and unknowable.

Thoreau's thawing sandbank is first and foremost an account—one of the very few accounts in literature—of interiority per se. It gives us access to the inside of things, to the inside of the earth, which happens at this spot to be turning itself inside out. In order to grasp fully the ambition and achievement of the passage, we must understand the degree to which we have been (and the further degree to which Thoreau's contemporaries were) conditioned to regard human work as the imposition of order upon the flux of materiality. Whether the work be the labor of the woman spinning wool, or of the farmer drawing his plow across the earth, or of the blacksmith beating iron into implements, all human productive processes tend to be seen as a bestowal or construction of form on the relative formlessness of nature. In giving form, we are inclined to lay great emphasis on the surface of things—on what can be seen, touched, changed. We have no access, either mental or physical, to the interior of things. If we split open a stone, all we can see are new surfaces of stone; if we dig into the earth, all we can see are the shafts and galleries we create; if we weave a blanket, as Elaine Scarry has said, we are making a second skin, a supplementary surface to cover the surface of the body. A great deal of mental productivity, too, is structured by these metaphors: when we think we either explore, delve, and investigate, or associate, knit, draw, and the like. The *inside* is something which we know to be there (within the sphere of stone we heft in our hand) but which we cannot experience immediately.

Nevertheless, we can assume that the interiority of the human body has been a constantly lived and experienced fact. We infer the inside of the stone, but we know the inside of our body. Recall that in his meditations on and celebrations of the body, Thoreau himself almost never dwells on the beauty of limbs, skin, hair, eyes. He writes about the senses and he writes about organs: "taste the world and digest it" is his advice to the poet.[22] Though the effort culminates in the sandbank chapter, all of *Walden* (or at least one side of its dialogue with itself) can be seen as repeated attempts to get at the interior—the inside—of the human frame. (Isn't this why he delights in turning his house inside out? And wasn't it Wilkinson's success in this attempt that Thoreau so much admired?)

Thoreau's description of the thawing sandbank derives its power from the fact that Thoreau is verging on an account of the inside of the earth; he is coming as close as one can, as close as anyone had come, to describing the interior. He is able to come close precisely because he is not splitting open a stone, but, rather, witnessing a site at which the earth turns itself inside out, expresses outwardly what it "so labors with . . . inwardly." "No wonder that the earth expresses itself outwardly in leaves," Thoreau writes, "it so labors with the idea inwardly" (p. 306). Thoreau's fanciful etymology thus places labor at the very core of nature's self-expression rather than as a human activity that sets itself up over and against nature: "(λειβω, *labor, lapsus,* to flow or slip down-ward, a lapsing: λοβος, *globus,* lobe, globe; also lap, flap, and many other words,) . . ." (p. 306). The earth is continually in labor, turning herself inside out. "True, it is somewhat excrementitious in its character, and there is no end to the heaps of liver lights and bowels, as if the globe were turned wrong side outward; but this suggests at least that Nature has some bowels, and there again is the mother of humanity." Birthing and defecating are in effect the same thing: the body turns itself inside out, the inside deposits on the surface what will eventually rot and com-post and become the interior out of which more will be born. "I feel as if I were nearer to the vitals of the globe, for this sandy overflow is something such a foliaceous mass as the vitals of the animal body." By witnessing this process in which the earth's body expresses outwardly "what it so labors with . . . inwardly," Thoreau is completing the prom-ise he made in "Higher Laws" to "descend into the body," except that no descent is necessary. The interior exfoliates, the interior labors to make itself visible and palpable. Rather than engage in an Aylmeresque project of cutting into the surface of things, or the body, Thoreau de-lights in the sandbank as a place where "the mother of humanity" re-veals "the secret of creative force." The sandbank is a place where we can witness not just an alternative mode of making but an alternative notion of value. The value of the sandbank is not to be described by as-signing to it a metaphysical characteristic plucked from a transcendental order, but by recognizing the self-expressive value of immanence. This value is immediately linked to labor, and not just to the labor of a woman, or the earth, giving birth, but to the labor of the body more generally, to Therien's labor and Thoreau's. In other words, this pas-sage makes explicit what is implied in the phrase "labor theory of value." Value occurs, or appears, when labor occurs, that is, when something turns itself "wrong side outward."

Again, Edward Everett's view of matter as "an unorganized, inani-mate, cold, dull, and barren thing" is instructive. Recall that in order to advance the superiority of mental labor, and specifically of inventions that will master nature, Everett felt obliged to disparage the body as "clay or dust"; "these substances seem to us to make the nearest ap-proach to the total privation of all the properties of the intellect" (*A Lec-ture on the Working Men's Party,* p. 15). By contrast, in the *Journal* pas-sage, which he revised for this section of *Walden,* Thoreau celebrates both the "thawing clay" of the human body and the "foecal and sterco-ral" "fertility" of the earth:

The earth I tread on is not a dead, inert mass. It is a body, has a spirit, is

organic, and is fluid to the influence of spirit, and to whatever particle of
that spirit is in me. She is not dead, but sleepeth. It is more cheering than
the fertility and luxuriance of vineyards, this fundamental fertility near to
the principle of growth. To be sure, it is somewhat foecal and stercoral.
So the poet's creative moment is when the frost is coming out in the
spring, . . .[23]

Although here, too, Thoreau's rhetoric is divided against itself when he
invokes transcendental values to account for immanent ones—the earth
has "spirit" and is "fluid to the influence of spirit"—the accent, I think,
must be placed on his effort to dispense with such an invocation. When
he writes that the earth "is a body, has a spirit, is organic," he is surely
equating these and collapsing the hierarchy that distinguishes and ranks
them. When he contrasts the "fertility and luxuriance of vineyards" with
a "fundamental fertility near to the principle of growth" he is surely trying to locate value within matter and the "poet's creative moment"
within his body.

But Thoreau's meditation on the sand foliage cannot be his only or
last word on the subject of creativity: if it were, he could not have written *Walden*—which, despite its manifold resistance to its own nature as
an artifact, stands before us as a crafted artifact, as a durable object in a
human, not a natural, world. Even in this passage, so extraordinarily
celebrative of creation as natural labor, an image of the traditional male
creator working on his creation from outside it makes an appearance: "I
am affected as if in a peculiar sense I stood in the laboratory of the Artist
who made the world and me,—had come to where he was still at work,
sporting on this bank, and with excess of energy strewing his fresh designs about" (p. 306). The artist of Kouroo—Thoreau's final, and for
that reason most privileged figuring of creativity—is even more supremely detached from himself, his body, and his work. He strives for
aeons to make something "perfect in all respects," and this effort en-
dows him "with perennial youth" (precisely, I would suggest, because
the motive behind that effort is a fear of old age and death). He has
been able to step out of time because he is eager to step out of his body.
And when the artist has put the "finishing stroke" to his work, it instantly transforms itself from a mere staff into an entire world. He has
undone and outdone nature. "He had made a new system in making a
staff, a world with full and fair proportions; in which, though the old
cities and dynasties had passed away, fairer and more glorious ones had
taken their places" (pp. 326–27). We are back to Aylmer's project of re-
placing nature, back to Sidney's poet who makes a "golden" world to
supplement nature's merely "brazen" one.

When Edward Everett disparages matter as "inanimate, cold, dull, and barren," and Nathaniel Greene claims that mechanical pursuits are essentially the "operation of mind upon matter," they seem to close the door upon the possibility that, since matter has its own being unto itself, its own value, the "knowledge of things" is a knowledge of valuable things. Consequently, mental work is seen as the highest form of work because the mental worker is not entangled in matter at all. Manual labor, by the same token, is accorded value only insofar as it takes an instrumental attitude toward matter, unlocking its secrets, mining it, ransacking it, exposing the interior of matter to the light of reason and the light of day so that content can be appropriated or used. I have argued that *Walden,* by contrast, begins to reopen the door on this possibility by developing a language in which matter has its own life, so to speak, and by being alert to occasions when matter turns itself inside-out, so that the interior is not pried open but reveals itself. But I have also suggested that, for Thoreau at least, the development of such a language also portends the foreclosure on another, the language of art-as-supplement. It would seem, in general, that Transcendence calls forth language as a way of bodying forth, however inadequately and even profanely, the invisible; whereas Immanence silences language because meaning is always here to announce itself to those who would listen (and the chatter of supplementary voices seems just to make hearing harder). While a writer may feel an affinity to manual labor because its knowledge of things is desirable, the knowledge of things seems to lead to a suspension of writerly work and to the absorption of the writer's expressive energy into the taciturn stolidity of workers like Therien.

I have said that the artist of Kouroo is Thoreau's last word on creativity, but perhaps it would be more accurate to say that this is *Walden*'s last word. *Walden* has been generated by Thoreau's inability to commit himself to either labor or work, expression or artifice, earth or world, body or mind; its most successful moments are those in which this dialectic is most fully dramatized. But such a dialectic is too exhausting to be sustained indefinitely. *Walden* is the last book Thoreau publishes in his lifetime. All the rest (that is, the *Journal*) is the kind of work Thoreau alludes to in *A Week*—an unwritten sequel, an unbounded promise with total "freedom of prospect" because it has no obligations to an audience. Its writing, always verging on speech to himself, is a private, naturalized labor that never contributes to the making of a world. In January, 1852, he meditates on the advantages of the journal form over the essay. "I do not know but thoughts written down thus in a journal might be printed in the same form with greater advantage than if the related ones were brought together into separate essays. They are now allied to life, and are seen by the reader not to be far-fetched. It is more simple, less artful." In the next entry he continues to explore the possibility—in these years a real one—of never finishing *Walden*, of leaving the *Journal* intact instead of ransacking it for material. "Perhaps I can never find so good a setting for my thoughts as I shall thus have taken them out of . . . Where else will you ever find the true cement for your thoughts? How will you ever rivet them together without leaving the marks of the file?"[24] The rivets and the file take us back seven years to the essay on Carlyle and Thoreau's contrast between the blacksmith's "thrashing of the anvil" and the haymaker's "true sunny perspiration." Only now the choice is not so much between blacksmithing and farming, or (to use Arendt's terms) "work" and "labor," as between publication and silence.

Thoreau's final product, the *Journal*, owes its existence not to an artificer like the artist of Kouroo, but to a process of exfoliation and growth like that embodied in the thawing sandbank. Until it was published decades after Thoreau's death, the *Journal* very nearly succeeded in achieving that impossible ontological status of existing only as a promise—that is, of existing and not existing at the same time. Moreover, the naturalized labor of its composition is appropriate to its subject, which is, increasingly and eventually almost exclusively, nature. "The poet says the proper study of mankind is man. I say, study to forget all that; take wider views of the universe. That is the egotism of the race. . . . I do not value any view of the universe into which man and the institutions of man enter very largely and absorb much of the attention."[25] The man who writes about nature does not labor to build a durable house, nor even to cultivate the earth and make it say one thing rather than another. He confines himself increasingly to "facts" and "observations," which he leaves alone rather than attempting to transform them into literature. "A fact truly and absolutely stated is taken out of the region of common sense and acquires a mythologic or universal significance. . . . Express it without expressing yourself." And eventually even this minimalistic writing can appear redundant and superfluous, since nature has ways of keeping her own records, or recording her own facts. She is "self-registering." The fittest work of the naturalized poet is, finally, silence.[26]

Afterword

Most of the writers I have discussed in this book employed, tested, and found inadequate the nineteenth-century's paradigmatic distinctions between manual and mental labor, body and mind, as ways of understanding their own and other persons' work. These writers sensed and explored a deep affinity between the apparently mental labor of writing and manual labor of different kinds—blacksmithing, house building, housework, mothering, field labor, growing beans, and so on. Their reasons for doing so varied, but in general their motive was erotic, in the broadest sense of that word. All turned to the bodily aspects and origins of their work as writers because they sensed that the body offered them a means of affiliating with others, or with the natural world. And yet, all these writers also resisted identifying their labor as purely or simply bodily. They saw the body as a source of pain, as both a constituent and a threat to their class, gender, or racial identity, and as a site and means of subjugation. Nor were they willing entirely to forego the privileges and obligations that devolved upon them as mental and spiritual laborers in a society that placed such labor at the top of its scale of values. Thus, in almost all cases, these writers' attraction to physical labor and the body was resisted both by their misgivings and by their loyalties to convention.

Both Hawthorne and Melville, for example, seemed to have experienced writing as an activity that isolated them socially and cramped the free play of their manifold sensuality. Both regarded physical labor—the labor of sailors, blacksmiths, artisans—as offering at least the possibility of an unrestricted, sensual self-expressiveness in work. But Melville's firsthand experience of the sailor's life and work introduced him to the fact that class politics intervenes in work; the sailor is the "bottom" on which the coach of society "rolls." The fact that the sailor is economically exploited and socially despised intrudes upon his workplace and too often spoils the corporeal satisfactions and erotic relations he might

241

enjoy there. Hawthorne found his limited experience of manual labor at Brook Farm equally discouraging, but his pessimism about physical labor as a model for artistic creativity seems to have had a more powerful source in the gender anxieties it promoted. Several of Hawthorne's fictions dramatize the insight that the value of physical labor rests finally on the value of the body and of matter. Although the theory of organic form presupposes that these do have value and offers the writer a chance to figure creativity as natural, physical, and bodily, the theory also threatens to demolish the male writer's identity as a disembodied creator of enduring artifacts—an identity to which Hawthorne remained strongly attached.

Stowe and Douglass, too, were drawn to the erotic (that is, to what Whitman called the "adhesive," to the affiliative rather than isolating) potentialities of writing figured as a kind of bodily labor. For Stowe, such a conception of authorial work allowed her both to practice writing as an extension of maternal labor and to empathize with the victimized body of the black slave. Both of these desires are expressed, for example, when she claims that her book was inspired by the death of her son Charley, a death which allowed her to see and experience for the first time what slave mothers experience almost as a matter of course. At the same time, however, Stowe personally experienced the pains and difficulties of embodied maternal labor and sought to revise, rather than reject, the Christian hierarchy that elevated mind and spirit over body and matter. Similarly, Frederick Douglass was drawn to the manual labor of slaves and to the songs that accompanied them. When in the 1845 *Narrative* he writes that he can lay his pen in the cracks of his feet, and still more when, in *My Bondage, My Freedom,* he explicitly locates his authorial origins in the "sable" body of his mother, a "field hand," he acknowledges his indebtedness to that body and that labor. It is an indebtedness through which he affiliates himself not only with his brethren still in bondage, but also with all free African Americans who are defined in the eyes of white Americans by their body, by the color of their skin. However, because this identity is to a considerable degree forced upon him, Douglass resists it, and in so doing he resists also the bodily aspects and origins of his work as a writer.

Resists but does not deny—and here I think is where the accent must lie for all of these writers. All of them participated in a process of destabilizing the conventional hierarchy of mind over matter, mental over manual labor. All of them responded to the social division of labor by sensing its erotic inadequacies and its political inequities. And many sought to broaden the reach of literature not by diffusing it through a transcendental order, but by focusing it through the prism of the human body.

Probably because the last twenty years have discouraged what little faith in progress I might once have had, I place neither intrinsic nor teleological value on this tendency. Whereas some interpreters of history might applaud it, and others (like Hannah Arendt) might see it as a mixed blessing at best, I hope only to have made it visible. Its visibility, I believe, makes possible a new perspective on both the content and form of a number of works of antebellum literature and perhaps also brings to light a more specifiable relation between writer and history, text and context, than most historicism has generated. I hope, finally, that my discussion of these writers' attempts to refigure the relation between the mental and bodily aspects of their own work has revealed the rich and complex ramifications of the paradigm out of which the meaning of work was more broadly constructed in the antebellum decades.

Those who still read and remember F. O. Matthiessen's *American Renaissance* will have realized by now that this book has been written under the sign of, but also in opposition to, that foundational text. Less explicitly than Matthiessen, but like him, I have been writing with a political agenda in mind: I turn to the American literature of the nineteenth century to recover and recreate the democratic possibilities of this country and its culture. I have focused on the subject of work because, to my mind, it is the exclusion or erasure of work from critical consciousness that enforces a separation of artist and audience, culture and community.

For Matthiessen, I would argue, the fundamental political problem confronting the critic in his role as a critic is that his work is fundamentally, ontologically different from the work performed by the common man with whom Matthiessen desired to affiliate himself. The difference Matthiessen assumes to be there is precisely the one absorbed, but also contested, by the nineteenth-century writers he and I have both discussed: it is the split between mental and manual labor. From this split emerge the contradictions in the project of *American Renaissance* Eric Cheyfitz has so astutely identified and explained. Matthiessen desires to combine the new criticism's sensitivity to the formal properties of a work of art with a historical or political consciousness which can negotiate between that work and the society which produced it and the society which consumes it. Matthiessen desires to celebrate the heroic and supranormal genius of the individual artist and, at the same time, to establish unbreakable bonds between that artist and the common working man. Matthiessen desires to affirm the values of craftsmanship and artisanry, but, at the same time, he desires to celebrate the democratic potentialities he locates in the theory of organic form. As Cheyfitz has written, the methodological tension between what Matthiessen calls "aesthetic values" and "background," a "tension . . . between historical and literary approaches . . . is still central to American studies today."[1]

The methodological approach of this book, like Matthiessen's, has sought to bring together historical "background" and formalist "aesthetics." It has tried to do so, however, not by merely yoking them, but in a way that reveals and does justice to their mutually constituting and illuminating properties. Specifically, it has attempted to do so by recovering within the term "aesthetics" not only the sensual, bodily characteristics of art but also the fact that *work* is what produces a work of art. When we take with full seriousness the obvious fact that a writer works, and when we see that the work of producing an artwork seems invariably to call into question the distinction between mind and body, mental and physical labor, the problem Matthiessen foundered on reconstitutes itself. It is still a problem, still something to look into and understand, but it is a problem that has promise because it is historical not ontological.

This is a point I want to emphasize. My attention to the activity of work as it reveals itself in a work of art, and particularly in an artwork's representation of work, has moved through the channels of the nineteenth-century's paradigmatic distinction between mind and body. But that paradigm will not endure forever; indeed, I believe it has already largely disintegrated. A study of work in the writing of late twentieth-century writers might move through a quite different paradigm. What will change more slowly, I suspect, will be the tendency not to study work at all, since the political and social investment in constructing the activities which constitute "art," "literature," and "culture" as something other than work remains very high. But in the long run, I believe, the project of continually recovering and recreating the democratic possibilities of literature, and of developing a critical vocabulary commensurate with that task, will depend upon our ability to see and think about work.

Notes

Introduction

1. Mark Twain, *The Adventures of Tom Sawyer* (Berkeley: University of California Press, 1980), p. 13.

2. The specific bibliographies of each of these topics will be found in the notes accompanying the following chapters.

3. Daniel T. Rodgers, *The Work Ethic in Industrial America, 1850–1920* (Chicago: University of Chicago Press, 1974).

4. See Jacob Riis, *How the Other Half Lives* (New York: Dover Publications, 1971); Walter A. Wyckoff, *The Workers: A Study in Reality,* 2 vols. (New York: Charles Scribner's Sons, 1898); Michael Denning, *Mechanic Accents: Dime Novels and Working-Class Culture in America* (New York: Verso, 1987), p. 4.

5. Lewis Hine, *Women at Work: 153 Photographs by Lewis Hine,* edited by Jonathan L. Doherty (New York: Dover Publications, 1981), p. 81.

6. Thus, one does not instantly agree with Charles Eliot Norton, who wrote in 1852 that "The most distinguishing characteristic of the literature of the present age is the attention which it bestows to that portion of society which is generally called 'the lower classes.'. . . From the folio report to the novel, the essay, and the poem, the claims of labor and the laborer are set forth with various power, but with a single object" ("Dwellings and Schools for the Poor," *North American Review* 74, no. 155 [April 1852]: 464.) By contrast, William Dean Howells's views seem closer to the mark: "The American public does not like to read about the life of toil. What we like to read about is the life of noblemen or millionaires; . . . if our writers were to begin telling us on any extended scale how mill hands, or miners, or farmers, or iron-puddlers really live, we should soon let them know that we do not care to meet with such vulgar and commonplace people" ("The Man of Letters as a Man of Business," in *Literature and Life: Studies* (New York: Harper and Co., 1911), p. 2. Note, however, that Norton's subject is "the *claims* of labor and the laborer," and Howells's "the *life* of toil." Neither man even considers the possibility of a literature that would take labor itself as a principal subject.

7. Frank Lentricchia, *Criticism and Social Change* (Chicago: University of Chicago Press, 1983), p. 80.

8. Ralph Waldo Emerson, *Collected Works,* vol. 2 of 4 vols. (Cambridge: Harvard University Press, 1979), p. 32.

9. In the Afterword to this book I suggest that what Eric Cheyfitz has deemed an unacknowledged tension in *American Renaissance*—a tension between Matthiessen's new-critical interest in formalism and his sociopolitical concern with the possibilities of a democratic literature and culture—might have been resolved or at least enriched if Matthiessen had looked more closely at work. If we take seriously the notion that writing is work, and that as work it is not ontologically different from all other kinds of work, then I believe we have a way to link formalist concerns with broader social and political concerns. See Eric Cheyfitz, "Matthiessen's *American Renaissance:* Circumscribing the Revolution," *American Quarterly* 41, no. 2 (June 1989): 341–61.

10. See F. O. Matthiessen, *American Renaissance* (New York: Oxford University Press, 1941); Perry Miller, *The New England Mind: From Colony to Province* (Cambridge: Harvard University Press, 1967), pp. 40–52; Henry Nash Smith, "Emerson's Problem of Vocation—A Note on 'The American Scholar,'" *The New England Quarterly* 12 (March–December 1939): 52–67; Sherman Paul, *The Shores of America* (Urbana: University of Illinois Press, 1958); William Charvat, *The Profession of Authorship in America, 1800–1870* (Columbus: Ohio State University Press, 1968); Walter Benn Michaels, "Romance and Real Estate," *Raritan* 2, no. 3 (1983): 66–87; Michael T. Gilmore, *American Romanticism and the Marketplace* (Chicago: University of Chicago Press, 1985); Mary Kelley, *Private Women, Public Stage: Literary Domesticity in Nineteenth-Century America* (New York: Oxford University Press, 1984); Kathryn Kish Sklar, *Catharine Beecher: A Study in American Domesticity* (New York: W. W. Norton Co., 1976); Gillian Brown, "Getting in the Kitchen with Dinah: Domestic Politics in *Uncle Tom's Cabin,*" *American Quarterly* 36, no. 4 (Fall 1984): 503–23.

11. See Karl Marx, *The Economic and Philosophic Manuscripts of 1844* (New York: International Publishers, 1982), and *Capital: A Critique of Political Economy, Volume I* (New York: Vintage Books, 1977); Charlotte Perkins Gilman, *Women and Economics: A Study of the Economic Relation between Men and Women as a Factor in Social Evolution* (New York: Harper and Row, 1966), and *Human Work* (New York: McClure, Phillips and Co., 1904); Sigmund Freud, *Civilization and Its Discontents* (New York: W. W. Norton and Co., 1961); Martin Heidegger, "The Origin of the Work of Art," *Poetry, Language, Thought* (New York: Harper and Row, 1971), pp. 15–88; Herbert Marcuse, *Eros and Civilization: A Philosophical Inquiry into Freud* (Boston: Beacon Press, 1955); Hannah Arendt, *The Human Condition* (Chicago: University of Chicago Press, 1958); Elaine Scarry, *The Body in Pain: The Making and Unmaking of the World* (New York: Oxford University Press, 1985).

12. Theodore Parker, "Thoughts on Labor," *The Dial* 1, no. 4 (April 1841): 497; Herman Melville, *Moby-Dick, or The Whale* (Evanston and Chicago: Northwestern University Press, 1988), p. 304; John Neal, *Address at the Maine Charitable Mechanic Association* (Portland: Charles Day and Co., 1838),

p. 77; quoted in O. B. Frothingham, *George Ripley* (Boston: Houghton Mifflin Co., 1882), p. 307; Alonzo Potter, *Political Economy, Its Objects, Uses, and Principles: Considered with Reference to the Condition of the American People* (New York: Harper and Co., 1841), p. 61; William Heighton, *An Address Delivered Before the Mechanics and Working Classes Generally of the City and County of Philadelphia* (1827), p. 4; Mrs. A. J. Graves. *Woman in America: Being an Examination into the Moral and Intellectual Condition of American Female Society* (New York: Harper and Bros., 1847), p. 29; Henry Bibb's narrative, in *Puttin' on Ole Massa: The Slave Narratives of Henry Bibb, William Wells Brown, and Solomon Northup,* compiled by Gilbert Osofsky (New York: Harper and Row, 1969), hereafter referred to as, Henry Bibb, *Narrative.*

13. Recently, however, the challenge of doing justice to the gendered aspects of labor has prompted labor historians to reconsider the complexity of labor itself as a category of human experience. See, for example, Ava Baron, "Gender and Labor History: Learning from the Past, Looking to the Future," in *Work Engendered: Toward a New History of American Labor,* edited by Ava Baron (Ithaca: Cornell University Press, 1991).

14. Ralph Waldo Emerson, *Early Lectures,* vol. 2 of 2 vols. (Cambridge: Harvard University Press, 1979), p. 124.

15. Emerson, *Collected Works,* vol. 1, p. 153.

16. Emerson's anxiety that his work might not be sufficiently masculine was brought to my attention by Joel Porte's *Representative Man: Ralph Waldo Emerson in His Times* (New York: Oxford University Press, 1979). The subject is further explored by David Leverenz, *Manhood and the American Renaissance* (Ithaca: Cornell University Press, 1989).

17. Emerson, *Collected Works,* vol. 1, p. 152.

18. Ralph Waldo Emerson, *Emerson's Works,* vol. 6 of 14 vols. (Boston: Houghton Mifflin Co., 1883), p. 16.

19. Theodor Adorno, "Culture, Criticism, and Society," in *Prisms* (Cambridge: MIT Press, 1967), pp. 19–34; Emerson, *Collected Works,* vol. 1, pp. 67, 150.

20. Ralph Waldo Emerson, *Journals and Miscellaneous Notebooks,* 16 vols., vol. 5, edited by Morton Sealts, Jr. (Cambridge: Harvard University Press, 1965), p. 206.

21. Nathaniel Hawthorne, *The Complete Works,* vol. 6 of 22 vols. (Boston: Houghton, Mifflin and Co., 1900), pp. 49–51.

22. William Ellery Channing, "Lecture on the Elevation of the Laboring Portion of the Community," in vol. 5 of *Works,* in 6 vols. (Boston: Walker, Wise, and Co., 1862), p. 176; *Catalog of the Fifth Exhibition of the Massachusetts Charitable Mechanic Association* (Boston: Dutton and Wentworth, 1847), p. 2; Nathaniel Hawthorne, *The Complete Works,* vol. 5, p. 315 and vol. 8, pp. 90, 91.

23. Richard H. Brodhead, *Hawthorne, Melville, and the Novel* (Chicago: University of Chicago Press, 1976), p. 53.

Chapter One

1. James J. Davis, *The Iron Puddler: My Life in the Rolling Mills and What Came of It* (New York: Grosset and Dunlap, 1922), unnumbered page in Preface.

2. Parker, "Thoughts on Labor," p. 497.

3. Ripley to Emerson, quoted in O. B. Frothingham, *George Ripley* (Boston: Houghton Mifflin Co., 1882), p. 307.

4. Emerson, *Collected Works*, vol. 1, p. 150. All further page references will be made in the text.

5. Theodore Weld, ed., *First Annual Report of the Society for the Promotion of Manual Labor in Literary Institutions* (New York: S. W. Benedict and Co., 1833), p. 120; L. A. Hine, *A Plea for Harmonic Education* (Cincinnati, 1856), p. 180. See also John C. Warren, *Physical Education and the Preservation of Health* (Boston: William D. Ticknor and Co., 1845).

6. Horace Greeley, "The Relations of Learning to Labor: A Commencement Address before the Literary Societies of Hamilton College, July 23rd, 1844," included in *Hints toward Reform* (New York: Harper and Co., 1850), p. 120.

7. Parker, "Thoughts on Labor," p. 515.

8. Norton, "Dwellings and Schools for the Poor," p. 464.

9. Figures are from Rodgers Taylor, *The Transportation Revolution, 1815–1860*, cited in Leo Marx, *The Machine in the Garden: Technology and the Pastoral Ideal in America* (New York: Oxford University Press, 1964), p. 215.

10. The literature on the history of labor and the laboring class in these decades is vast. I have relied primarily on: John Commons and Associates, *History of Labor in the United States* (New York: Augustus M. Kelley, 1966); Norman Ware, *The Industrial Worker, 1840–1860* (Chicago: Quadrangle Books, 1964); Walter Hugins, *Jacksonian Democracy and the Working Class: A Study of the New York Workingmen's Movement, 1829–1837* (Stanford: Stanford University Press, 1960); Alan Dawley, *Class and Community: The Industrial Revolution in Lynn, Massachusetts* (Cambridge: Harvard University Press, 1976); Joseph Dorfman, *The Economic Mind in American Civilization, 1606–1865* (New York: Viking Press, 1946); Bruce Laurie, *Working People of Philadelphia* (Philadelphia: Temple University Press, 1980), and *Artisans into Workers: Labor in Nineteenth-Century America* (New York: Hill and Wang, 1989); Paul G. Faler, *Mechanics and Manufacturers in the Early Industrial Revolution: Lynn, Massachusetts, 1786–1860* (Albany: State University of New York Press, 1981); Thomas Dublin, *Women at Work: The Transformation of Work and Community in Lowell, Massachusetts, 1826–1860* (New York: Columbia University Press, 1979); Edward Pessen, *Most Uncommon Jacksonians: The Radical Leaders of the Early Labor Movement* (Albany: State University of New York Press, 1967); Nancy F. Cott, *The Bonds of Womanhood: "Woman's Sphere" in New England, 1790–1835* (New Haven: Yale University Press, 1977); Paul E. Johnson, *A Shopkeeper's Millennium: Society and Revivals in Rochester, New York, 1815–1837* (New York: Hill and Wang, 1984); and Sean

Wilentz, *Chants Democratic: New York City and the Rise of the American Working Class, 1788–1850* (New York: Oxford University Press, 1984). On professionalism: Daniel C. Calhoun, *Professional Lives in America: Structure and Aspiration, 1750–1850* (Cambridge: Harvard University Press, 1965); Donald M. Scott, *From Office to Profession: The New England Ministry, 1750–1850* (Philadelphia: University of Pennsylvania Press, 1978); Daniel T. Rodgers, *The Work Ethic in Industrial America, 1850–1920* (Chicago: University of Chicago Press, 1974).

11. Statistics cited in Michael T. Gilmore, *American Romanticism and the Marketplace,* p. 4.

12. Quoted in Perry Miller, *The New England Mind: From Colony to Province* (Cambridge: Harvard University Press, 1967), p. 41.

13. Quoted in Rodgers, *The Work Ethic,* p. 8.

14. Ibid., pp. 1–29.

15. Thomas Carlyle, *Past and Present* (London: J. M. Dent), p. 189. All further references will be made in the text.

16. Adam Smith, *An Inquiry into the Nature and Causes of the Wealth of Nations,* vol. 1 of 2 vols. (Oxford: Clarendon Press, 1976), p. 51.All further references will be made in the text.

17. Quoted in Ronald L. Meek, *Studies in the Labor Theory of Value* (New York: Monthly Review Press, 1956), p. 124.

18. J. N. Cardozo, *Notes on Political Economy* (Charleston: 1826), p. 8. A useful account of antebellum political economy can be found in Michael J. L. O'Connor, *Origins of Academic Economics in the United States* (New York: Columbia University Press, 1944). O'Connor notes that "especially in the period following 1825, the labor literature was significant enough to awaken marked academic concern" (p. 73).

19. Quoted in Meek, *Studies in the Labor Theory of Value,* p. 40.

20. Quoted in Commons, *History of Labor in the United States,* p. 307.

21. Ibid., p. 309. For a brief but excellent account of the ideological contest over the labor theory of value, see Paul G. Faler, *Mechanics and Manufacturers,* pp. 175–79.

22. Jared Sparks, *The North American Review* 19, no. 45 (October 1824): 328.

23. This is not to say that classes were actually formed by this paradigm or that its terms corresponded exactly to social realities. Indeed, antebellum writers like Everett and Parker were apt to point out that the dichotomy of mental and manual labor was false to almost all kinds of work: the surgeon works with both brain and hand, so does the painter, and so, even, does the common day-laborer. But notwithstanding their awareness of its inaccuracy, these writers made use of the dichotomy to structure their analyses of work. The paradigm also functioned ideologically as the broadest and most reliable indicator of class identity. My findings here help specify the "broad ideological context" in which, as Sean Wilentz argues, class consciousness is mutually and dialectically constituted (*Chants Democratic,* p. 14). Though arrived at by a different path, my findings

confirm Stuart M. Blumin's uncovering of "the importance of the manual-non-manual dichotomy in shaping social perceptions and values" (p. 131). See *The Emergence of the Middle Class: Social Experience in the American City, 1760–1900* (Cambridge: Cambridge University Press, 1989), especially chapter 4: "Republican Prejudice: Work, Well-being, and Social Definition."

24. Edward Everett, *A Lecture on the Working Men's Party* (Boston: Gray and Bowen, 1831), p. 3. All further references will be made in the text.

25. William Ellery Channing, "Lecture on the Elevation of the Laboring Portion of the Community," p. 176.

26. Theodore Sedgwick, *Public and Private Economy* (New York: Harper and Bros., 1836), p. 272.

27. Emerson, *Early Lectures*, vol. 2, p. 233.

28. William Heighton, *An Address to the Members of Trade Societies, and to the Working Classes Generally* (Philadelphia, 1827), p. 4. All further page references will be made in the text.

29. William Heighton, *The Principles of Aristocratic Legislation, Developed in an Address Delivered to the Working People of the District of Southwark, and Townships of Moyamensing and Passyunk* (Philadelphia: J. Coates, 1828), pp. 9–10. All further page references will be made in the text.

30. Heighton, *An Address . . .*, p. 8.

31. Seth Luther, *An Address to the Working-Men of New-England on the State of Education and on the Condition of the Producing Classes in Europe and America* (Boston: 1832), pp. 9–10. All further page references will be made in the text.

32. This contradiction does not pass unregistered. One of Heighton's addresses bears for its epigraph the following passage from Ecclesiastes: "Then said I, Wisdom is better than Strength; Nevertheless, the poor man's wisdom is despised, and his words are not heard." The first half of this sentence conforms nicely to the central argument of the address—namely, that important as the "strength" of their manual labor might be, workers must also acquire "wisdom." But the second half of the epigraph moves in the opposite direction: it suggests not that the manual laborer should acquire a wisdom now monopolized by the rich, but that the rich (that is, the nonmanual laborers of the world) should respect, not "despise," the wisdom the manual laborer *already* possesses. This notion, however, is never taken up and elaborated in the "Address." William Heighton, *An Address Delivered before the Mechanics and Working Classes Generally, of the City and County of Philadelphia, at the Universalist Church, in Callowhill Street, on Wednesday Evening, November 21, 1827.*

33. A recent account of the manual laborer's bodily knowledge, or knowledge of "things," can be found in Shoshana Zuboff's *In the Age of the Smart Machine: The Future of Work and Power* (New York: Basic Books, 1988). Zuboff argues that the body plays a dual role in the work process: it is "the scene and source of effort" and "a source of skill."

34. Neal, *Address at the Maine Charitable Mechanic Association*, p. 77.

35. Mark Erlich, *With Our Hands* (Philadelphia: Temple University Press, 1986), p. xii.

36. Alfred Sohn-Rethel, *Intellectual and Manual Labor: A Critique of Epistemology* (London: Methuen and Co., 1978), p. 38. All further page references will be made in the text.

37. Quoted in Charles Alpheus Bennett, *History of Manual and Industrial Education up to 1870* (Peoria, IL: Manual Arts Press, 1926), pp. 68–69, 80. These difficulties point to the problem Theodor Adorno has expressed as "the original sin" of culture—namely, that it "originates in the radical separation of mental and physical work" and thereby conceals the material origins of its own being. Even cultural criticism, Adorno warns, insofar as it is a project in self-consciousness and mentality, is likely to reproduce this delusion. See Adorno, *Prisms*, p. 26.

38. Davis, *The Iron Puddler,* p. 30.

39. Calvin Colton, *The Rights of Labor* (New York: A. S. Barnes, 1846), p. 4.

40. Christopher Clark, ed., *The Diary of an Apprentice Cabinetmaker: Edward Jenner Carpenter's "Journal"* (Worcester, MA: American Antiquarian Society, 1988), pp. 340–41.

41. Surprisingly, for all their interest in the working class and in the social transformations effected by industrialism, neither George Lippard nor George Foster attempts to represent or analyze manual labor. Indeed, their texts can be taken as classic instances of the ways attention is diverted from work at the moment work presses toward visibility. In *New York by Gas-Light,* for example, Foster chaperons his readers to the "Bowling and Billiard Saloons," "The Ice-Creameries," "The Dance House," the "Theatres and Public Amusements," of New York, but not to workshops, factories, or other places of work. Even when he is focusing on a form of work, as when he writes about prostitution, he does not write about the activity *as* work but as something else (usually vice). See George C. Foster, *New York by Gas-Light and Other Urban Sketches,* edited by Stuart M. Blumin (Berkeley: University of California Press, 1990).

42. A. J. H. Duganne, *The Gospel of Manual Labor* (Boston: William Filmer, 1849), p. 7. All further page references will be made in the text.

43. Elaine Scarry has suggested that the novel (or at least the British and continental novel) has a "natural affinity" with work and is by nature especially suited to the representation of physical labor. See "Work and the Body in Hardy and Other Nineteenth-Century Novelists," *Representations* 3 (Summer 1983): 90–123. Although on this point and several others our views are substantially different—Scarry is interested in labor mainly as a self-objectifying activity while I am trying to get at it as a subjective condition or experience—in general I am deeply indebted to her recovery of work as a subject of critical inquiry. More particularly, my own linkage of the body and work was made possible largely by my encounter both with this article and with her *The Body in Pain* (New York: Oxford University Press, 1985). Other treatments of work which had a formative influence on my thinking include: Hannah Arendt, *The Human Condition*

(Chicago: University of Chicago Press, 1958); Harry Braverman, *Labor and Monopoly Capital* (New York: Monthly Review Press, 1974); Charlotte Perkins Gilman, *Human Work* (New York: McClure, Phillips and Co., 1904); Karl Marx, *Capital* (New York: Vintage Books, 1977), and *Economic and Philosophical Manuscripts* (New York: International Publishers, 1964).

44. Herman Melville, *Moby-Dick, or The Whale* (Evanston, IL: Northwestern University Press, 1988), pp. 303–4.

45. [Anonymous], "Poetry for the People," *The Democratic Review* (September 1843): 267.

46. Emerson's famous celebration of a democratized culture is found, of course, in "The American Scholar," in vol. 1 of *Collected Works,* p. 67. See also, for example, [Anonymous], "On the Consideration Due to the Mechanical Arts," *The New England Magazine* (July 1831): 1–10.

47. Henry David Thoreau, *Walden* (Princeton: Princeton University Press, 1971), pp. 146–47. All further page references will be made in the text.

Chapter Two

1. Ralph Waldo Emerson, "The Transcendentalist," in *Collected Works,* vol. 1, p. 216.

2. Joseph Harrison, Jr., *The Ironworker and King Solomon* (Philadelphia: J. B. Lippincott and Co., 1868), pp. 39–43.

3. Michael Denning, *Mechanic Accents: Dime Novels and Working-Class Culture in America* (New York: Verso, 1987).

4. Edward Foucaud, *The Book of Illustrious Mechanics* (New York: Appleton and Co., 1847), pp. 10–11. See also Timothy Claxton, *Memoirs of a Mechanic* (Boston: George W. Light, 1839). On the cultural function of mechanics' libraries as instruments of social control, see Denning, *Mechanic Accents,* p. 48. See also Sidney Ditzion, "Mechanics' and Mercantile Libraries," *Library Quarterly* 10, no. 2 (April 1840): 192–219.

5. Paul Faler provides a brief account and points to the need for a fuller historical account of the term "mechanic" in *Mechanics and Manufacturers,* pp. 179–82.

6. Timothy Walker, "Defense of Mechanical Philosophy," *The North American Review* 33, no. 72 (July 1831): 122–27. All further page references will be made in the text.

7. F. D. Huntington, *Hands: Brain: Heart: An Address Delivered before the Mass. Charitable Mechanic Association on the Occasion of their Eighth Exhibition, Sept. 24, 1856* (Boston: Rand and Avery, 1856), p. 5. For a brief and helpful history of the Massachusetts Charitable Mechanic Association, see Gary J. Kornbluth, "From Artisans to Businessmen: Master Mechanics in New England" (Ph.D. diss., Princeton University, 1983).

8. *Catalog of the First Exhibition and Fair of the Massachusetts Charitable Mechanic Association* (Boston: Dutton and Wentworth), p. 7. All further page references will be given in the text.

9. Edward Everett, *An Address Delivered before the Massachusetts Charitable Mechanic Association, 20th September, 1837, on the Occasion of their First Exhibition and Fair* (Boston: Dutton and Wentworth, 1837), p. 6. All further page references will be given in the text.

10. *Catalog of the Fifth Exhibition of the Massachusetts Charitable Mechanic Association* (Boston: Dutton and Wentworth, 1847). All page references will be given in the text.

11. Adorno, *Prisms*, p. 26.

12. *Catalog of the Eighth Exhibition and Fair of the Massachusetts Charitable Mechanic Association*, unnumbered page. All further page references will be given in the text.

Chapter Three

1. Quoted in Barbara Novak, *American Painting of the Nineteenth Century: Realism, Idealism, and the American Experience* (New York: Harper and Row, 1979), p. 151.

2. Quoted in T. J. Clark, *Image of the People: Courbet and the 1848 Revolution* (Princeton: Princeton University Press, 1982), p. 80.

3. Ibid., p. 80.

4. The dualism of Wellingborough/Redburn has been discussed by a number of critics. See, for example, Terence Lish, "Melville's *Redburn*," *English Language Notes* 5 (December 1967): 113–20. A useful overview of early criticism of *Redburn* is provided by James Schroeter, "*Redburn* and the Failure of Mythic Criticism," *American Literature* 39, no. 3 (November 1967): 279–97. My own reading of the novel developed out of a seminar taught by Sacvan Bercovitch at Harvard in the fall of 1986.

5. Nathaniel Hawthorne, *The Complete Works*, vol. 7, p. 51.

6. Herman Melville, *Redburn: His First Voyage*, edited by Harrison Hayford, Herschel Parker, and G. Thomas Tanselle (Evanston, IL: Northwestern University Press, 1969), p. 11. All further page references will be made in the text.

7. Herman Melville, *White-Jacket, or The World in a Man-of-War*, edited by Harrison Hayford, Herschel Parker, and G. Thomas Tanselle (Evanston, IL: Northwestern University Press, 1970), p. 375.

8. See Channing, "Lecture on the Elevation of the Laboring Portion of the Community," in vol. 5 of *Works*, p. 154. Melville's account of conventional social attitudes toward sailors (here and in chapter 29) is strikingly similar to George Little's in his *Life on the Ocean, or Twenty Years at Sea* (Boston: Waite, Pierce, and Co., 1844), p. 369: "Not many years have elapsed since sailors were considered a class of isolated beings, scarcely worthy to be ranked among the lowest and most degraded of human kind;—when it might truly have been said, that 'no man cared' either for their souls or their bodies; and even up to this hour, there are many in our community who look upon poor Jack as a kind of wild animal, dangerous to society, and who ought not to be suffered to roam at large."

9. Karl Marx, *Writings of the Young Marx on Philosophy and Society,* edited by Lloyd D. Easton and Kurt H. Guddat (New York: Anchor Books, 1967), p. 292.

10. Herman Melville, *The Letters of Herman Melville,* edited by Merrell R. Davis and William H. Gilman (New Haven: Yale University Press, 1960), pp. 90–91.

11. Melville, *Letters,* pp. 95–96.

12. Hawthorne, *The Complete Works,* vol. 8, pp. 72–73.

13. Quoted in *The Utopian Vision of Charles Fourier: Selected Texts on Work, Love, and Passionate Attraction,* translated and edited by Jonathan Beecher and Richard Bienvenue (Boston: Beacon Press, 1971), p. 41.

14. Timothy Shay Arthur, *Ten Nights in a Bar-Room* (Boston: L. P. Crown and Co., 1854), p. 42.

15. The notable exception to this rule was Orestes Brownson, who saw and argued clearly that the middle class was the real oppressor of the working class and that improvement in working-class conditions would have to be achieved through political struggle rather than cultural "elevation." See "The Laboring Classes," *The Boston Quarterly Review* (July 1840): 358–95.

16. See Joel Porte, *Representative Man: Ralph Waldo Emerson in His Times* (New York: Oxford University Press, 1979); and Ben Barker-Benfield, "The Spermatic Economy: A Nineteenth-Century View of Sexuality," in *The American Family in Social-Historical Perspective,* edited by Michael Gordon (New York: St. Martin's Press, 1973).

17. Emerson, *Collected Works,* vol. 6, p. 74.

18. Ibid., vol. 1, p. 160.

19. Ibid., p. 153.

20. Ibid., p. 150.

21. Emerson, *Early Lectures,* vol. 2, p. 124.

22. Emerson, *Collected Works,* vol. 1; p. 152.

23. Ibid., p. 173.

24. Ibid., p. 207.

25. Ibid., vol. 2, p. 82.

26. Herman Melville, "Bartleby the Scrivener: A Tale of Wall Street," in *The Piazza Tales and Other Prose Pieces, 1839–1860,* edited by Harrison Hayford, Alma A. MacDougall, and G. Thomas Tanselle (Evanston, IL: Northwestern University Press, 1987), p. 21. All further references will be made in the text.

27. Parker, "Thoughts on Labor," pp. 502–3.

28. See, for example, Leo Marx, "Melville's Parable of the Walls," *Sewanee Review* 61 (1953): 602–27; Michael T. Gilmore, *American Romanticism and the Marketplace,* pp. 132–45.

29. Melville, *White-Jacket,* p. 375.

30. See also Robert K. Martin, *Hero, Captain, and Stranger: Male Friendship, Social Critique, and Literary Form in the Sea Novels of Herman Melville* (Chapel Hill: University of North Carolina Press, 1986). Martin focuses on the

"political implications of sexuality" but not on work as the matrix within and through which those implications are enacted.

31. In his discussion of Melville's attitudes toward sexuality, Martin argues (persuasively, I think) that Melville drew a sharp distinction between "buggery, or sodomy, and homosexuality, opposing the former and approving the latter, which meant, in effect, mutual masturbation. . . . Melville knew that his feelings had a sexual basis, but he wanted that sexuality expressed in a way that for him conveyed mutuality and sharing rather than power and possession" (p. 63).

32. Melville, *Moby-Dick*, p. 416.

Chapter Four

1. Thomas Starr King, "The Earth and the Mechanic Arts," in *Substance and Show, and Other Lectures*, edited by Edwin P. Whipple (Boston: James R. Osgood and Co., 1877), p. 278.

2. Henry David Thoreau, *A Week on the Concord and Merrimack Rivers* (Princeton: Princeton University Press, 1980), p. 380. All further page references will be made in the text.

3. Thoreau's concern with work begins early and figures in numerous essays, lectures, and reviews, including: "The Commercial Spirit of Modern Times" (1837), "Paradise (To Be) Regained" (1843), "Thomas Carlyle and His Works" (1845), and "Getting a Living" (1854), not to mention *A Week* and *Walden*. Thoreau delivered various versions of the lecture, "Getting a Living" throughout the 1850s; the work was published posthumously in 1863 as "Life without Principle."

4. Henry David Thoreau, "Carlyle and His Works," in *Early Essays and Miscellanies*, edited by Joseph J. Moldenhauer and Edwin Moser (Princeton: Princeton University Press, 1975), p. 224. All further page references will be given in the text.

5. I am indebted to Sherman Paul's account of Thoreau's problem of vocation (*The Shores of America*, pp. 16–25); but whereas Paul suggests that Thoreau managed to resolve the problem as he wrote *A Week*, I argue that the problem intensified as it led Thoreau into questions about the nature and meaning of work in general. I am indebted also to J. Lyndon Shanley's *The Making of "Walden"* (Chicago: University of Chicago Press, 1957), and Linck C. Johnson's *Thoreau's Complex Weave: The Writing of "A Week on the Concord and Merrimack Rivers" with the Text of the First Draft* (Charlottesville: University Press of Virginia, 1986), and to Robert Sattelmeyer's most useful *Thoreau's Reading: A Study in Intellectual History with Bibliographical Catalogue* (Princeton: Princeton University Press, 1988).

6. *United States Magazine and Democratic Review* (September 1843): 269, 268. Further page references to this article will be given in the text.

7. Hannah Arendt, *The Human Condition* (Chicago: University of Chicago Press, 1958).

8. Ibid., pp. 96–101.

9. Richard Slotkin, in *Regeneration through Violence: The Mythology of the American Frontier, 1800–1860* (Middletown, CT: Wesleyan University Press, 1973), writes that "The informing metaphor of Thoreau's vision is the struggle between two modes of perception, that of the hunter and that of the farmer" (p. 519). Since his concern is with the mythology of the frontier, however, Slotkin does not link this dialectic to Thoreau's engagement with antebellum (re)evaluations of the meaning of labor. As I hope I have made clear, the contest in Thoreau's imagination between "two modes of perception" devolves not only from his position between two situations (settlement and frontier), but from a more immediate indecision about two ways of making, or two methods of composition—artifice and generation.

10. Quoted in Paul, *The Shores of America*, p. 17.

11. A useful summary of the ways various writers handled the Dustan (or Dustin, or Duston) narrative can be found in Robert D. Arneau, "The Story of Hannah Duston: Cotton Mather to Thoreau," *American Transcendental Quarterly* 18 (1973): 19–23. See also Johnson, *Thoreau's Complex Weave,* pp. 155–57.

12. In *Walden,* Thoreau elaborates the myth of a fall from hunting-gathering into systematic agriculture as follows: "But lo! Men have become the tools of their tools. The man who independently plucked the fruits when he was hungry is become a farmer; and he who stood under a tree for shelter, a housekeeper" (p. 37).

13. King, "The Earth and the Mechanic Arts," p. 278.

14. Eric Sundquist, in *Home as Found: Genealogy and Authority in Nineteenth-Century American Literature* (Baltimore: Johns Hopkins University Press, 1979), also sees Thoreau trying to "naturalize" his writing, but his explanation is fundamentally different from mine. Sundquist writes, for example, that: "The violence of the masculine is countered by the commanding effort of the feminine, and in many respects Thoreau, like Whitman, finds the artist the perfect union of the two" (p. 70). I, on the other hand, maintain that Thoreau realizes that "perfect union" is unattainable and knows that in order to be a naturalized poet he must jettison many traditional characteristics of masculinity. In *A Week,* at least, the masculine is definitely subordinated to the feminine.

James McIntosh, too, sees that Thoreau "means not only that the book is about the outdoors but also that he has tried to imitate in it the fecundity, variety, and secret inner unity of nature" (p. 138). McIntosh sees Thoreau caught in a dialectic with nature: "Thoreau wants to be involved with nature; yet he feels that he is apart from it, either because he values the distinctiveness of his human state, or because he distrusts the nature he confronts, or both" (p. 9). I offer another explanation: Thoreau will not achieve the relation with nature he seeks until he is willing to forsake human creativity as expressed through artifice and make only as nature makes. He approaches such a commitment to natural making (or generation) throughout *A Week* and *Walden,* but he stakes himself to it only in the *Journal.* In general, McIntosh focuses on Thoreau's dramatization of central problems of Romanticism whereas I argue that his engagement with nature is inseparable from his concern with the central social and political concern of his day—work. See James McIntosh, *Thoreau as Romantic Naturalist: His Shifting Stance toward Nature* (Ithaca, NY: Cornell University Press, 1974).

15. Sir Philip Sidney, *An Apology for Poetry* (Indianapolis: Bobbs-Merrill Co., 1970), p. 15.

16. I owe this perspective on the *Journal* to Sharon Cameron's *Writing Nature: Henry Thoreau's "Journal"* (New York: Oxford University Press, 1985).

Chapter Five

1. Terry Eagleton, *The Ideology of the Aesthetic* (Oxford: Basil Blackwell, 1990), p. 13.

2. Ibid., p. 13.

3. Most criticism of these stories has read them in relation to Romantic principles or aesthetics. See, for example, Millicent Bell, *Hawthorne's View of the Artist* (New York: State University Press of New York, 1962), pp. 127–34, 182–85, and 193–94; Mary E. Ruckler, "Science and Art in Hawthorne's 'The Birth-mark,'" *Nineteenth-Century Fiction* 41, no. 4 (March 1987): 445–61; Sheldon W. Liebman, "Hawthorne's Romanticism: 'The Artist of the Beautiful,'" *ESQ: A Journal of the American Renaissance* 22, no. 2 (1976); Sarah I. Davis, "Margaret Fuller's 'Canova' and Hawthorne's 'Drowne's Wooden Image,'" *American Transcendentalist Quarterly* 49 (Winter 1981).

4. Nathaniel Hawthorne, *The Complete Works* (Boston: Houghton, Mifflin and Co., 1900), vol. 5, p. 315. All further page references will be made in the text.

5. Ibid., vol. 4, p. 52. All further references will be made in the text.

6. Ibid., vol. 4, p. 104.

7. Few critics have attempted to place these stories in a historical context. One notable exception is June Howard's "The Watchmaker, the Artist, and the Iron Accents of History: Notes on Hawthorne's 'The Artist of the Beautiful,'" *ESQ: A Journal of the American Renaissance* 28 (1st. Quarter 1982). Howard sees the story as "a complex response to a complex historical situation" (p. 1) and notices that "while Owen's occupation in one sense represents iron and industry . . . in another sense it represents a diminishing craft" (p. 5). However, she defines this situation exclusively in terms of industrialism's perceived threat to the imagination and does not explore the ways in which the story dramatizes antebellum cultural concern about the meanings of and relations among manual, intellectual, and artistic work.

8. As we have seen, the term "mechanic" was remarkably elastic. Usually it referred to those who performed some skilled manual labor, but at times it was applied more generally to all kinds of manual laborers—as, for example, when Whitman addresses himself to "butchers, sailors, stevedores, and drivers of horses—to ploughmen, wood-cutters, marketmen, carpenters, masons, and laborers—to workmen in factories—and to all in These States who live by their

daily toil! Mechanics!" (Quoted in M. Wynn Thomas, *The Lunar Light of Whitman's Poetry* [Cambridge: Harvard University Press, 1987], p. 78.)

9. Many efforts have been made to decode the meaning of "Aminadab" by focusing on its biblical source or on the possibility that it is an anagram. A useful overview which also provides literary antecedents for Hawthorne's use of the name can be found in Thomas Pribek, "Hawthorne's Aminadab: Sources and Significance," *Studies in the American Renaissance* 1987: 177–86. Pribek points out that a number of authors (Goldsmith, Bullock, Middleton) gave the name to servants or to what we would now call working-class characters. Nathan Cervo suggests, convincingly, that we read the name "Georgiana" as the "Greek *Ge* (earth) and *ergon* (work, enterprise) . . ." Nathan Cervo, "Hawthorne's 'The Birthmark," *Explicator* 42, no. 4 (Summer 1984): 19.

10. Nathaniel Hawthorne, *The Blithedale Romance* (New York: Penguin Books, 1983), p. 66. Hawthorne's letters from Brook Farm express disappointment, then cynicism, about the project of unifying mental and manual labor. "Even my Custom House experience was not such a thraldom and weariness; my mind and heart were freer. Oh, belovedest, labor is the curse of this world, and nobody can meddle with it, without becoming proportionately brutified." "The real Me was never an associate of the community; there has been a spectral Appearance there, sounding the horn at daybreak, and milking the cows, and hoeing potatoes, and raking hay, toiling and sweating in the sun, and doing me the honor to assume my name." "Belovedest, I doubt whether I shall succeed in writing another volume of Grandfather's Library, while I remain at the farm. I have not the sense of perfect seclusion, which has always been essential to my power of producing anything. . . . It will be good to have a longer interval between my labor of the body and that of the mind." Hawthorne's letters are included in Henry W. Sams, ed., *Autobiography of Brook Farm* (Englewood Cliffs, NJ: Prentice-Hall, Inc., 1958), pp. 33–35.

11. Quoted in M. H. Abrams, *The Mirror and the Lamp: Romantic Theory and the Critical Tradition* (New York: Oxford University Press, 1953), pp. 172–73. My account of organicist aesthetics is drawn largely from Abrams, pp. 156–83.

12. Thomas Carlyle, *Critical and Miscellaneous Essays,* vol. 2 of 5 vols. (New York: Charles Scribner's Sons, 1900), p. 74, pp. 59–61.

13. Martin Heidegger, "The Origin of the Work of Art," in *Poetry, Language, Thought,* pp. 68–71.

14. Rebecca Harding Davis, *Life in the Iron Mills* (New York: The Feminist Press, 1985), p. 19. All further page references will be made in the text.

15. James J. Davis, *The Iron Puddler,* p. 30.

Chapter Six

1. Susan Warner, *The Wide, Wide World* (New York: The Feminist Press, 1987), p. 72. All further page references will be made in the text.

2. Mary P. Ryan, *The Empire of the Mother: American Writing about Domesticity, 1830–1860* (New York: Oxford University Press, 1982), p. 97.

3. Jane Tompkins, *Sensational Designs: The Cultural Work of American Fiction, 1790–1860* (New York: Oxford University Press, 1985).

4. See, for example, Barbara Welter, "The Cult of True Womanhood, 1820–1860," *American Quarterly* 18, no. 2 (Summer 1966): 151–74; Nancy Cott, *The Bonds of Womanhood,* pp. 63–70, 128–35; Gillian Brown, *Domestic Individualism: Imagining Self in Nineteenth-Century America* (Berkeley: University of California Press, 1990), pp. 63–79.

5. Tompkins, *Sensational Designs,* p. 25.

6. Lydia Maria Child, *The Mother's Book* (Boston: Carter and Hendee, 1831), p. 20.

7. Ryan, *Empire of the Mother,* p. 56.

8. Ibid., pp. 24–90.

9. Quoted in Barbara Welter, *Dimity Convictions: The American Woman in the Nineteenth Century* (Athens: Ohio University Press, 1976), p. 48.

10. Cott, *The Bonds of Womanhood,* p. 72.

11. Quoted in Richard H. Brodhead, "Sparing the Rod: Discipline and Fiction in Antebellum America," *Representations* 21 (Winter 1988): 72.

12. See, especially, Gillian Brown, *Domestic Individualism,* pp. 63–64, in which Brown argues that "domestic rhetoric expunged the corporeality of women's work."

13. Quoted in Ryan, *Empire of the Mother,* p. 79.

14. Quoted in Welter, *Dimity Convictions,* p. 39.

15. Ibid., p. 38.

16. Maria J. McIntosh, *Woman in America: Her Work and Her Reward* (New York: Appleton and Co., 1850), p. 24. All further page references will be made in the text,

17. Mrs. A. J. Graves, *Woman in America: Being an Examination into the Moral and Intellectual Condition of American Female Society* (New York: Harper and Bros., 1847), p. 29. All further page references will be made in the text.

18. Catharine Beecher, *Treatise on Domestic Economy* (Boston: Marsh, Capen, Lyonn, and Webb, 1841), p. 26. All further page references will be made in the text.

19. Ryan, *Empire of the Mother,* p. 98.

20. Quoted in Carroll Smith-Rosenberg, "Puberty to Menopause: The Cycle of Femininity in Nineteenth-Century America," reprinted in *Clio's Consciousness Raised: New Perspectives on the History of Women,* edited by Mary S. Hartman and Lois Banner (New York: Octagon Books, 1976), p. 24.

21. Henry C. Wright, *Marriage and Parentage* (Boston, 1855), p. 55. All further page references will be made in the text.

22. Orson Fowler, *Creative and Sexual Science* (New York: National Publishing Co., 1870), pp. 754–55.

23. Elizabeth Blackwell, *The Laws of Life, with Special Reference to the Physi-*

cal Education of Girls (New York: George P. Putnam, 1852), p. 15. All further page references will be made in the text.

24. Harriet Beecher Stowe, *Household Papers and Stories* (New York: AMS Press, 1967), p. 334. All further page references will be made in the text.

25. See Karl Marx, *The Economic and Philosophic Manuscripts of 1844* (New York: International Publishers, 1982), pp. 108–9, and *Capital,* vol. 1 (New York: Vintage Books, 1977), p. 284; Elaine Scarry, *The Body in Pain,* pp. 168–71.

26. Margaret Ossoli Fuller, *Woman in the Nineteenth Century* (New York: W. W. Norton and Co., 1971), p. 29.

Chapter Seven

1. Nina Baym, *Woman's Fiction: A Guide to Novels by and about Women in America, 1820–1870* (Ithaca, NY: Cornell University Press, 1978), pp. 32–33.

2. Ibid., p. 22.

3. Catharine Maria Sedgwick, *A New England Tale* (New York: George P. Putnam and Co., 1852), p. 35. All further page references will be made in the text.

4. See Daniel Scott Smith, "Family Limitations on Sexual Control and Domestic Feminism," *Feminist Studies* 1, no. 3–4 (Winter–Spring 1973): 40–57.

5. Mary Kelley, *Private Woman, Public Stage: Literary Domesticity in Nineteenth-Century America* (New York: Oxford University Press, 1984), pp. 286–87. Sedgwick and Warner are quoted by Kelley, pp. 286–87.

6. Baym, *Woman's Fiction,* p. 11.

7. Tompkins, *Sensational Designs,* pp. 149–60.

8. Child, *The Mother's Book,* p. 89.

9. Quoted in Cott, *The Bonds of Womanhood,* p. 89.

10. John S. C. Abbott, *The Mother at Home* (New York: American Tract Society, 1833), p. 65.

Chapter Eight

1. Harriet Beecher Stowe, *Uncle Tom's Cabin, or Life Among the Lowly* (Harmondsworth: Penguin Books Ltd., 1981), p. 393. All further page references will be made in the text.

2. As my use of the word "power" indicates, I am indebted to Jane Tompkins's chapter on Stowe, "Sentimental Power: *Uncle Tom's Cabin* and the Politics of Literary History" in *Sensational Designs: The Cultural Work of American Fiction, 1790–1860* (New York: Oxford University Press, 1985), pp. 122–46.

3. Child, *The Mother's Book,* p. 19.

4. Quoted in Annie Fields, *The Life and Letters of Harriet Beecher Stowe* (Boston: Houghton Mifflin Co., 1898), p. 104. My understanding of Stowe's family life is based on Mary Kelley's account in "At War with Herself: Harriet Beecher Stowe as a Woman in Conflict within the Home," *American Studies* 19, no. 2 (1978): 23–40.

5. Quoted in Fields, *The Life and Letters of Harriet Beecher Stowe*, p. 163. All further page references will be made in the text.

6. Harriet Beecher Stowe, *Works*, vol. 8 of 16 vols. (New York: AMS Publishers, 1969), p. viii.

7. Harriet Beecher Stowe, "The Woman Who Does Her Own Work," in *Household Papers and Stories* (Boston: Houghton, Mifflin, and Co., 1896), p. 85. All further page references will be made in the text.

8. Margaret Ossoli Fuller, *Woman in the Nineteenth Century*, p. 115.

9. Stowe, "What is a Home?" in *Household Papers*, p. 39.

10. Charlotte Perkins Gilman, *Human Work* (New York: McClure, Phillips and Co., 1904), p. 204. All further page references will be made in the text.

11. Gillian Brown offers a complementary and compelling reading of *Uncle Tom's Cabin* as a drama of resistance both to the threat (to domesticity) of the marketplace and to the views (on domesticity) of Stowe's sister, Catharine Beecher. See "Getting in the Kitchen with Dinah: Domestic Politics in *Uncle Tom's Cabin,*" *American Quarterly* 36, no. 4 (Fall 1984): 503–23.

12. Quoted in E. Bruce Kirkham's indispensable study, *The Building of Uncle Tom's Cabin* (Knoxville: University of Tennessee Press, 1977), p. 66. All further page references will be made in the text.

13. Henry David Thoreau, *Walden*, p. 101.

14. Mary O'Brien, "Feminist Theory and Dialectical Logic," in *Feminist Theory: A Critique of Ideology*, edited by Nannerl O. Keohane, Michelle Z. Rosaldo, and Barbara C. Gelpi (Chicago: University of Chicago Press, 1982), p. 109.

15. Philip Fisher, *Hard Facts: Form and Setting in the American Novel* (Oxford: Oxford University Press, 1985), p. 98.

16. Ralph Waldo Emerson, *Journals and Miscellaneous Notebooks*, 16 vols., vol. 4, edited by Morton Sealts (Cambridge: Harvard University Press, 1964), p. 335.

17. Stowe's commitment to motherhood implicates her, however, in a discourse of racialism in which the mother figure plays a crucial role. Indeed, for Stowe race is the one social distinction that is essential, not contigent, and as such as it is profoundly threatening to her view of society as one organic whole. See Laura Doyle's *Bordering on the Body: The Racial Matrix of Modernism* (New York: Oxford University Press, forthcoming).

18. Marcuse, *Eros and Civilization*, pp. 35–37.

19. Child, *The Mother's Book*, p. 4.

20. Edward Everett, *An Address Delivered before the Massachusetts Charitable Mechanic Association, 20 Sept., 1837, on the Occasion of their First Exhibition and Fair* (Boston: Dutton and Wentworth, 1837), p. 8.

Chapter Nine

1. See Kenneth Burke, *Language as Symbolic Action: Essays on Life, Literature, and Method* (Berkeley: University of California Press, 1966), pp. 3–24.

My thinking about the expressivity of the body, and about the mother figure as a potent example of that expressivity, has its source in conversations with Laura Doyle and in her notion of "intercorporeity" particularly.

2. Paul Valéry, *The Art of Poetry* (New York: Vintage Books, 1961), pp. 71–72.

3. William Wordsworth, "The Solitary Reaper," in *The Poetical Works of William Wordsworth* (New York: Oxford University Press, 1933), p. 289.

4. Frederick Douglass, *Narrative of the Life of Frederick Douglass, An American Slave* (New York: Penguin Books, 1982), p. 57.

5. Ibid., p. 58.

6. Mary Prince, "The History of Mary Prince, A West Indian Slave," in *The Classic Slave Narratives,* edited by Henry Louis Gates (New York: New American Library, 1987), p. 195.

7. Quoted in Norman Yetman, ed., *Life Under the 'Peculiar Institution': Selections from the Slave Narrative Collection* (New York: Holt, Rinehart, and Winston: 1970), pp. 134 and 156.

8. Ibid., p. 58.

9. Henry Bibb, *Narrative,* p. 44.

10. Elizabeth Keckley, *Behind the Scenes; of Thirty Years a Slave and Four Years in the White House* (New York: Oxford University Press, 1988), p. 46.

11. "White Slavery," *The Democratic Review* 11, no. 52 (September 1842): 261.

12. Thoreau, *Walden,* p. 7.

13. Frederick Law Olmsted, *A Journey in the Seaboard Slave States in the Years 1853–1854, with Remarks on their Economy,* 2 vols. (New York: G. P. Putnam and Sons, 1904), vol. 1, p. 20. All further page references will be made in the text.

14. Thomas Carlyle, *Critical and Miscellaneous Essays,* vol. 4 of 5 vols., pp. 355–56.

15. Elizabeth Fox-Genovese and Eugene Genovese, *Fruits of Merchant Capital: Slavery and Bourgeois Property in the Rise and Expansion of Capitalism* (New York: Oxford University Press, 1983), p. 292.

16. Josiah Henson, *The Life of Josiah Henson, Formerly A Slave, Now An Inhabitant of Canada, as Narrated by Himself* (Boston: Arthur D. Phelps, 1849), p. 8. In *To Tell a Free Story: The First Century of Afro-American Autobiography, 1760–1865* (Urbana: University of Illinois Press, 1986), William Andrews observes that Henson's and several other "work ethic" narratives based their appeal to Northern sensibilities on slavery's hostility to the work ethic and its indifference to contractual relations between master and slave (p. 112).

17. Quoted in Yetman, *Peculiar Institution,* p. 47.

18. Quoted in George P. Rawick, *The American Slave: A Composite Autobiography,* vol. 4 of 10 vols. (Westport, CT: Greenwood Publishing Co., 1973), pp. 1 and 5.

19. Quoted in Yetman, *Peculiar Institution,* p. 74.

20. Bruce Jackson, *Wake Up Dead Man: Afro-American Worksongs from Texas Prisons* (Cambridge: Harvard University Press, 1972), pp. 24–25, 4, and 9.

21. Quoted in Rawick, *The American Slave,* p. 45.

22. Linda Brent, in Gates, ed., *The Classic Slave Narratives,* pp. 241–44.

23. See James E. Newton and Ronald L. Lewis, eds., *The Other Slaves: Mechanics, Artisans, and Craftsmen* (Boston: G. K. Hall, 1978), p. 179. Newton and Lewis make clear that although slave artisans like Pennington were few in proportion to the total number of slaves, their impact on Southern culture and on slave culture was greater than their numbers might suggest.

24. James W. C. Pennington, *The Fugitive Blacksmith* (Westport, CT: Negro University Press, 1971), pp. 8–9.

25. Quoted in Lawrence Levine, *Black Culture and Black Consciousness: Afro-American Folk Thought from Slavery to Freedom* (New York: Oxford University Press, 1977), p. 5.

26. Quoted in Leslie Howard Owens, *This Species of Property: Slave Life and Culture in the Old South* (New York: Oxford University Press, 1976), pp. 173–74.

27. Quoted in Owens, *Species of Property,* p. 165.

28. Levine, *Black Culture,* p. 6.

29. Ibid., pp. 3–7.

30. Owens, *Species of Property,* p. 164.

31. Eugene Genovese, *Roll, Jordan, Roll: The World the Slaves Made* (New York: Vintage Books, 1976), p. 324. Although we disagree at a number of points, I am indebted to Genovese's brief but richly suggestive account of slave work and the slaves' work ethic (pp. 285–324).

32. Levine, *Black Culture,* p. 18.

33. Imamu Amiri Baraka, *Blues People* (Westport, CT: Greenwood Press, 1963), p. 18.

34. Jackson, *Wake Up, Dead Man,* p. 2. All further page references will be made in the text.

35. Valéry, *The Art of Poetry,* pp. 66–67.

36. William Francis Allen, Charles Pickard Ware, Lucy McKim Garrison, eds., *Slave Songs of the United States* (1867, 1st ed.; New York: Peter Smith, 1951, reprint), pp. 2–3.

Chapter Ten

1. Frances E. W. Harper, *Iola Leroy* (Boston: Beacon Press, 1987), p. 251.

2. W. E. B. DuBois, *The Souls of Black Folk,* in *Three Negro Classics,* edited by John Hope Franklin (New York: Avon Books, 1965), p. 378.

3. Andrews, *To Tell a Free Story,* pp. 214–39.

4. Frederick Douglass, *My Bondage, My Freedom,* (Urbana: University of Illinois Press, 1987), p. 242. All further page references will be made in the text.

5. Smith even provides a scientific theory to explain why Douglass's drama of self-elevation and self-culture does not entail abandonment of a past that has been located mainly in the body and its labors. "Naturalists tell us that a full grown man is a resultant or representative of all animated nature on this globe; beginning with the early embryo state, then representing the lowest forms of

organic life, and passing through every subordinate grade or type, until he reaches the last and highest—manhood" (p. 17). Thus, Douglass is great precisely in that he embodies the entire spectrum of what exists, from matter to spirit, from body to mind; his achievement (like that of all great men, according to Smith) is not that he transcends, but that he includes, or contains. This is another version of the Thoreauvian and Whitmanesque wish that the sentient knowledge of the body and its labors might be accorded their full value and seen not just as a threshold to higher development, but as essential components of any complete man. "In like manner, and to the fullest extent, has Frederick Douglass passed through every gradation of rank comprised in our national make-up, and bears upon his person and upon his soul every thing that is American" (p. 17).

6. Quoted in Newton and Lewis, eds., *The Other Slaves,* p. 205.

7. Pauline Hopkins, *Contending Forces: A Romance Illustrative of Negro Life North and South* (New York: Oxford University Press, 1988), p. 32. All further page references will be made in the text.

8. The argument which follows owes much to Arnold Rampersad's "Slavery and the Literary Imagination: DuBois's *The Souls of Black Folk*" in *Slavery and the Literary Imagination,* edited by Deborah E. McDowell and Arnold Rampersad, (Baltimore: Johns Hopkins University Press, 1989), pp. 104–24.

9. W. E. B. DuBois, *The Gift of Black Folk, the Negroes in the Making of America* (New York: AMS Press, 1971), pp. 53–54.

10. DuBois, *The Gift of Black Folk,* p. 77.

11. DuBois, *The Souls of Black Folk,* p. 278.

Chapter Eleven

1. Heidegger, "The Thing," in *Poetry, Language, Thought,* p. 181.

2. My approach to *Walden* as a work of philosophical importance is indebted to Stanley Cavell's *The Senses of Walden* (New York: Viking Press, 1972) and to Sharon Cameron's *Writing Nature: Henry Thoreau's "Journal"* (New York: Oxford University Press, 1985). I have benefitted also from John P. Diggins's early and important essay, "Thoreau, Marx, and the 'Riddle' of Alienation," *Social Research* 39, no. 4 (Winter 1972). Diggins argues that Thoreau is more radical than Marx, at least philosophically, insofar as he aims to *evaluate* work, not just repossess it.

3. Thoreau, *Walden,* p. 91. All further page references will be made in the text.

4. Thoreau, *Early Essays and Miscellanies,* p. 242. All further page references will be made in the text.

5. Emerson, *Emerson's Works,* vol. 6, p. 41.

6. But here the ethical problem of right living recapitulates the procedural problems inherent in the theory (and aesthetic practice) of organic form: if the process of building (or writing) as one should is so simple and natural as to be "unconscious," there appears to be no need for conscious deliberation, for craft.

Insofar as aesthetics is predicated on the need for conscious, deliberate, even rational choice, Thoreau's program of natural living seems to make ethics impossible. He attempts to solve this problem by arguing that, while building is an outgrowth of living, living is also an outgrowth of building (see p. 51).

7. James McIntosh also employs Arendt's terms to explain Thoreau's activities at Walden, but whereas I see Thoreau attempting to collapse the difference between work and labor McIntosh argues that "Thoreau is both *animal laborans* and *homo faber;* he participates in nature while he hoes beans, and he formally structures his experience while away from nature by writing 'The Bean Field'; . . ." McIntosh, *Thoreau as Romantic Naturalist,* p. 254.

8. John Locke, *Of Civil Government* (South Bend, IN: Gateway Editions, 1955), p. 22. All further page references will be given in the text.

9. In *The Body in Pain,* Elaine Scarry argues that "While pain is a state remarkable for being wholly without objects, the imagination is remarkable for being the only state that is wholly its objects." These postulates enable Scarry to propose that "pain and imagining are the 'framing events' within whose boundaries all other perceptual, somatic, and emotional events occur; thus, between the two extremes can be mapped the whole terrain of the human psyche."

Work, Scarry argues, is the activity that mediates between these two states, as suggested by the fact that the term is used "at once as a near synonym for pain, *and* as a near synonym for created object." Meaningful work, therefore, is work that permits self-objectification; meaningless or painful work obstructs it. "The more it [work] realizes and transforms itself in its object, the closer it is to the imagination, to art, to culture; and the more it is unable to bring forth an object or, bringing it forth, is then cut off from its object, the more it approaches the condition of pain" (pp. 161–70).

It should be clear by now that Thoreau's re-vision of work sharply challenges such a view: Thoreau is to a considerable extent pained by the degree to which his work objectifies itself, himself, and the natural world. Ideally, as Cameron has shown, his work would merely present, not re-present; to use Scarry's terms, it would merely "enter" rather than "supplement" the natural world.

10. The relative invisibility of work to contemporary literary criticism is registered in the fact that Walter Benn Michaels, in "*Walden*'s False Bottoms," does not allude to this passage. Focusing on ontological and textual "bottomlessness" in *Walden,* Michaels's otherwise brilliant account of *Walden*'s search for "authority" overlooks the mysteriousness of the working class and its physical labor as a specific antebellum site of "bottomlessness." See Walter Benn Michaels, "*Walden*'s False Bottoms," *Glyph* 1 (1977): 132–49.

11. See Michael West, "Scatology and Eschatology: The Heroic Dimensions of Thoreau's Wordplay," in *PMLA,* 1989 (October 1974): 1043–64. This article was the first to provide a historical framework (West's emphasis is on nineteenth-century physiology and medicine) within which to place Thoreau's ambivalent attitudes toward the body. It was West who pointed me toward Thoreau's reading of James Garth Wilkinson's *The Human Body and Its Connection with Man.*

12. Henry David Thoreau, *Writings*, vol. 3 of 20 vols. (Boston: Houghton Mifflin, Co., 1906) p. 36.

13. Richard Slotkin, in *Regeneration through Violence*, discusses precisely these issues and provides an answer which, while true as far as it goes, fails to appreciate *Walden*'s (albeit tentative and often contradicted) embrace of physicality. He writes: "this sensuality, expressed in lust for the kill or sexual fever, is the source of the 'generative energy,' the creative power of man. To destroy it is to destroy man himself. What, then, is the alternative? . . . For Thoreau the answer is like that of Timothy Flint: the sublimation of sensual procreative passion, the discipline and training of it to acts of restrained and creative violence, as in the composition of poetry or the greedy observation of birds" (p. 531). While it is true that Thoreau sublimates his sexual passions, much more emphasis must be placed on his willingness to experience asexual (that is, nonprocreative) sensuality—a condition Freud himself establishes as prior to the social regimentation of sensuality and the channeling of varied and inchoate desires into heterosexual monogamy for procreation. By attributing so much importance to one form of sensuality, Slotkin is led to conclude that "The triumph of the hunt at Walden is thus intellectual rather than physical or mytho-sexual, ending with the acquisition of an Indian-like manner of perception, in which objects—animals, trees, rocks, clouds, water—become totally identified with their archetypes" (p. 532). The "alternative" for Thoreau should be figured not just as sublimation but as a more radical choice to align himself with the generative powers of nature rather than with a traditional, masculinist sexuality that opposes itself to, and seeks to dominate, nature.

14. Emerson, *Collected Works*, vol. 1, p. 9.

15. Ibid., p. 8.

16. Thoreau, *Journal*, vol. 2, p. 451.

17. James John Garth Wilkinson, *The Human Body and Its Connection with Man* (Philadelphia: Lippincott, Grambo and Co., 1851), p. 62. All further page references will be given in the text.

Wilkinson dedicated his book to Henry James, Sr., who six years earlier had named one of his sons (Garth Wilkinson) after him. Henry James, Jr., had little patience for the doctor. In a letter to his mother (8 April 1879), he writes: "I am sorry to say I was taken about nine days ago by one of those diabolical attacks of pain in my head which I have occasionally had before. . . . Not knowing what else to do I sent for Dr. Wilkinson, who, however, I am sorry to say, rendered me though he came three times, no assistance whatever—though he consented to accept a goodly fee." After another attack, about a year later, James reports that "I had this time a less metaphysical physician than poor old Wilkinson, who assuaged my pain with considerable promptitude." Henry James, *Letters*, Leon Edel, ed., Vol. 2 of 6 vols. (Cambridge, MA: Harvard University Press, 1975), pp. 228, 294.

18. James McIntosh observes: "There is evidence that while he was writing *Walden* he [Thoreau] reconsidered his moments of passionate commitment to *phusis*, recognizing that nature as growth did not in itself supply a framework

adequate to all his experience, and perhaps suspecting that these moments were tinged with undisciplined eroticism" (p. 250). This is certainly true, but as noted above, Thoreau's ambivalence toward the body (and nature, and matter) is registered also in numerous antebellum works of physiology, biology, and geology. For example, in a work Thoreau apparently read, J. B. Stallo argues that "Dead matter as such, waiting for the breath of life, does not exist . . . The whole theory of two independent factors of existence, Mind and Matter, force and inertia, is an absurdity" (*General Principles of the Philosophy of Nature* [Boston: Wm. Crosby and H. P. Nichols, 1848], pp. 35, 46).

Whereas McIntosh sees Thoreau moving "increasingly" away from nature, I read *Walden* as Thoreau's final effort to compromise between the demands of artifice and the appeal of naturalized labor. In "Thoreau and Coleridge's *Theory of Life*," *Studies in the American Renaissance* 1985: 269–84, Robert Sattelmeyer and Richard A. Hockes argue that Thoreau's reading of Coleridge's book (in late 1848) helped him make this transition from writing literature to what Cameron would call "writing nature." His reading "came just at the beginning of a subtle but profound shift in Thoreau's stance toward nature, a shift that amounted to adopting the study of natural history, along with writing, as the principal occupation of his life. In this context, Coleridge's treatise offered him a philosophical underpinning for this work, and more importantly provided him with a bridge between the idealism of his youth and the detailed and scientific study of nature that occupied his maturity" (p. 275).

19. Walt Whitman, *Leaves of Grass*, edited and with an introduction by Malcolm Cowley (New York: Penguin Books, 1959 and 1977 [1st ed. 1855]), p. 48.

20. Thoreau, *Writings*, vol. 3, p. 246.

21. Ibid., p. 276.

22. Ibid., p. 85.

23. Ibid., p. 165.

24. Ibid., p. 239.

25. Ibid., p. 271.

26. Ibid., p. 85, pp. 390–91. I feel obliged to acknowledge again my indebtedness to Sharon Cameron's reading of the *Journal* in *Writing Nature*.

Afterword

1. Cheyfitz, "Matthiessen's *American Renaissance*," p. 356.

Index